IMAGES
of America

BRIDGETON

IN AND AROUND THE OLD COUNTY TOWN

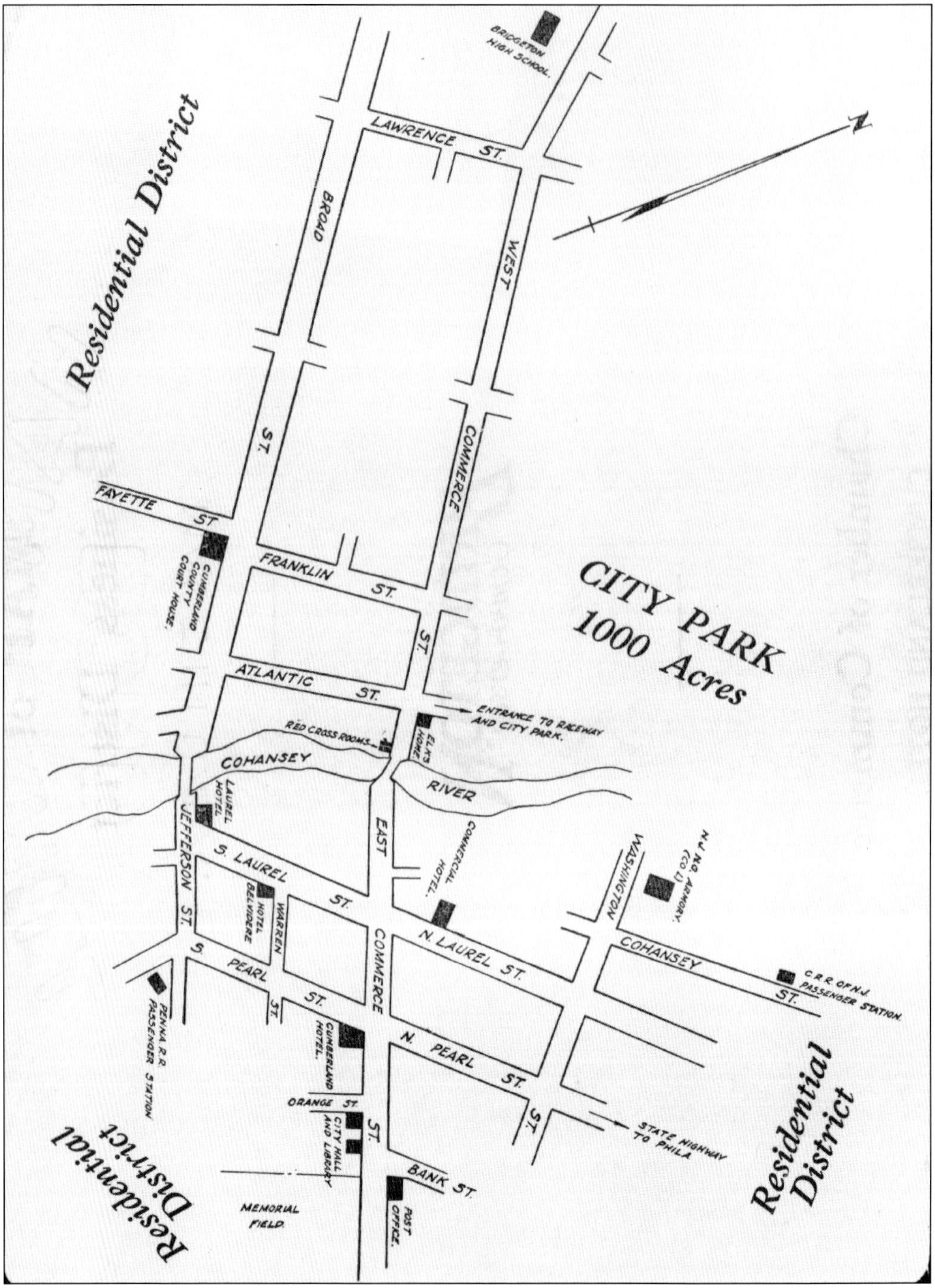

A MAP OF BRIDGETON IN THE LATE 1920s. By the time the late 1920s came along, the local chamber of commerce, then headquartered at the Cumberland Hotel, was promoting the town as the "Gem-o'-Jersey." This map, intended for visiting business people, depicts the passenger stations of the Central Railroad of New Jersey and the West Jersey and Seashore branch of the Pennsylvania Railroad, along with public buildings, hotels, civic and fraternal organizations, and the neighborhoods flanking the business district.

IMAGES
of America

BRIDGETON
IN AND AROUND THE OLD COUNTY TOWN

Bill Chestnut

ARCADIA
PUBLISHING

ISBN 978-0-7385-6328-2

Published by Arcadia Publishing
Charleston, South Carolina

Printed in the United States of America

Library of Congress Catalog Card Number: 2008927255

For all general information contact Arcadia Publishing at:
Telephone 843-853-2070
Fax 843-853-0044
E-mail sales@arcadiapublishing.com
For customer service and orders:
Toll-Free 1-888-313-2665

Visit us on the Internet at www.arcadiapublishing.com

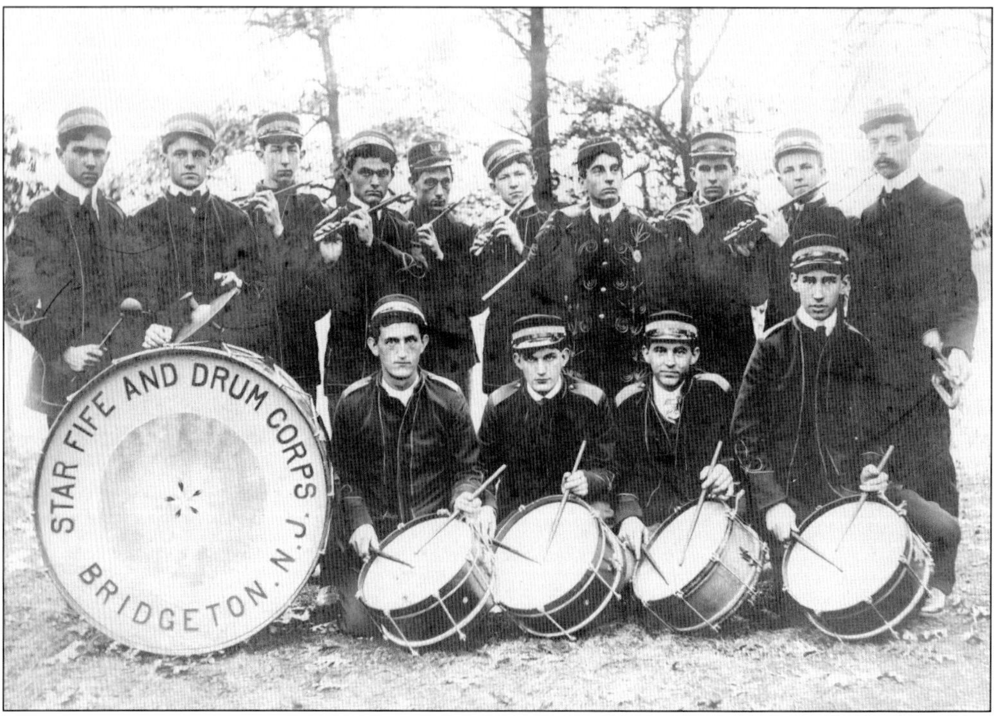

Contents

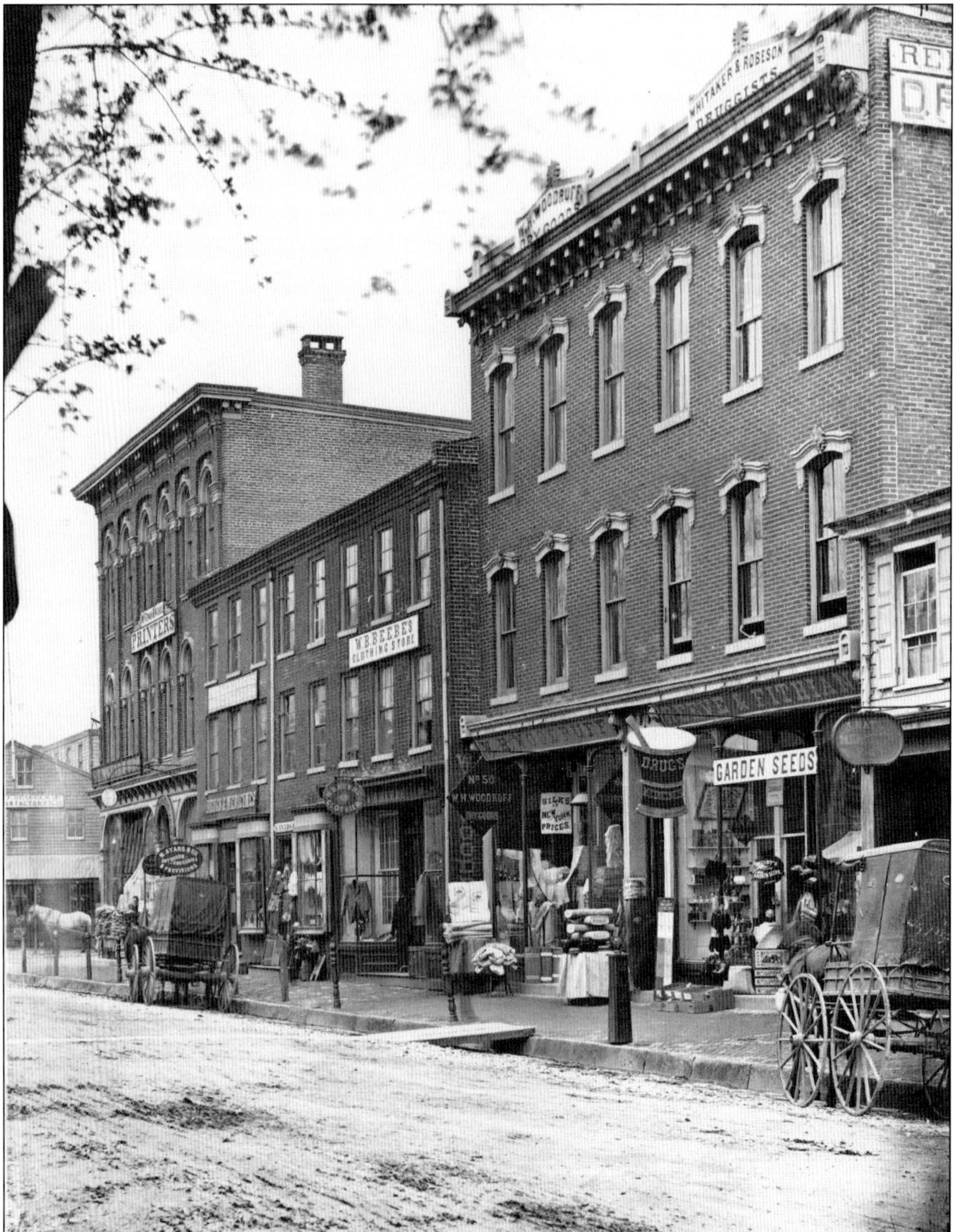

COMMERCE STREET LOOKING EAST TOWARDS LAUREL STREET, 1876–1880. The approximate date of this remarkable photograph taken during the Victorian era can be ascertained by the known locations of businesses during that time. Another clue comes from the fact that numbers for homes and businesses did not come into use until 1876. The tall building on the corner is S.E. McGear & Brother Dry Goods, which still dominates the intersection. When new in 1871, it was promoted as being the largest store in New Jersey south of Trenton.

Introduction

Founded on the Cohansey River in 1686 by Quaker Richard Hancock at a site long favored by the Native American Lenni Lenapes, the settlement that eventually became known as Bridgeton grew slowly at first. But when a bridge was erected at the present-day site of Commerce Street by 1716, and it became the County Town after Cumberland broke away from Salem in 1748, its future was assured.

Blessed by its location and its ambitious and talented population, Bridgeton became among the most prosperous communities in New Jersey after the Civil War. Not only did people come to the courthouse on the Broad Street hill to conduct business, but over the years the town became home to numerous industries, including shipbuilding, canning, glass, iron, and textile manufacturing, as well as the smaller enterprises that were needed to support the larger ones.

An 1882 promotional piece about the town declared: "The benefits of Bridgeton as a manufacturing center are plainly manifest. The streets are well laid out and to a great extent heavily shaded with maple, linden, elm and other trees. Unlike many manufacturing towns, where trade is done principally through factory stores, Bridgeton has numerous mercantile houses, embracing all lines of business . . . with as large and varied a stock as can be found in larger cities. To a very great extent the citizens own their own dwellings, which are neatly built . . ."

When it came to the establishment of an infrastructure to continue the community's growth, Bridgeton was always on the cutting edge of technology. A steamboat company was established in 1845 and a side-wheel paddle steamer known as the *Cohansey* ran regularly to Philadelphia. In 1857 the Bridgeton Gas Light Company was organized and residents were able to utilize what was then the latest in illumination technology.

On July 24, 1861, a railroad from Woodbury to Bridgeton was completed—an event that was considered to be among the greatest in the town's history. Still another important occasion was marked on December 18, 1877, when the city waterworks began operation for the first time. Equipped with street hydrants, it allowed a first-class fire department to serve the town.

The first known use of electricity for the purpose of illumination in Bridgeton, probably with arc lamps, was in August 1879 when a circus came to town. During the early 1880s, experiments were made with electric street lights. The Bridgeton Electric Light Company was founded in April 1886, a remarkably early date for the establishment of a utility of this nature. Local residents first were able to enjoy electric trolley car service during the summer of 1893, another relatively early innovation.

Bridgeton's importance also stems from the fact that between 1789 and 1913 it served as the Federal Port of Entry for most of South Jersey. In fact, the last customs house to be erected here continues in public use today as the city hall annex. Now recognized as New Jersey's largest historic district, nearly every corner of Bridgeton reflects its remarkable past.

Bill Chestnut
1996

Acknowledgments

Thanks to the many early photographers who worked in Bridgeton, we have an impressive picture of the city's past. As early as 1849, Franklin Ferguson advertised locally that he was capable of taking "daguerreotype likenesses." By 1864, Edwards & Ogden operated their Excelsior Photograph Gallery in Grosscup's Hall.

Victorian-era professional photographers in Bridgeton included Isaac H. Bowen, active in business about 1881, and William E. Service, who took over the studio of M.C. Edwards in 1878 and continued to work into the early twentieth century. About 1885 A.F. Brooks operated a studio, while in the 1890s William W. Seeler worked here. Right about that time a group of talented amateurs formed the Bridgeton Camera Club. By the late 1890s and into the early 1900s, the great Harvey W. Porch (1869–1954) was at work. His images were preserved by his son, Everett Porch.

Other early twentieth-century local professionals included Emerson B. Garrison and Daniel V. Ward. In the era immediately following World War I, prominent Bridgeton photographers were Milton F. Champion and John T. Roberts, who was followed in the family business by his son, Thomas G. Roberts. Many of the Roberts photographs are published in this book for the first time thanks to Margaret Roberts.

Rare photographs also were contributed to this volume by the Bridgeton Antiquarian League, whose president is Joe DeLuca. Others who helped to make this effort a reality are Don Wentzel, Tom Lane, Frank Stubbins, Jack Lippincott, Ben Turner, Dale Wettstein, Budd Ware, Jay Gandy, Florence Bacon, Gary Hewitt, Jerry MacDonald, Clem Lowe, Warren Robinson, Bill Harris, Jack West, Fred Hovermann, the McCormick-Penfield family, Tom Connelly, John Fuyuume (of the Seabrook Cultural Center), the late Henry Jones, Betty Lewis, Alan Woodruff, Lenny Wasserman, and especially Charlie Pedrick, the crown prince of all Bridgeton memorabilia collectors.

One

Matters of Civic Pride

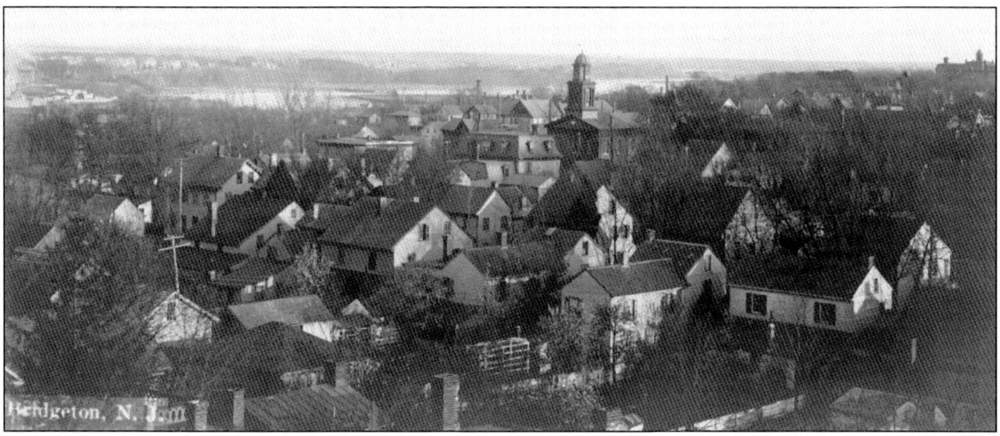

A PANORAMA OF THE COUNTY TOWN. An unidentified photographer climbed the tower of the Presbyterian church on West Commerce Street to capture this scene before 1909. The steeple in the center is the old 1844 Cumberland County Courthouse. The South Jersey Institute can be seen on the horizon.

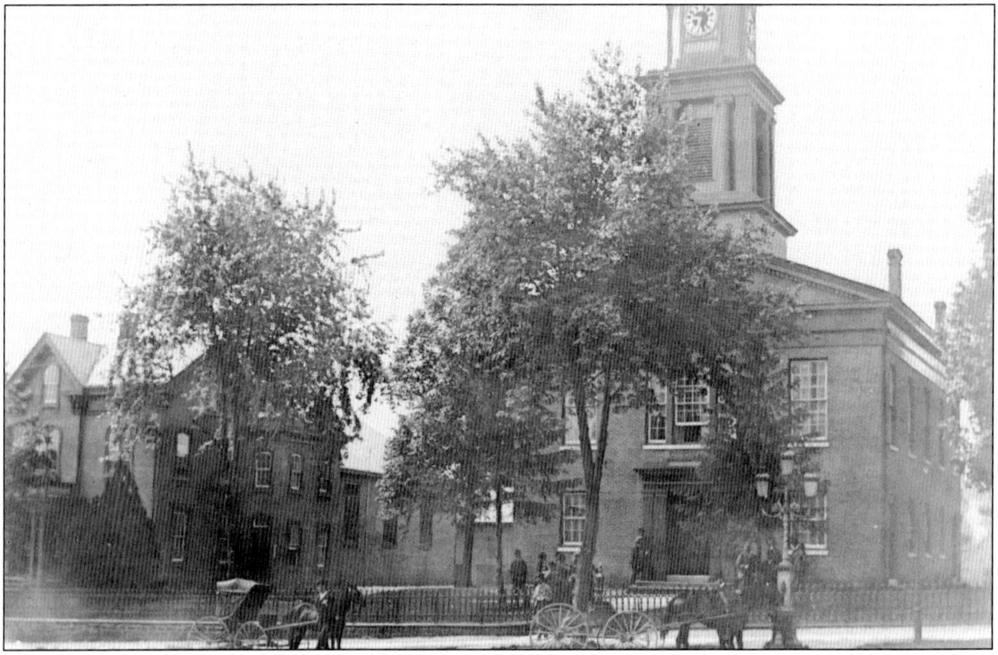

THE BROAD STREET HILL. Carriages line up in front of the 1844 Cumberland County Courthouse in this scene from the Pedrick collection which dates about 1905. At left is the 1866 sheriff's residence and jail, demolished in the early 1970s, which was satirically referred to as Peacock's Hotel.

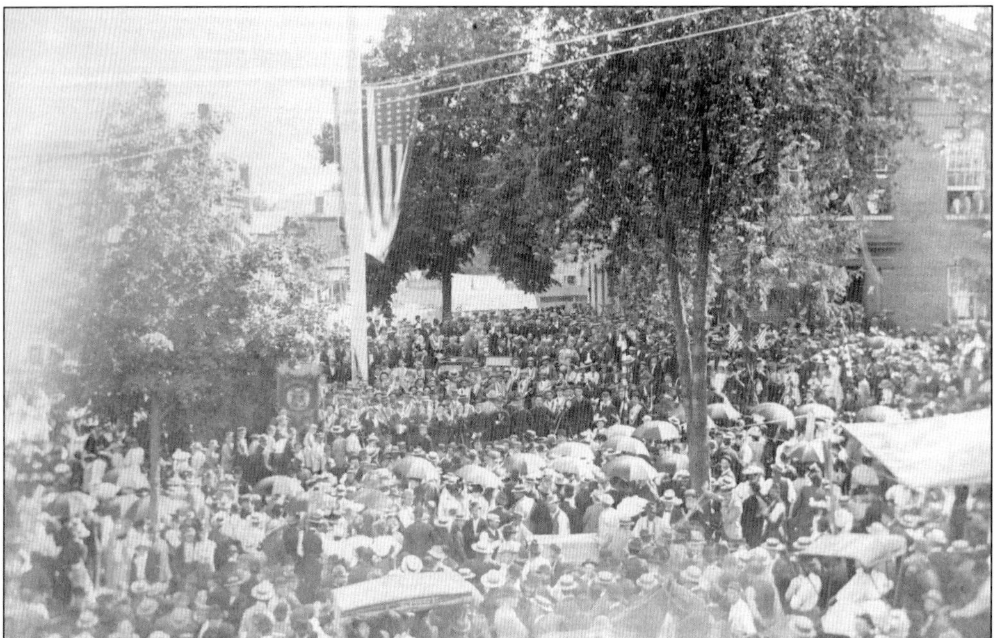

A GATHERING AT THE OLD COURTHOUSE. Among the earliest surviving outdoor photographs of Bridgeton is this scene in front of the 1844 courthouse on the Broad Street hill, probably taken on the Fourth of July. The number of stars on the flag suggests a date from the late 1860s to the mid-1870s.

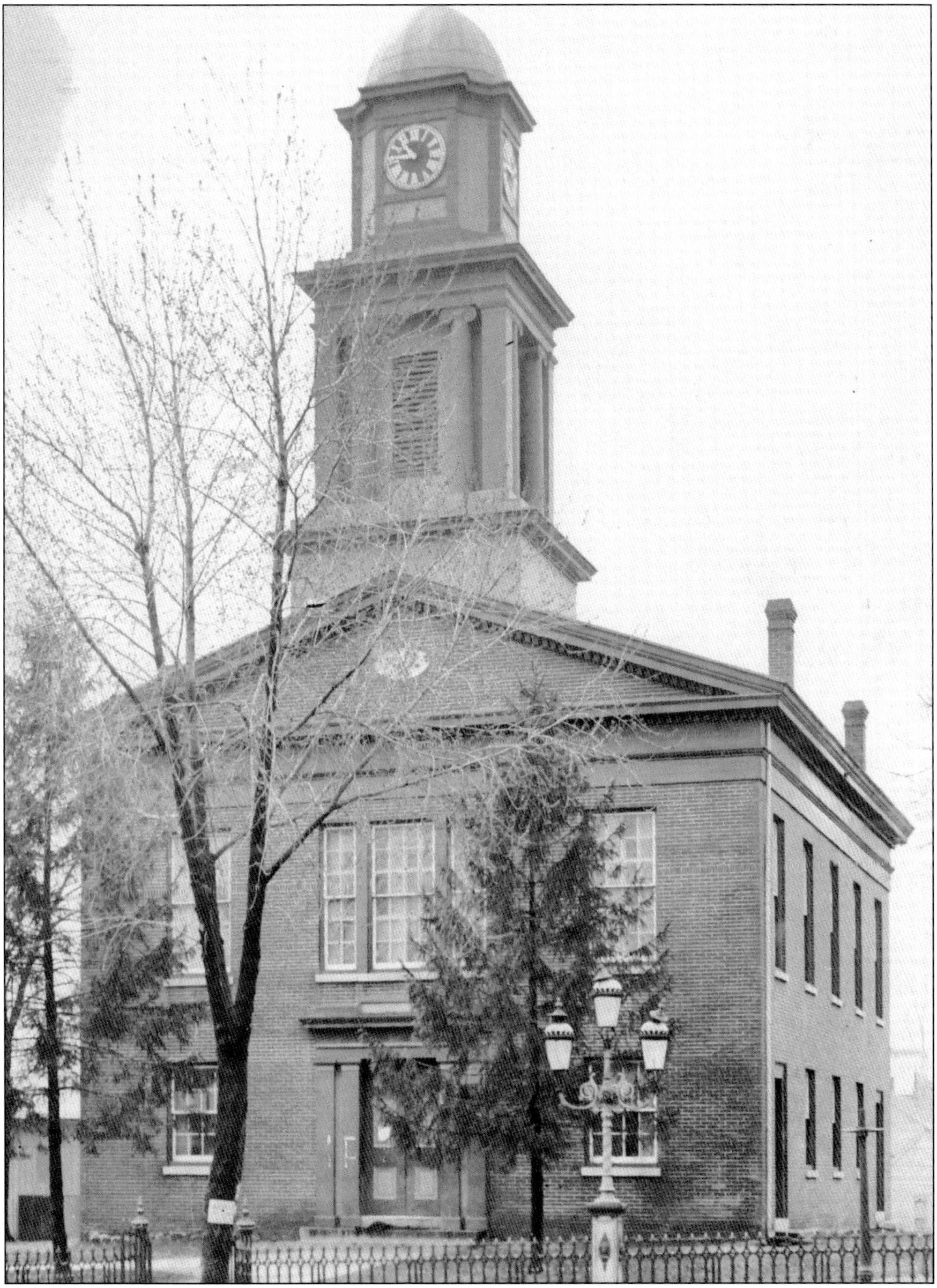

THE 1844 CUMBERLAND COUNTY COURTHOUSE, BROAD AND FAYETTE STREETS. Shortly after the courthouse was originally erected, the citizens of Bridgeton banded together to raise funds for a clock to be placed in its tower. The timepiece was built about 1846 by Lukens and Thompson of Norristown, Pennsylvania, whose senior member, Lukens, earlier had constructed another clock for Philadelphia's Independence Hall. When the new courthouse was erected in 1909, the timepiece was refurbished and installed in the new tower.

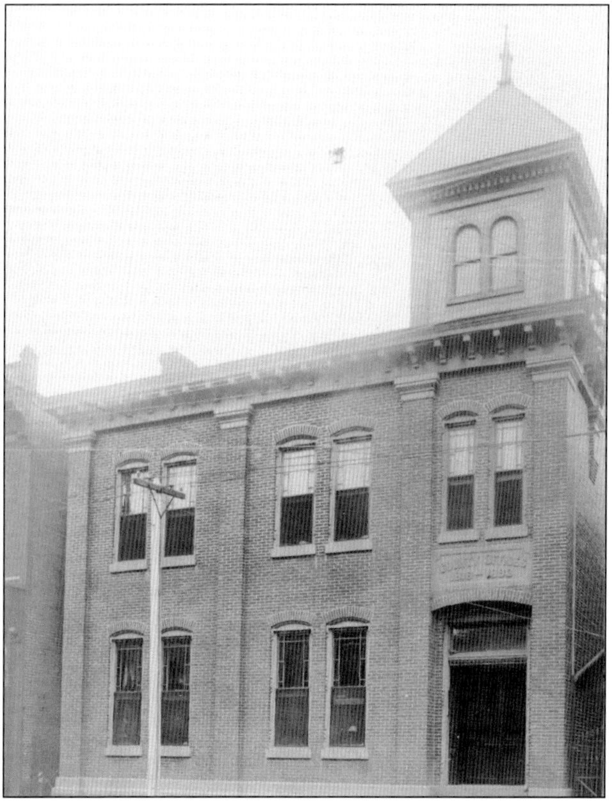

CUMBERLAND COUNTY OFFICES, 1890. Located on the south side of East Commerce Street between Laurel and Pearl Streets, this structure housed the offices of the county clerk on the first floor and the county surrogate on the upper level. The building survives and is in commercial use.

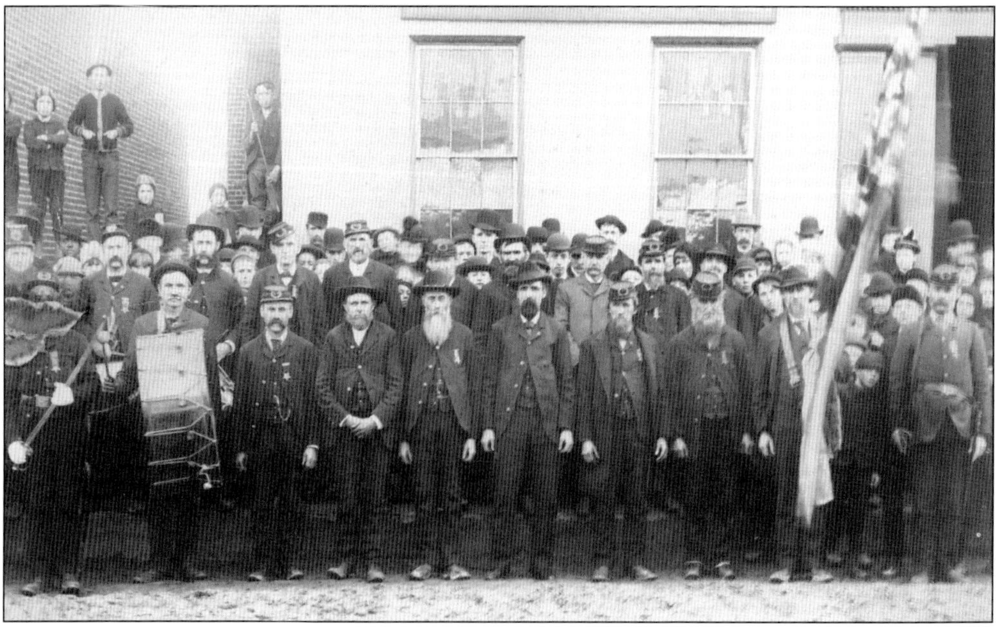

THE OLD COUNTY OFFICE BUILDING. Members of the Grand Army of the Republic Civil War veterans organization gather for a group portrait by the photographic team of Keller & Fleetwood in front of the 1816 county building at 78–80–82 East Commerce Street, probably in the 1880s.

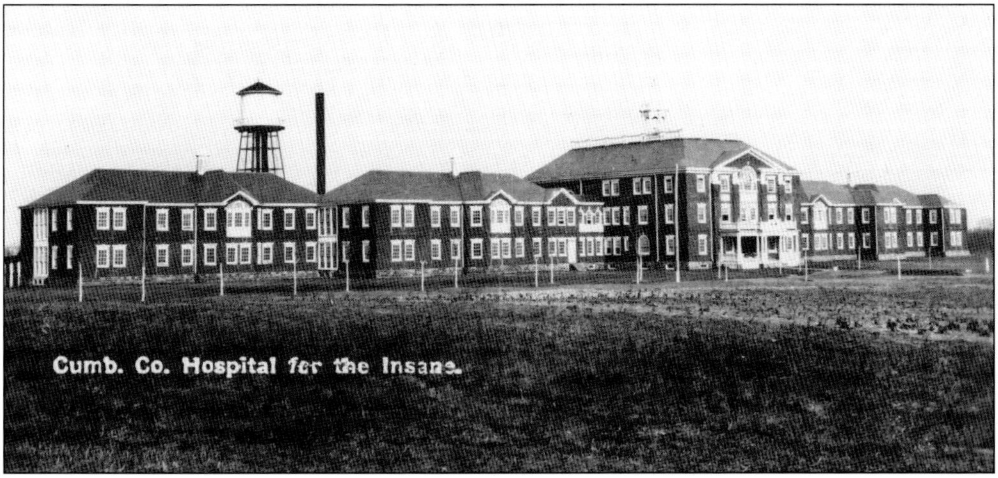

THE CUMBERLAND COUNTY HOSPITAL FOR THE INSANE. Erected in 1899 and 1900 on Cumberland Drive in Hopewell Township, this Neoclassical structure, later known as the county hospital, was designed to house those diagnosed with mental illnesses. It closed in 1982, and burned ten years later.

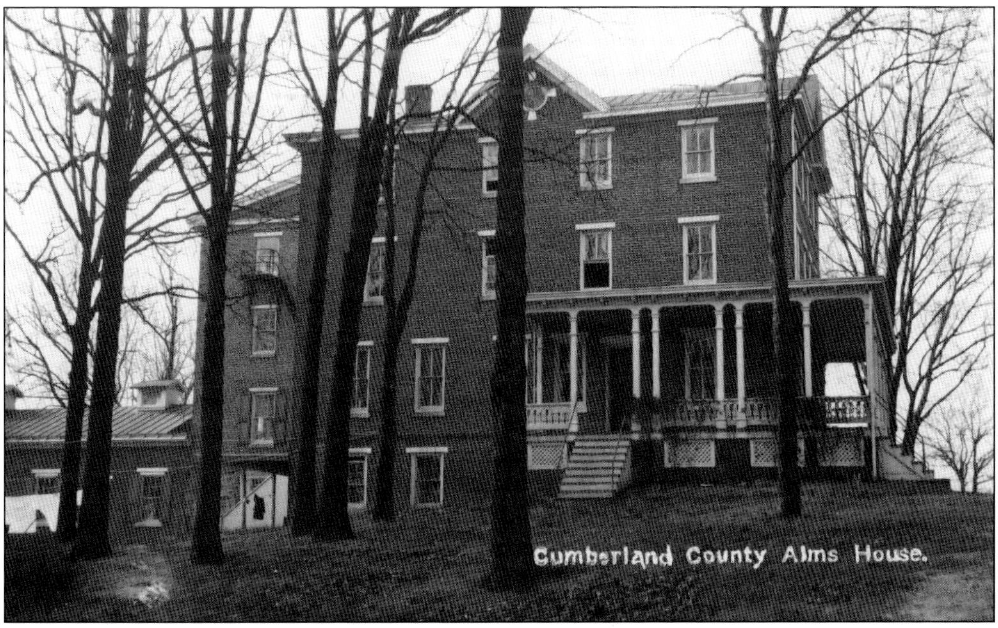

"YOU'LL DRIVE US TO THE POOR HOUSE." That's the refrain frequently heard by spendthrift children from their parents. There actually was a poor house, erected in 1851 as the Cumberland County Alms House, opposite the county hospital complex in Hopewell Township.

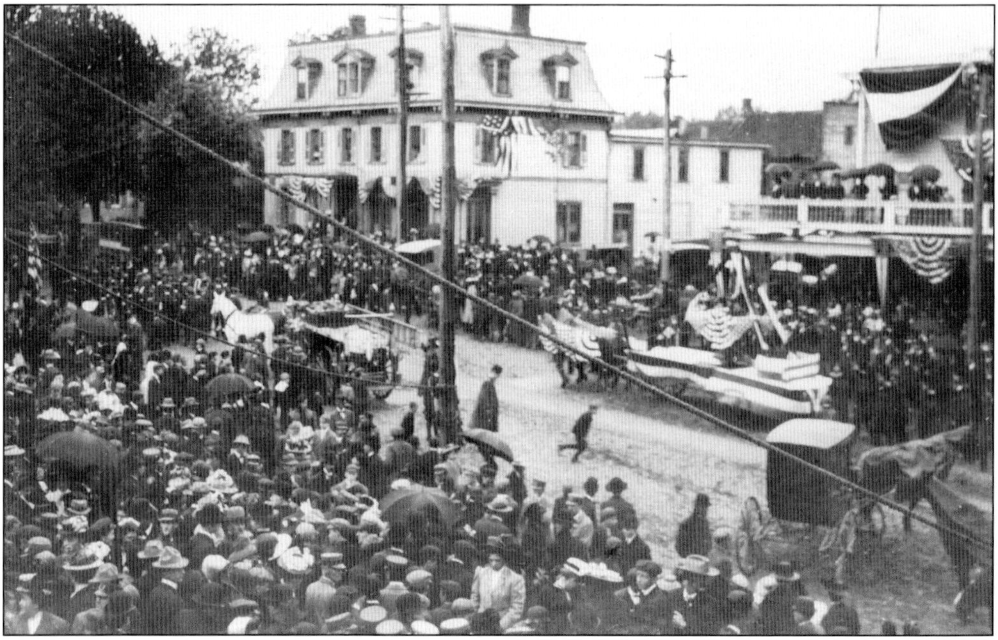

BEGINNING THE NEW COURTHOUSE. A huge crowd gathers on Bridgeton's Broad Street hill to see the cornerstone for the new Cumberland County Courthouse delivered in 1909. In the background at Franklin Street is the flag-bedecked Colonel David Potter House, now gone.

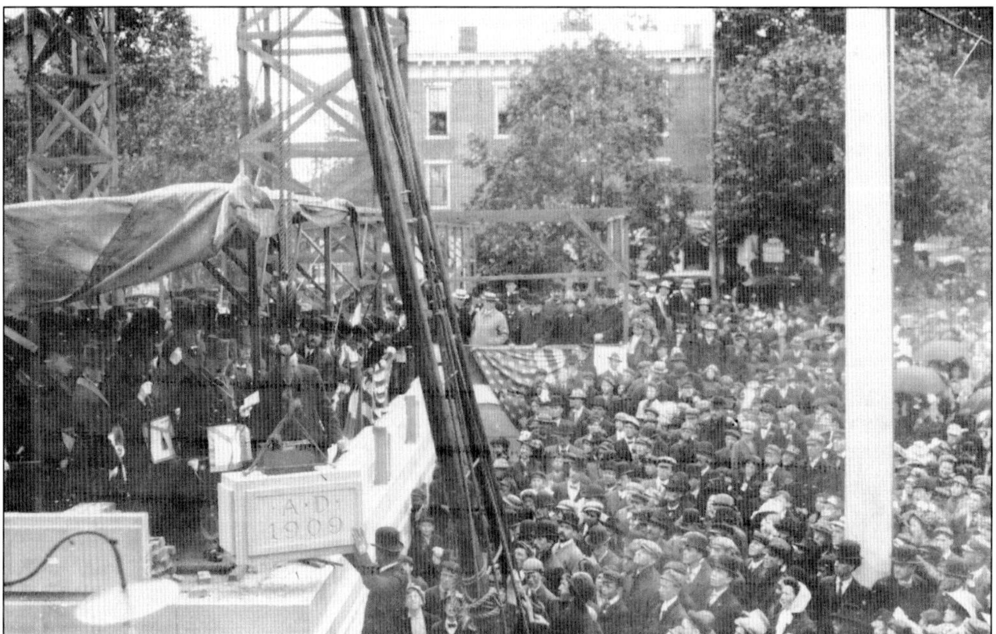

LAYING THE CORNERSTONE. At Broad and Fayette Streets, dignitaries attired in top hats and bowlers assist in swinging the "A.D. 1909" cornerstone into position in this photograph from the Pedrick collection. Soon the new Cumberland County Courthouse would rise.

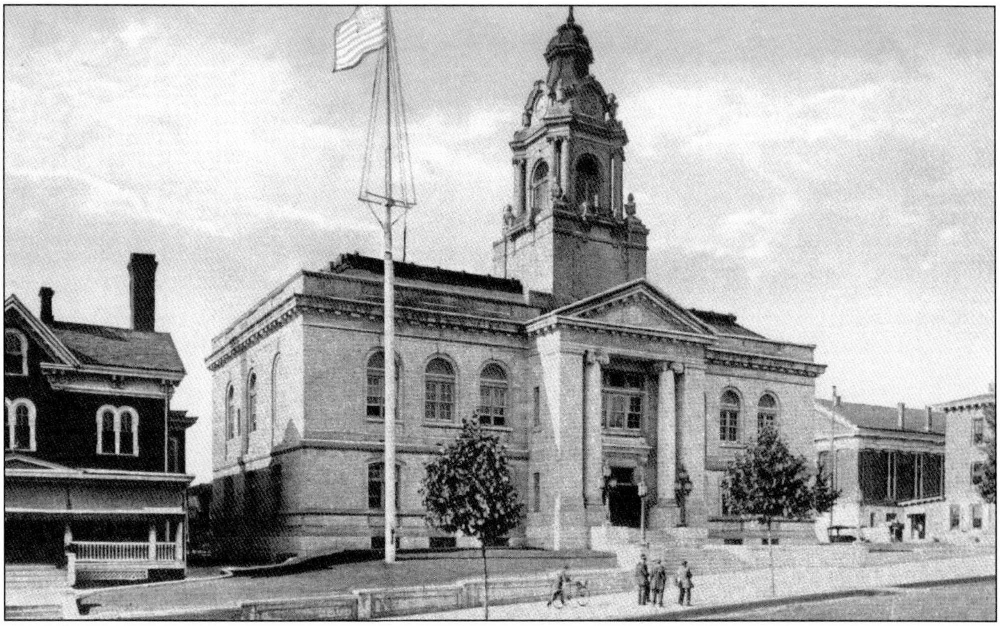

THE 1909 CUMBERLAND COUNTY COURTHOUSE. Although the present courthouse takes its name from "MCMIX," the Roman numeral inscribed over its main entrance, the structure actually did not open until November 1910. It was designed by the firm of Watson & Huckle and built by Harry H. Hankins.

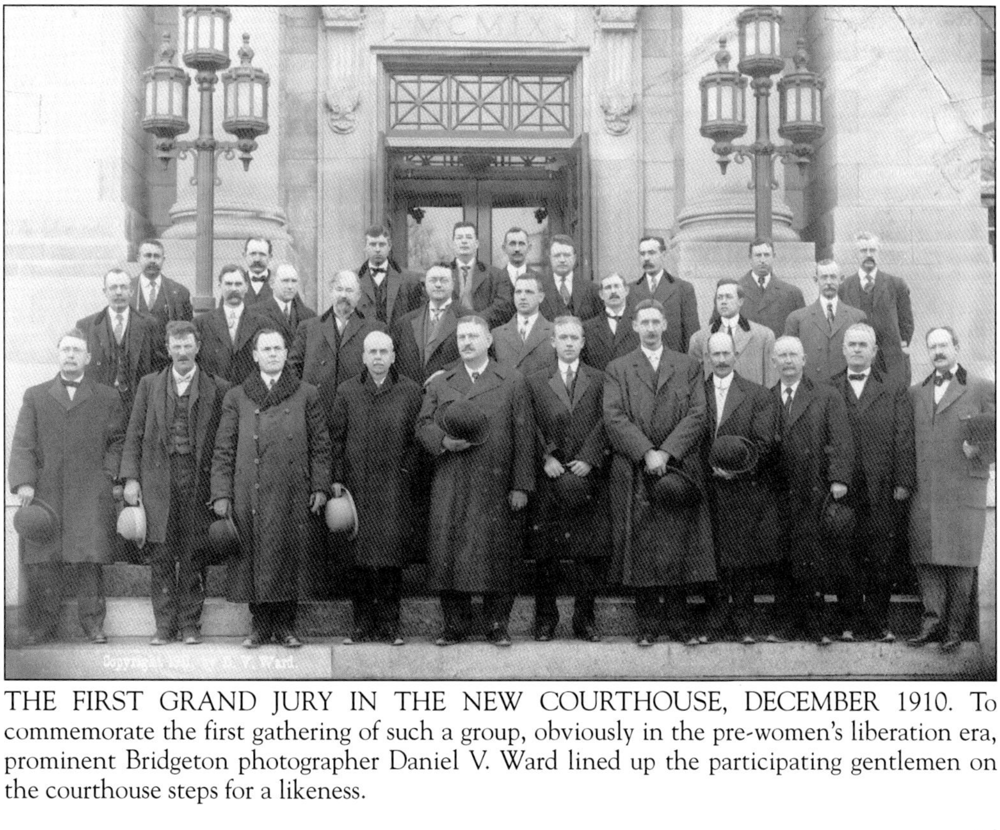

THE FIRST GRAND JURY IN THE NEW COURTHOUSE, DECEMBER 1910. To commemorate the first gathering of such a group, obviously in the pre-women's liberation era, prominent Bridgeton photographer Daniel V. Ward lined up the participating gentlemen on the courthouse steps for a likeness.

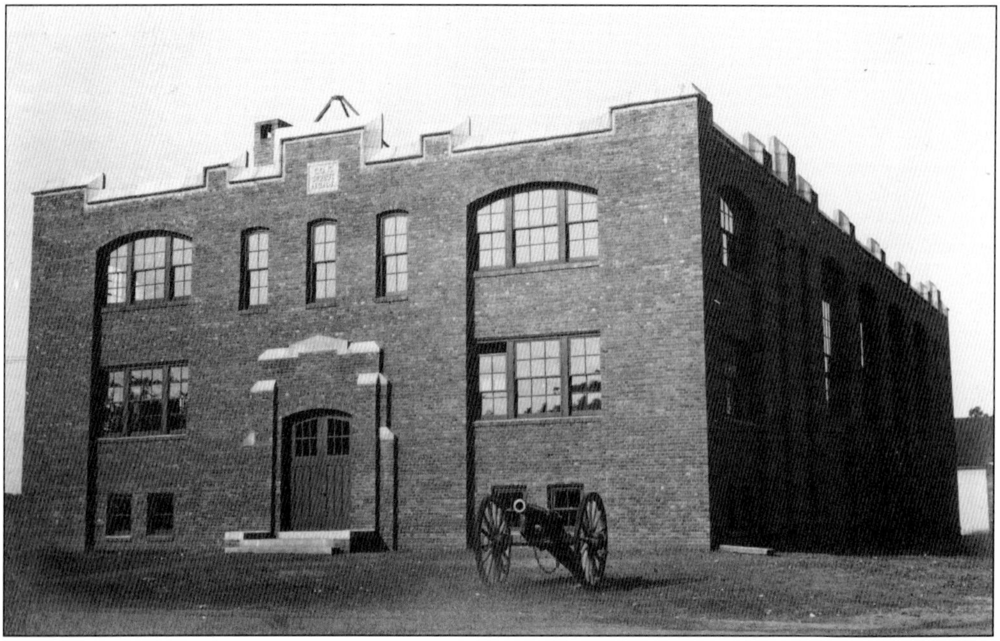

COMPANY K, 3RD REGIMENT ARMORY. Completed in 1914, this structure on Washington Street served as the base for the local unit of the New Jersey National Guard. It is also where many troops departed for World War I and, a quarter-century later, for World War II.

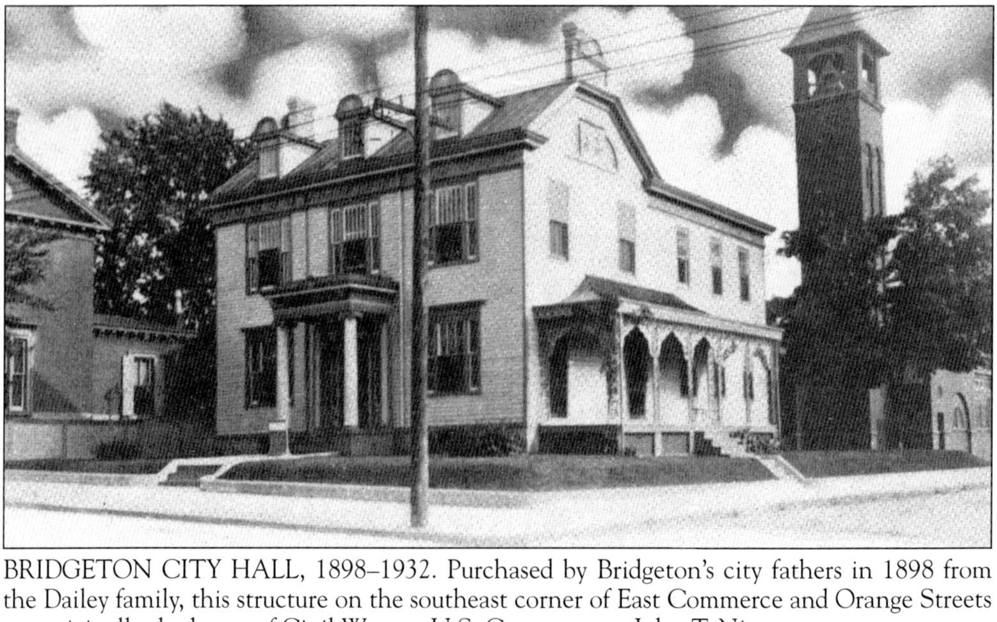

BRIDGETON CITY HALL, 1898–1932. Purchased by Bridgeton's city fathers in 1898 from the Dailey family, this structure on the southeast corner of East Commerce and Orange Streets was originally the home of Civil War-era U.S. Congressman John T. Nixon.

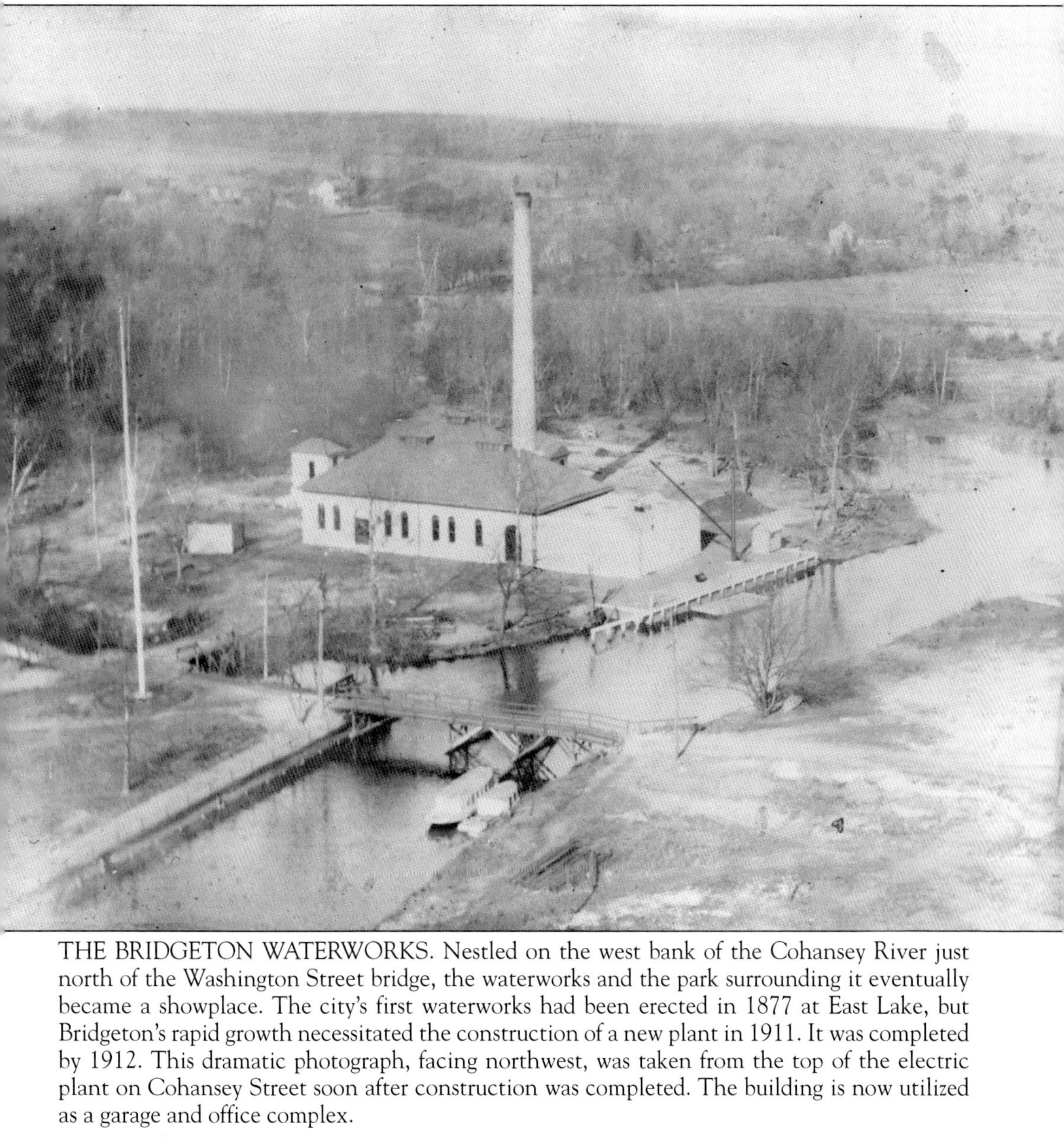

THE BRIDGETON WATERWORKS. Nestled on the west bank of the Cohansey River just north of the Washington Street bridge, the waterworks and the park surrounding it eventually became a showplace. The city's first waterworks had been erected in 1877 at East Lake, but Bridgeton's rapid growth necessitated the construction of a new plant in 1911. It was completed by 1912. This dramatic photograph, facing northwest, was taken from the top of the electric plant on Cohansey Street soon after construction was completed. The building is now utilized as a garage and office complex.

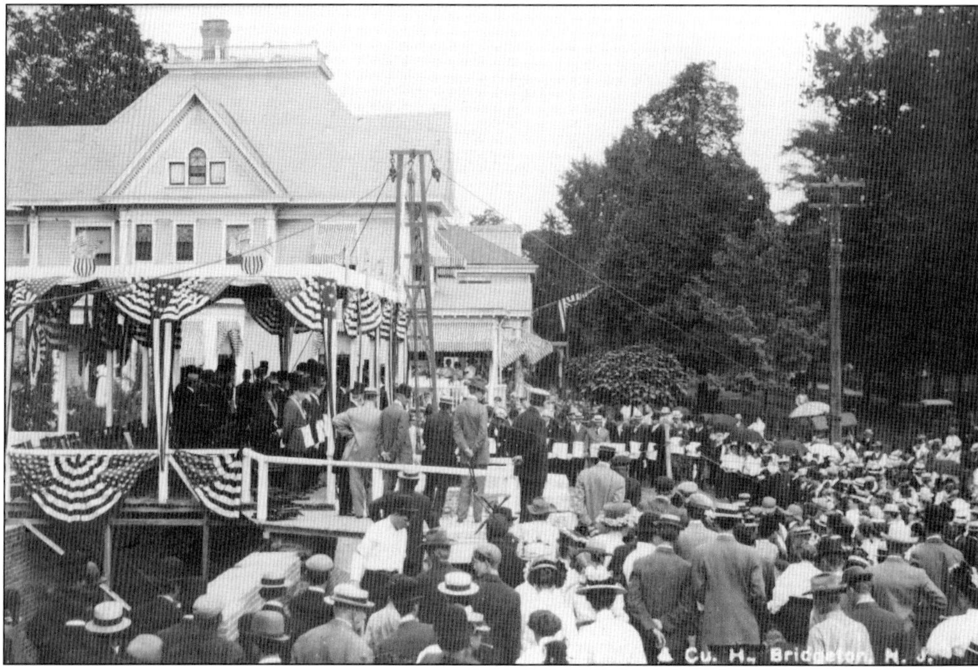

THE LAYING OF THE FEDERAL BUILDING CORNERSTONE. A large crowd assembles at the corner of East Commerce and Bank Streets to see the cornerstone laying for the new federal building in September 1909. Excavation of the foundation was carried out with horses pulling scoops.

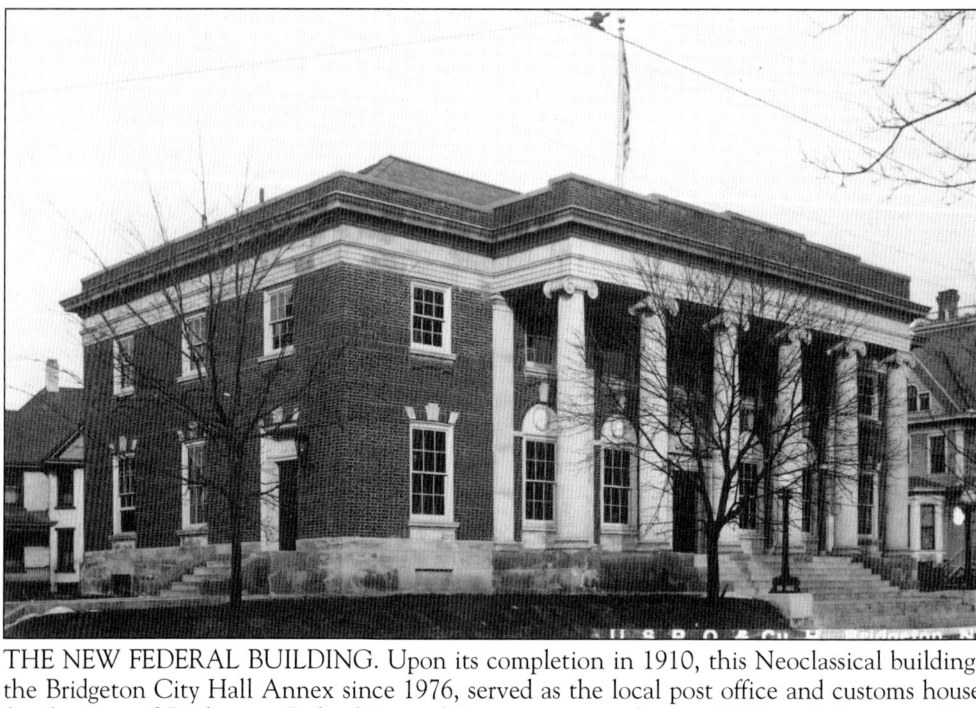

THE NEW FEDERAL BUILDING. Upon its completion in 1910, this Neoclassical building, the Bridgeton City Hall Annex since 1976, served as the local post office and customs house for the Port of Bridgeton. Federal Port of Entry status was lost in 1913, and the post office abandoned the site in 1970.

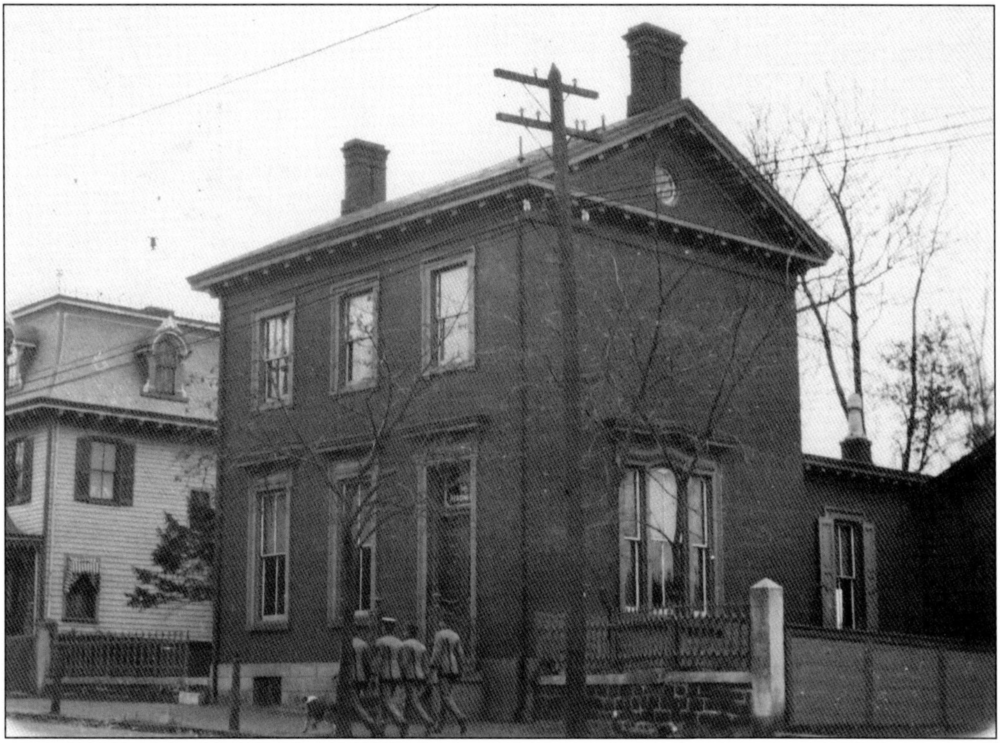

THE BRIDGETON FREE PUBLIC LIBRARY. Built in 1816 at East Commerce and Bank Streets as the original home of the Cumberland National Bank (the first bank in New Jersey south of Camden), this building began a new life in 1901 as what was then called the Bridgeton Library Association.

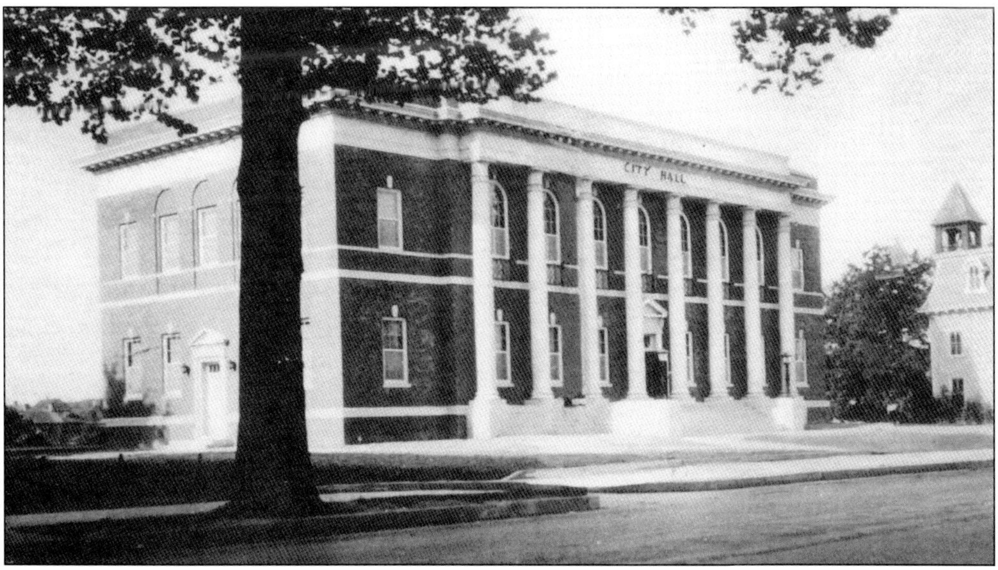

BRIDGETON CITY HALL, 1932. It had become evident that city hall had outgrown the capacity of its original structure several doors west on East Commerce Street, and the City of Bridgeton erected this building during the administration of Mayor Linwood W. Erickson, despite the fact that the city and the country were in the midst of the Great Depression.

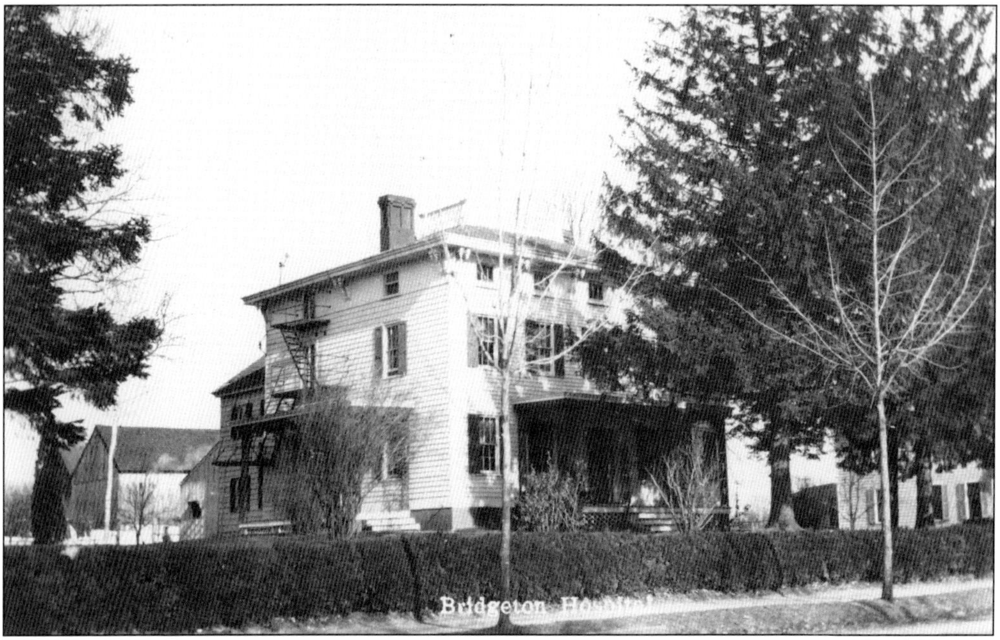

BRIDGETON HOSPITAL, 1899. Thanks to the original efforts of a group of local women, the doors to this structure, formally a private home on Irving Avenue, opened for the hospital's first patient in July 1899. Moved later to a nearby site, it was demolished in 1972.

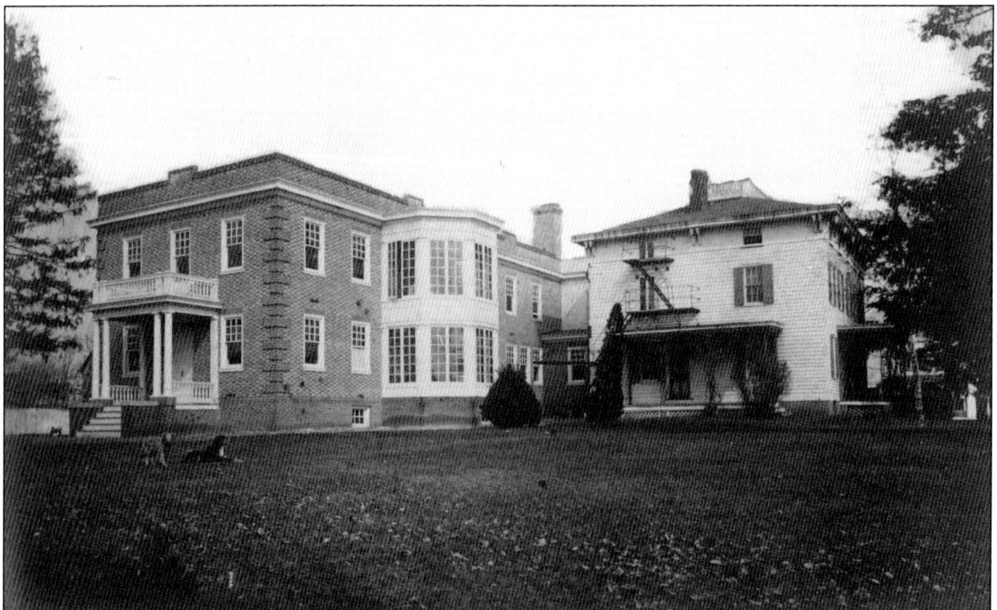

THE NEW HOSPITAL ANNEX, 1910. As a result of rapid growth, the hospital association erected a brick annex facing Magnolia Avenue in 1910. It featured a beautiful solarium, which enabled patients to sun themselves even during winter months.

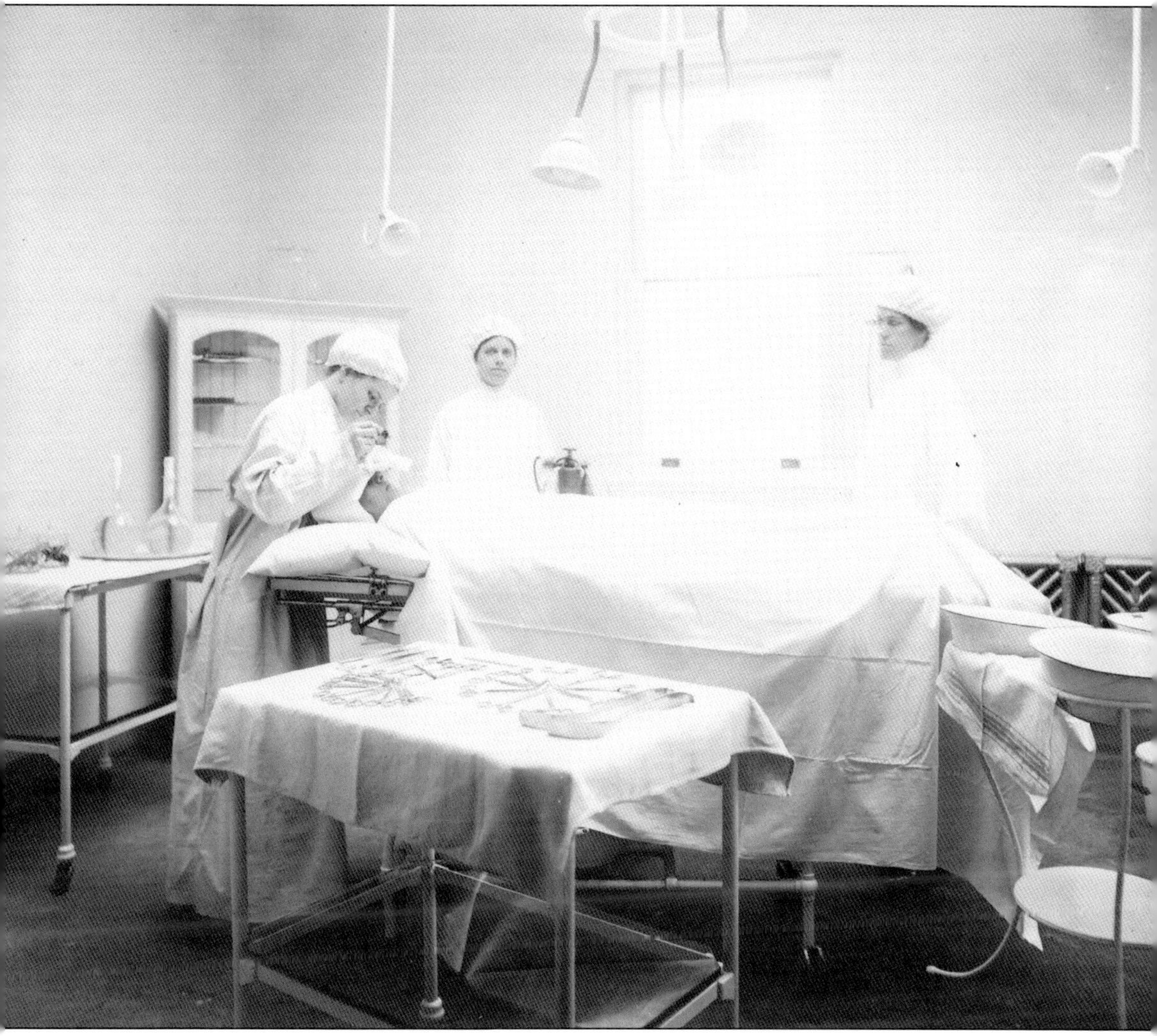

CUTTING-EDGE TECHNOLOGY. A group of nurses prepares a patient for an operation by administering drops of ether around the time of World War I. On the table can be seen an assortment of surgical tools, while overhead are state-of-the-art lighting fixtures. The doctor, perhaps delayed by a house call, has not arrived yet. In the hospital's earliest days a rule stated, "All convalescent free patients, who are able and not particularly exempted from such duty . . . shall assist the nurses in their respective wards when directed to do so . . ."

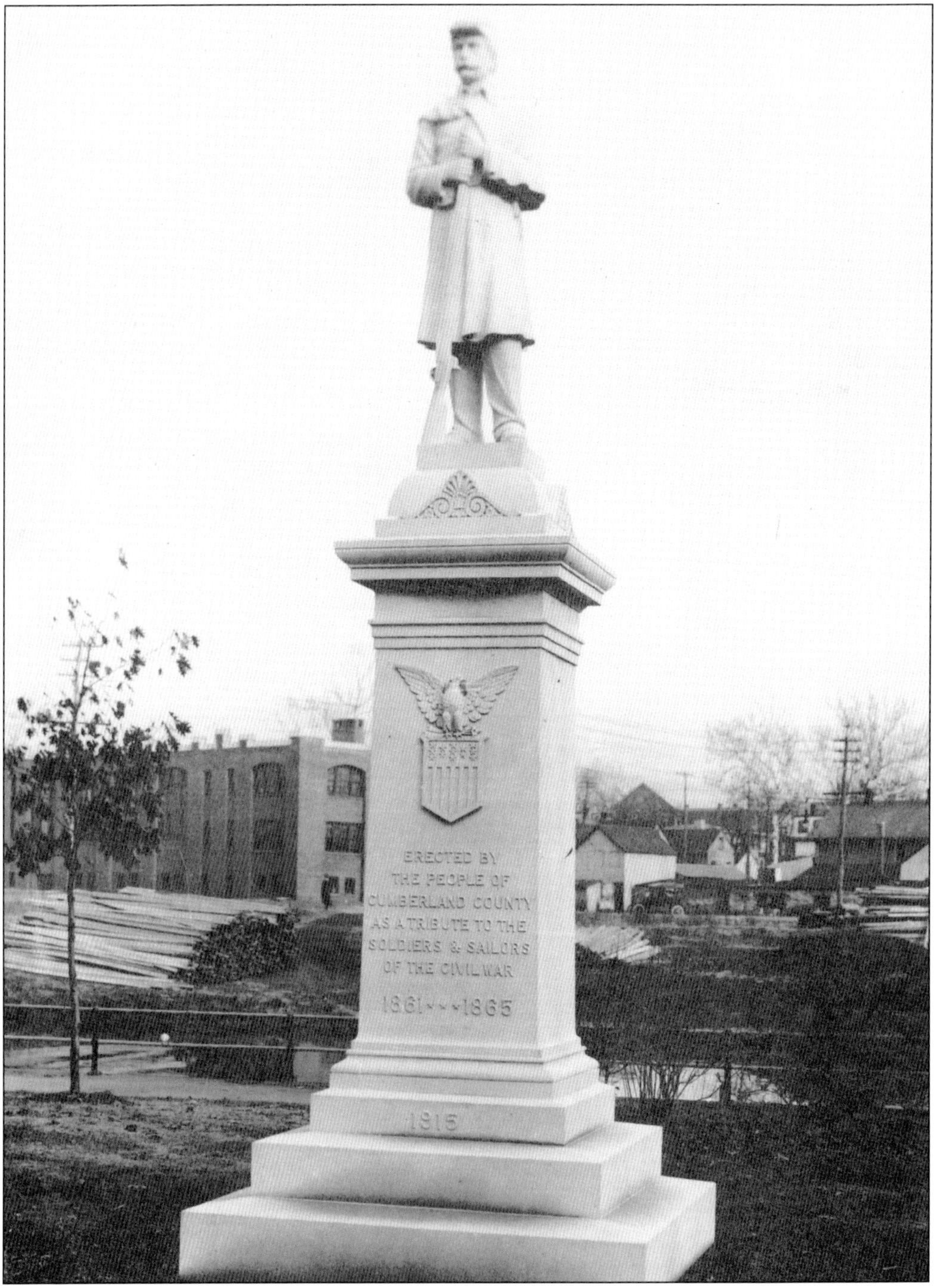

A CIVIL WAR BREAKS OUT AGAIN. When the city fathers decided to place this statue in the Morningside section of the Bridgeton City Park in 1915, surviving veterans of the Civil War objected. They wanted it to be placed adjacent to the Cumberland County Courthouse, in a more prominent location, but their demands fell on deaf ears. In the background, on the opposite side of the Cohansey River, can be seen the armory building. Decades later, the statue was moved to the waterworks section of the park where it remains today.

Two

Takin' Care of Business

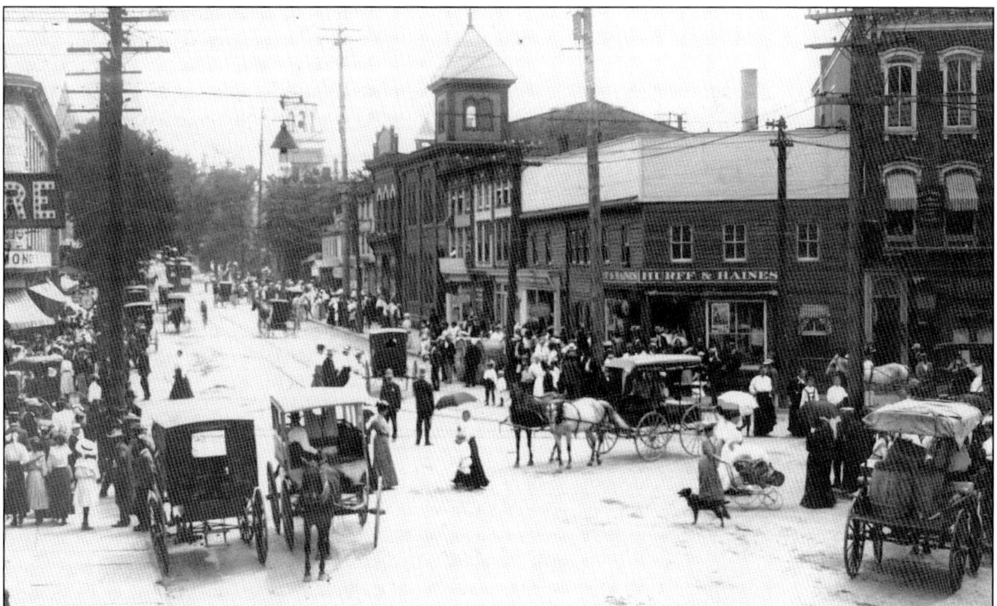

THE BUSINESS OF BRIDGETON IS BUSINESS. The intersection of Laurel and Commerce Streets is thronged with pedestrians and horse-drawn vehicles in this 1908 scene from the Pedrick collection. The 1890 county office building cupola dominates the diminutive skyline.

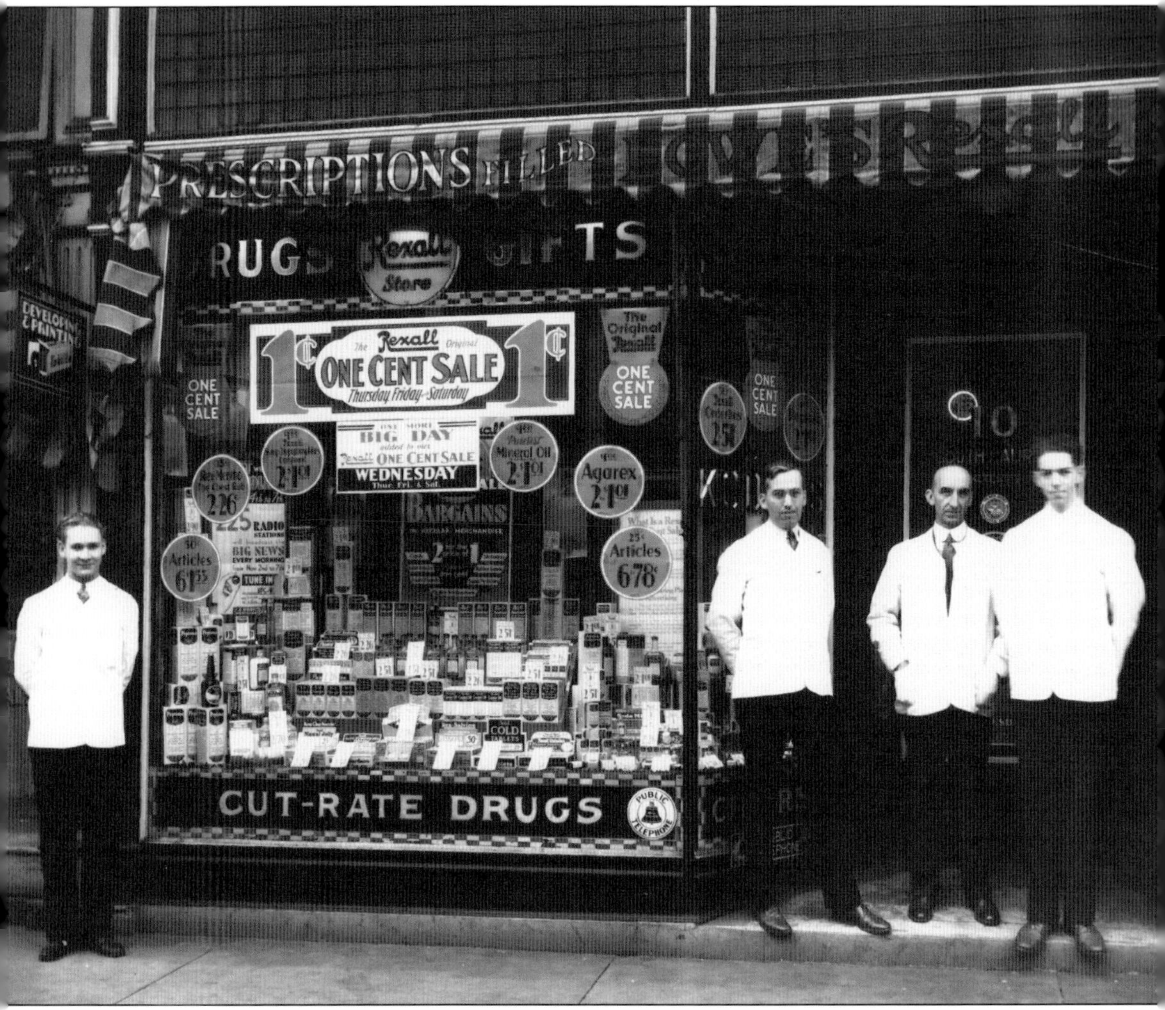

LOWE'S REXALL DRUGS, 10 SOUTH LAUREL STREET. In November 1931, photographer J.T. Roberts captured the exterior of a typical Depression-era drugstore that was doing its best to survive difficult times. From left to right are: soda jerk Joe Dailey, owner-pharmacist Clement W. Lowe, pharmacist Eugene Morton, and soda jerk Ralph Phillips (who later became a physician). In 1935, the business moved to the opposite side of the street. Note that the store advertised a public telephone, an important fixture in an era when many homes still lacked such luxuries.

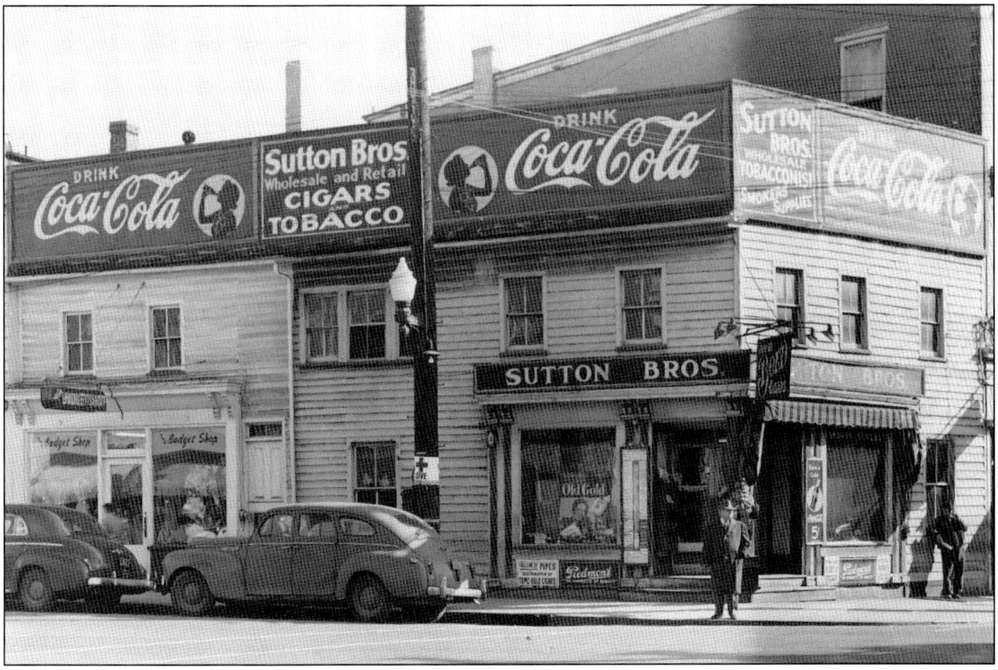

THE CORNER CIGAR STORE. Since before the Civil War, the southeast corner of Commerce and Laurel Streets had been the site of a cigar store, complete with Pompey, the store's mascot. By the 1940s the enterprise was owned by Sutton Brothers, as revealed in this photograph by Gene Wallace.

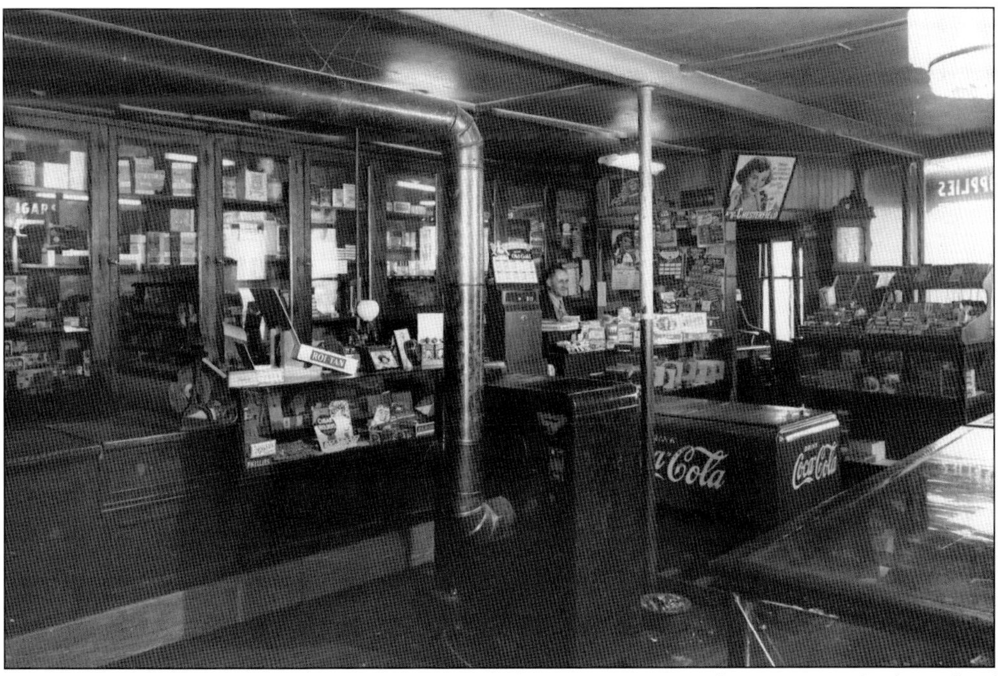

NO PLACE TO KICK THE HABIT. In 1943 the Surgeon General's report on the hazards of smoking was still several decades in the future and Americans freely indulged themselves with all sorts of tobacco products. The interior of Sutton Brothers indicates the brands for sale then.

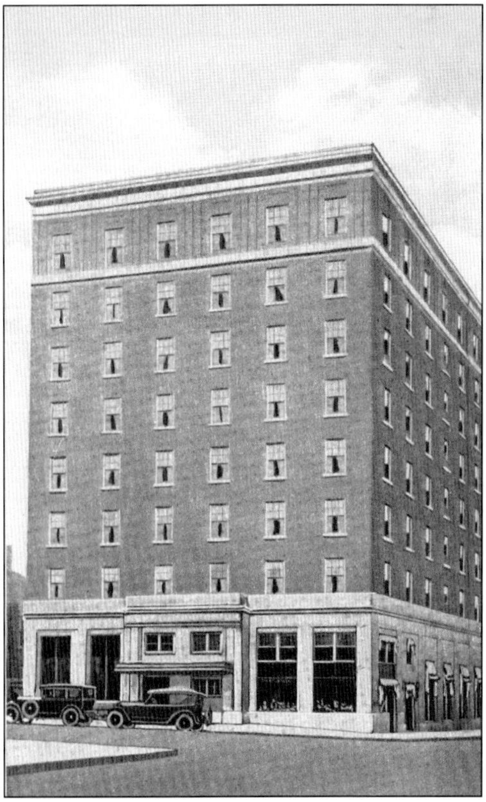

"MEET ME AT THE CUMBERLAND." That was a familiar phrase in Bridgeton after the Cumberland Hotel opened on the southeast corner of Commerce and Pearl Streets in 1924. The hotel was named after the British Duke of Cumberland.

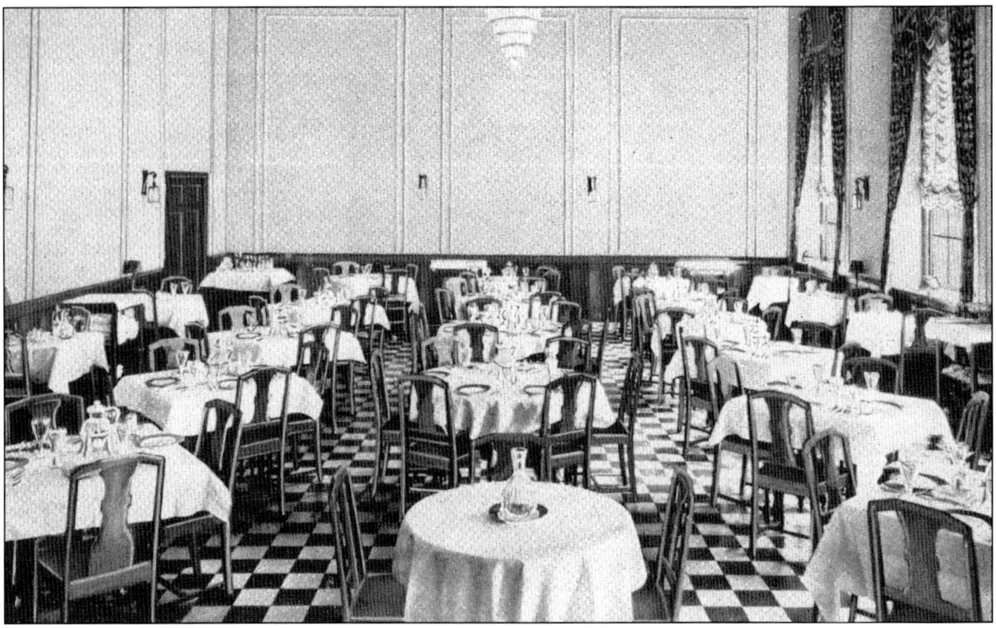

A NICE PLACE TO EAT. The main dining room of the Cumberland Hotel appeared this way during its first decades of operation. The menu featured many local products, including oysters from the nearby Delaware Bay. In later years the room was remodeled to reflect changing fashion.

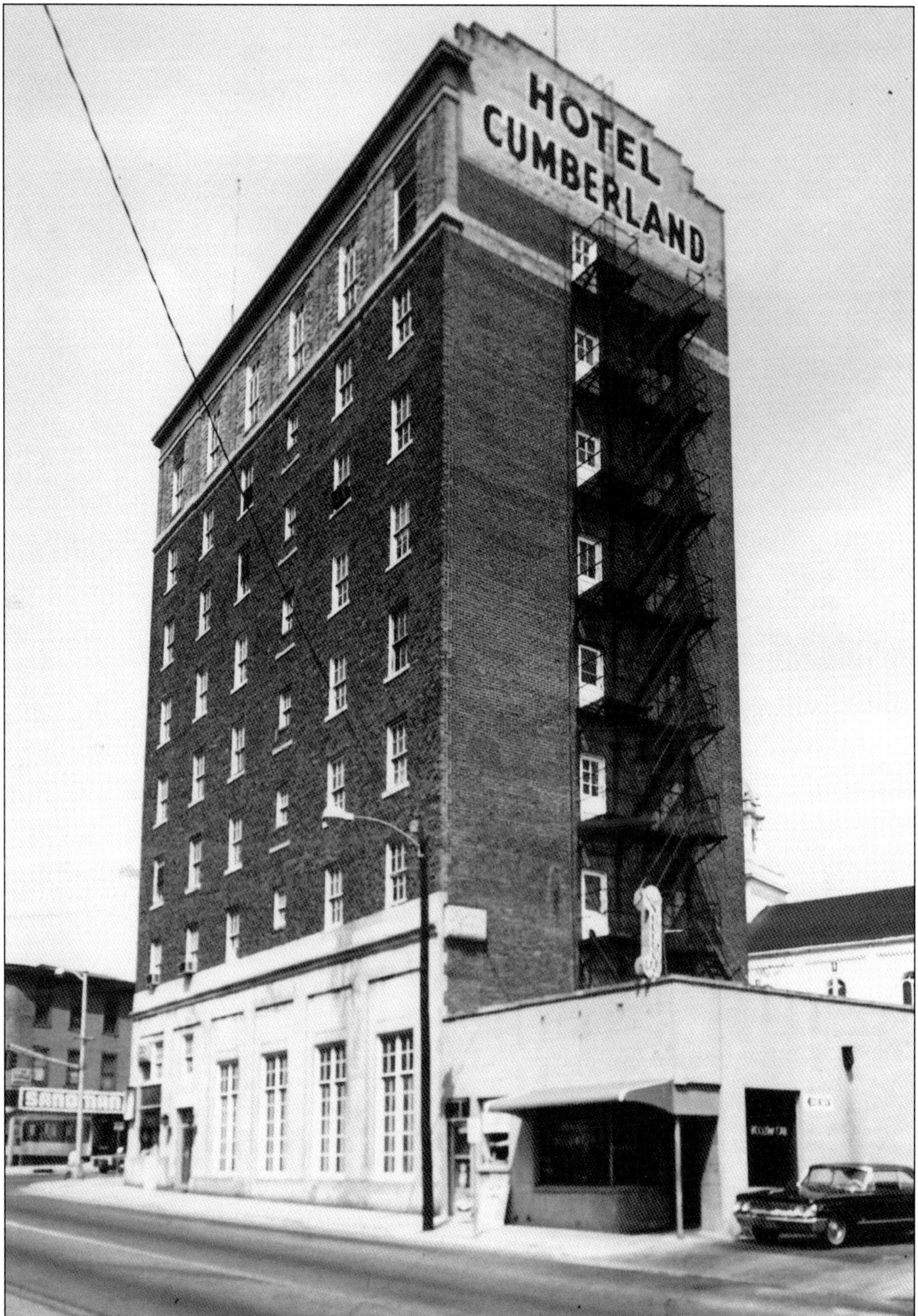

FADED GLORY. By the time the 1960s came along, the once-elegant Cumberland Hotel had become somewhat seedy. Seen here looking north along Pearl Street with a Yellow Cab stand close at hand, the hotel was only a few years away from its date with the wrecking ball in 1971.

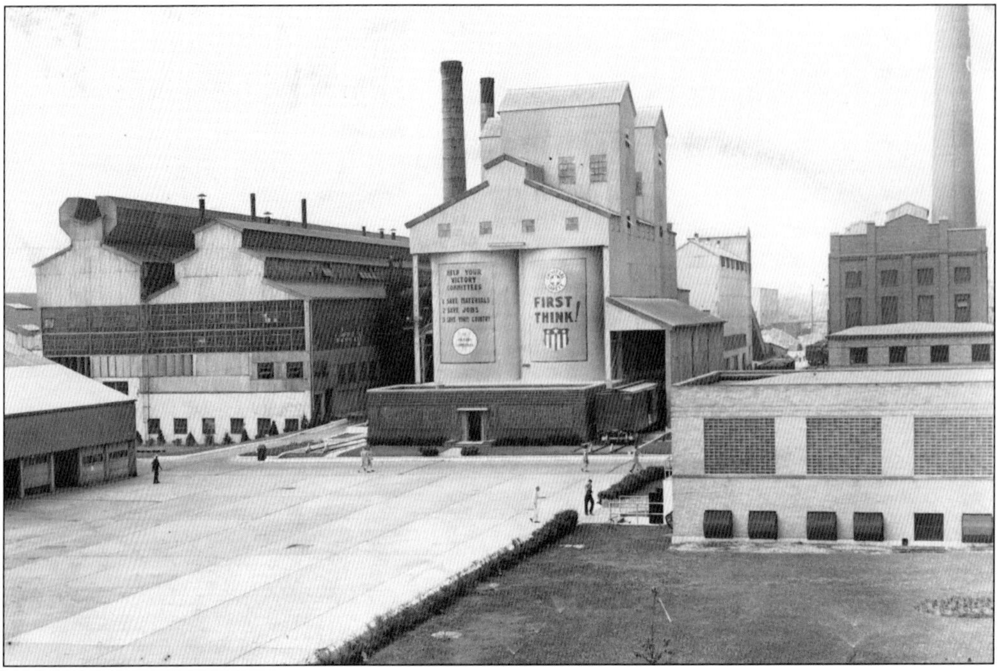

CONTRIBUTING TO THE WAR EFFORT. Once the largest glass bottle plant in America, Bridgeton's Owens-Illinois contributed to the war effort during World War II by manufacturing containers for food. A slogan on the batch house urges workers to "Save Materials, Save Jobs, Save Your Country."

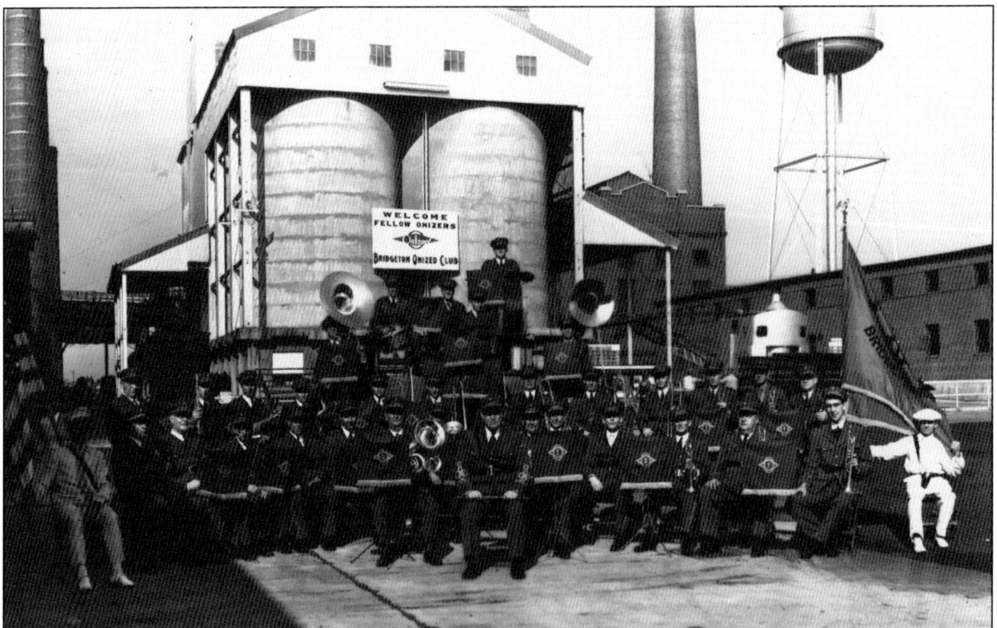

THE ONIZED CLUB BAND. Bridgeton's Owens-Illinois management was paternalistic and its club provided recreational opportunities for employees' families. In 1936, J.T. Roberts photographed the glass plant's band, which had been established four years earlier.

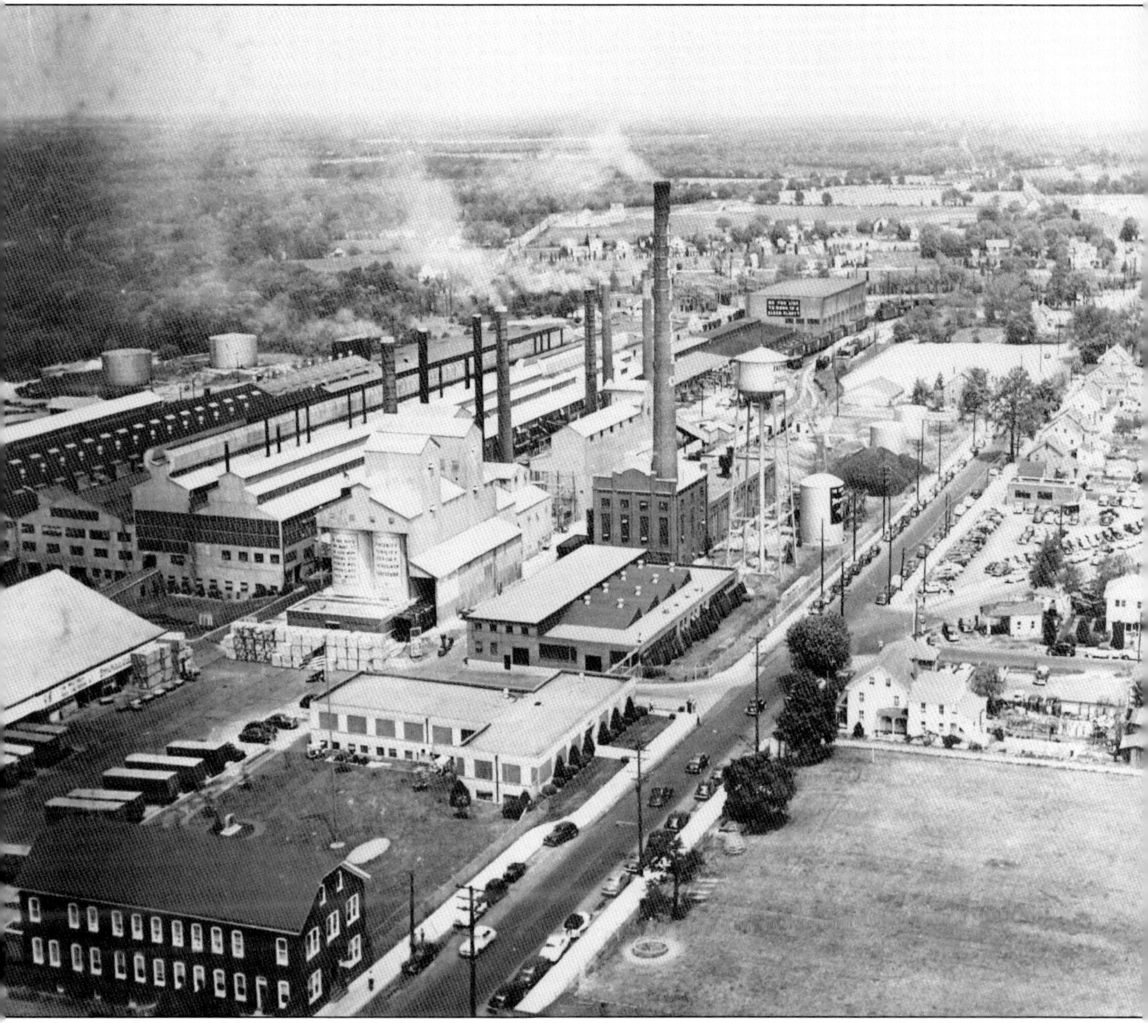

WHEN SMOKE MEANT PROSPERITY. An airplane swooped low over North Laurel Street to capture this view of the Owens-Illinois plant about 1950. In the lower left foreground is the Onized Club building, which early in the century had housed the offices of the old Cumberland Glass Works. Next to it is the plant's newer Art Deco-style office, which opened in 1936. In the right foreground is the baseball field that was donated to the people of Bridgeton by the Clark-Shoemaker family. The plant stopped manufacturing glass in 1984.

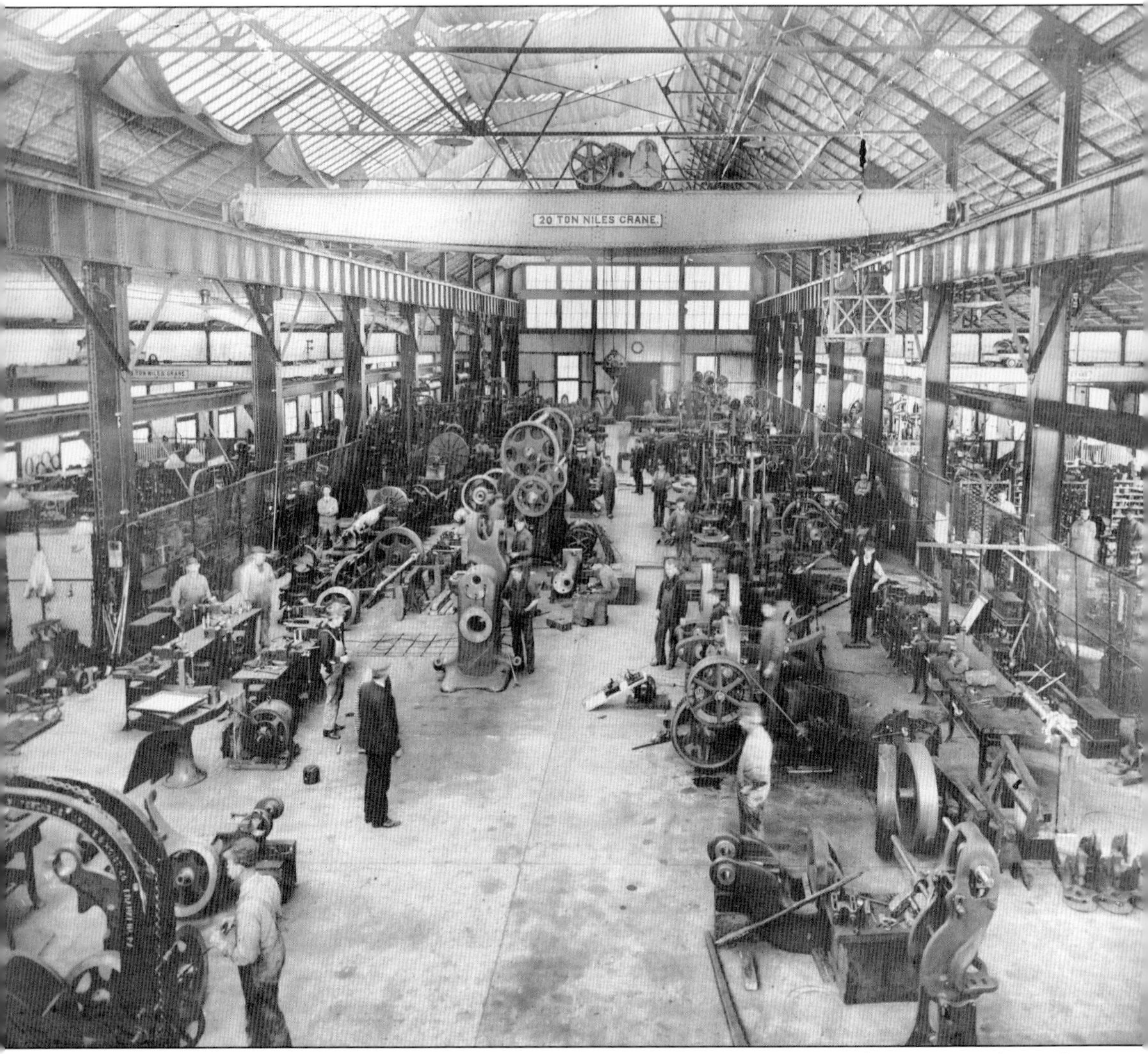

INSIDE THE FERRACUTE PLANT. Workers are as busy as bees as they swarm about the interior of the 1904 Ferracute Machine Company plant on East Commerce Street in this photograph taken when the structure was relatively new. Among the most famous products of the plant were presses used to strike coins. Until recently, one was still in operation at the United States Mint in Philadelphia. Plant owner Oberlin Smith once entertained ambitions of becoming the director of the mint. The plant ceased local operations in 1968.

BUILT TO LAST AN ETERNITY. Some of the presses produced by Ferracute were enormous, as was this one that was probably manufactured early in this century. Its macabre purpose was to stamp out metal coffins, one of which can be seen here.

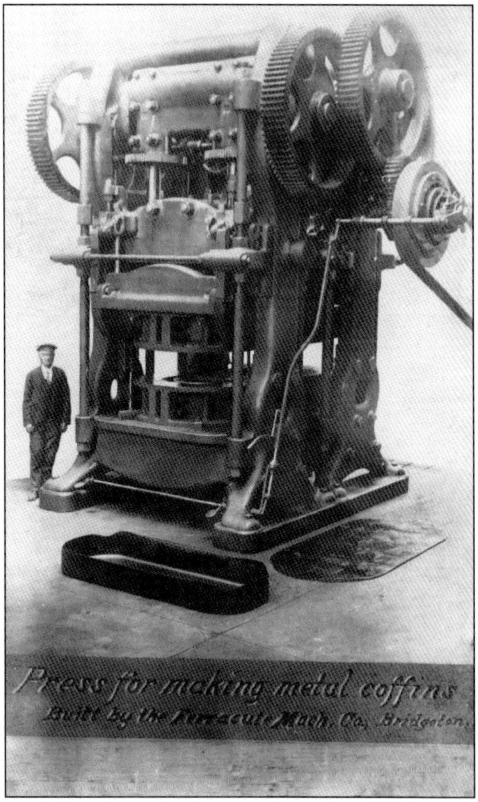

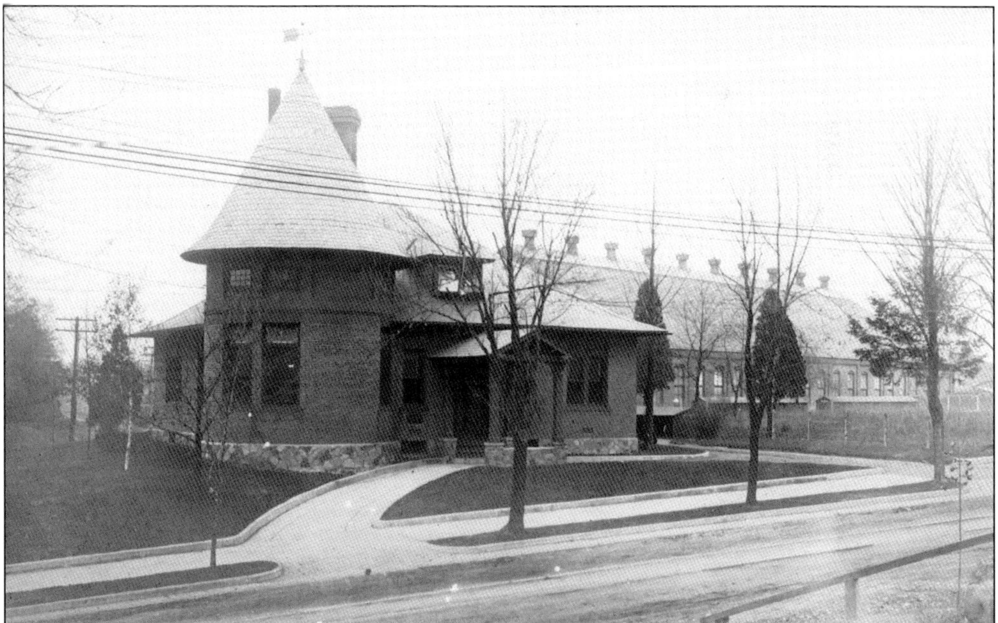

OBERLIN SMITH'S OFFICE, 1904. Among Bridgeton's most admired personalities, Ferracute owner Oberlin Smith built this Queen Anne-style office for himself on East Commerce Street as part of his new plant complex. A brilliant inventor, he was the father of magnetic recording.

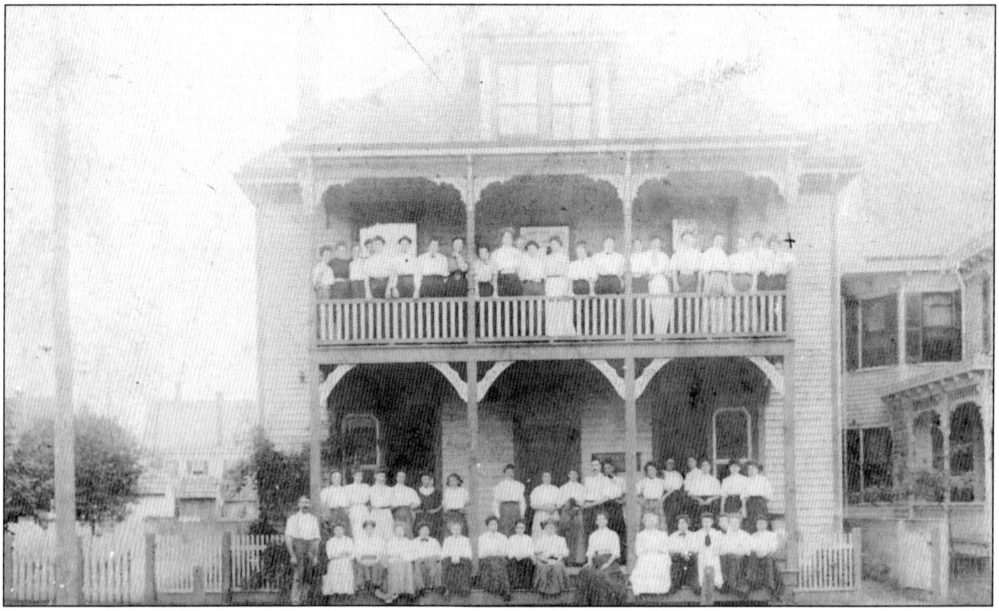

WARE'S SHIRT FACTORY, 1907. The mostly female staff of Casper G. Ware's shirt factory at 48–50 Elmer Street took a break from their labors to line up for this extremely rare photograph from the Pedrick collection. Up to sixty employees worked for the firm at one time.

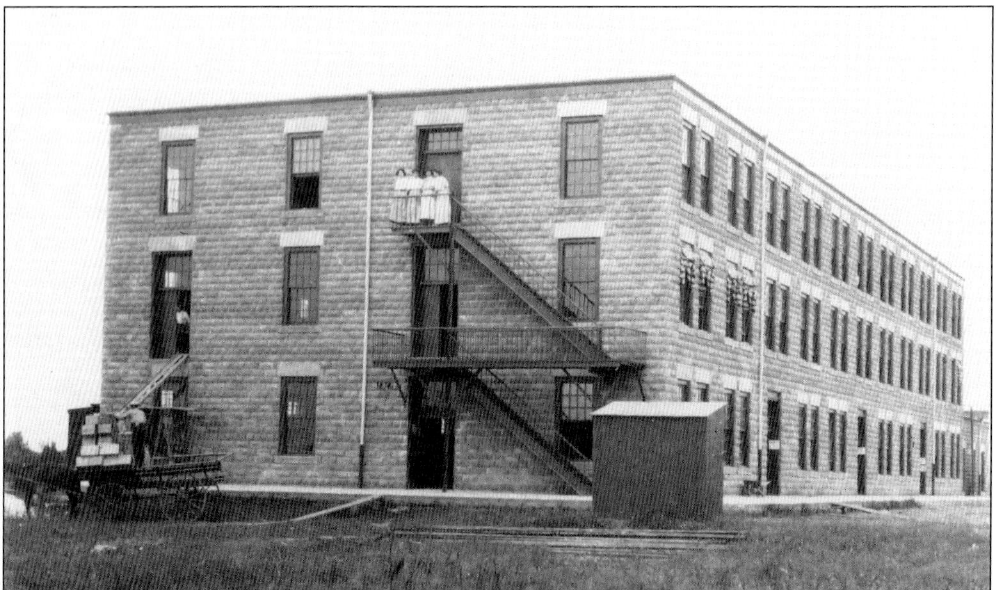

THE AMERICAN CAN COMPANY. Constructed just after the turn of the century, this plant, located near the intersection of North Bank and Penn Streets, produced state-of-the-art tin cans for Bridgeton's important food processing industry. It burned in 1976.

THE CUMBERLAND NAIL AND IRON SPIKE MACHINE. Reportedly in operation between 1881 and 1899, this machine manufactured wrought-iron wharf spikes that were shipped to the far corners of America. After the plant in which it is pictured was demolished, the machine was preserved as a relic.

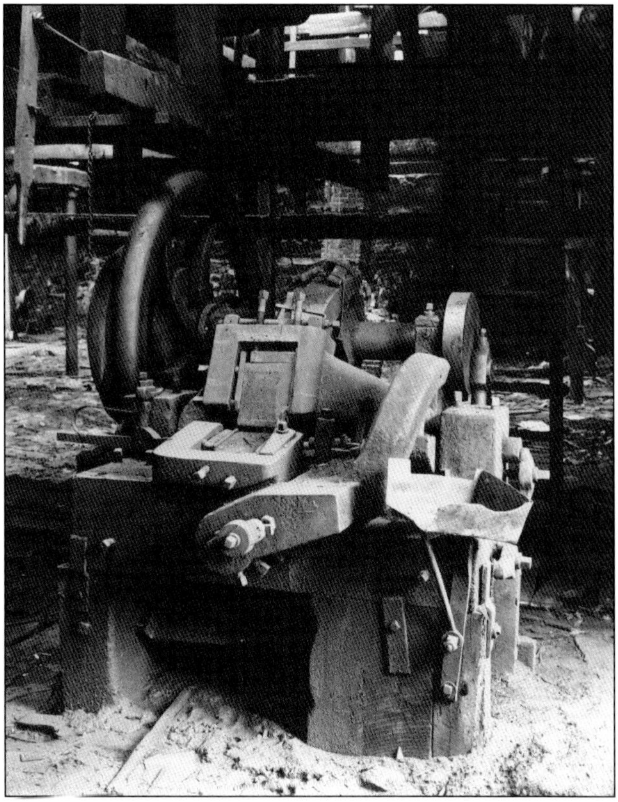

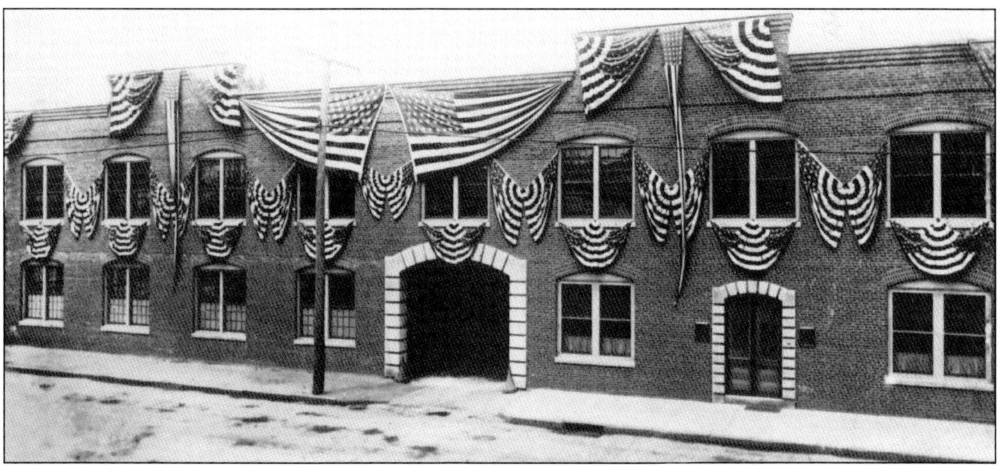

THE BRIDGETON CONDENSED MILK COMPANY, 1910. Located at 106–112 Cohansey Street, this facility produced evaporated milk marketed in small cans for consumption in homes and restaurants. The complex burned in 1992. Daniel Ward took this photograph which is now in the Pedrick collection.

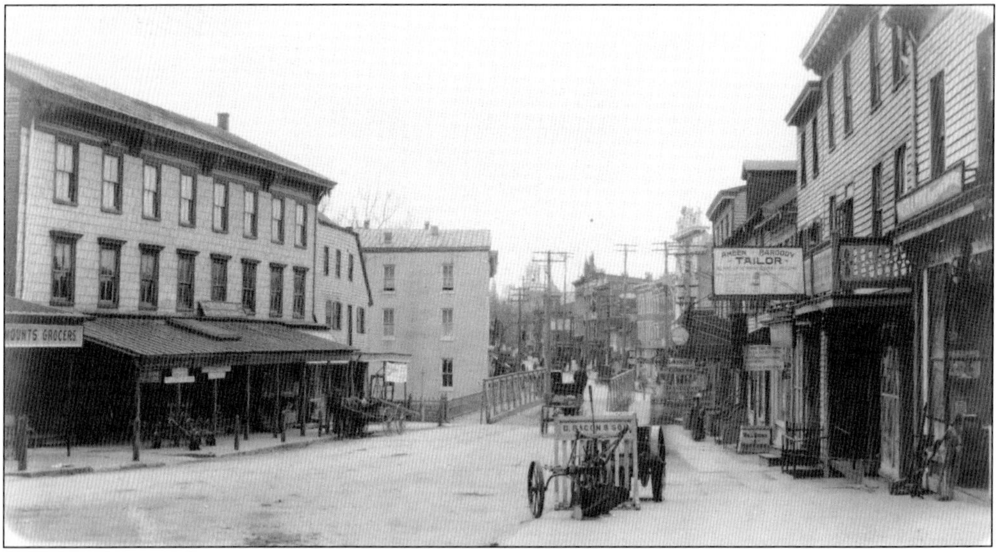

WEST COMMERCE STREET AT THE BRIDGE. At the right in this c. 1905 view are Bridgeton's famous Seven Sisters, which together comprise what is arguably the oldest commercial row in the Delaware Valley. The strip was known as Prosperity Row in the 1840s. Across the street is Civil War-era Sheppard's Hall.

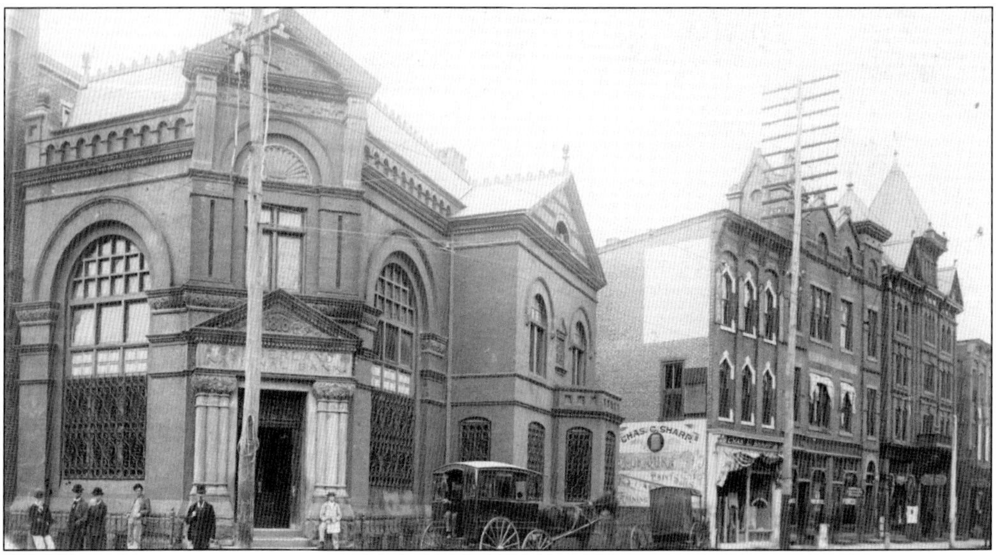

NORTH LAUREL STREET ABOVE COMMERCE STREET. Dominating the northwest corner is the Richardsonian Romanesque-style Cumberland National Bank, built in 1886. Other businesses include the Charles C. Sharp paint and wallpaper store, the post office, Pioneer Printing, and the old Hotel Cumberland.

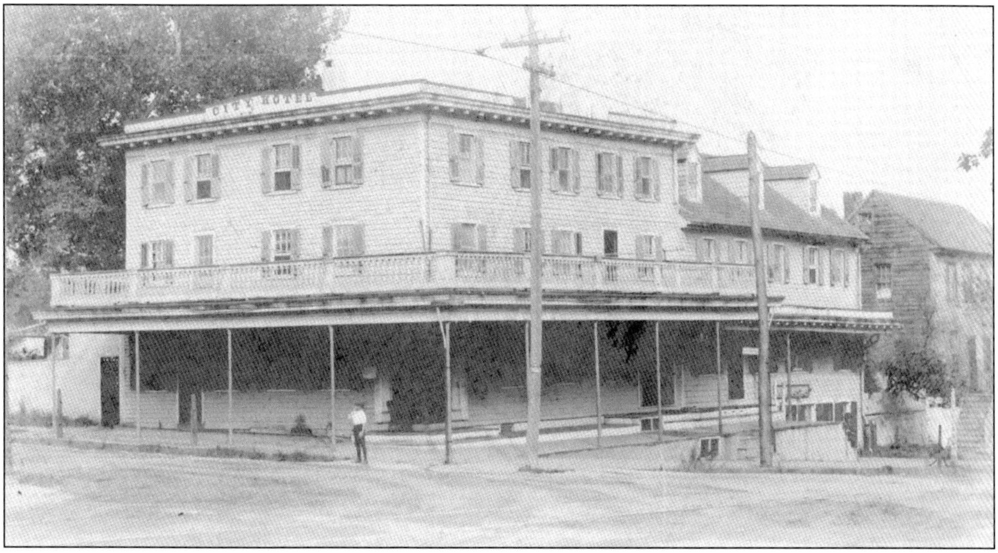

AN OLD WATERING SPOT. In 1835 this tavern opposite the courthouse on the Broad Street hill was known as the Lafayette Hotel. At that time it had been serving customers for a half-century. During Victorian times it was dubbed the City Hotel, and today it is the Hillcrest Tavern-Coach Room.

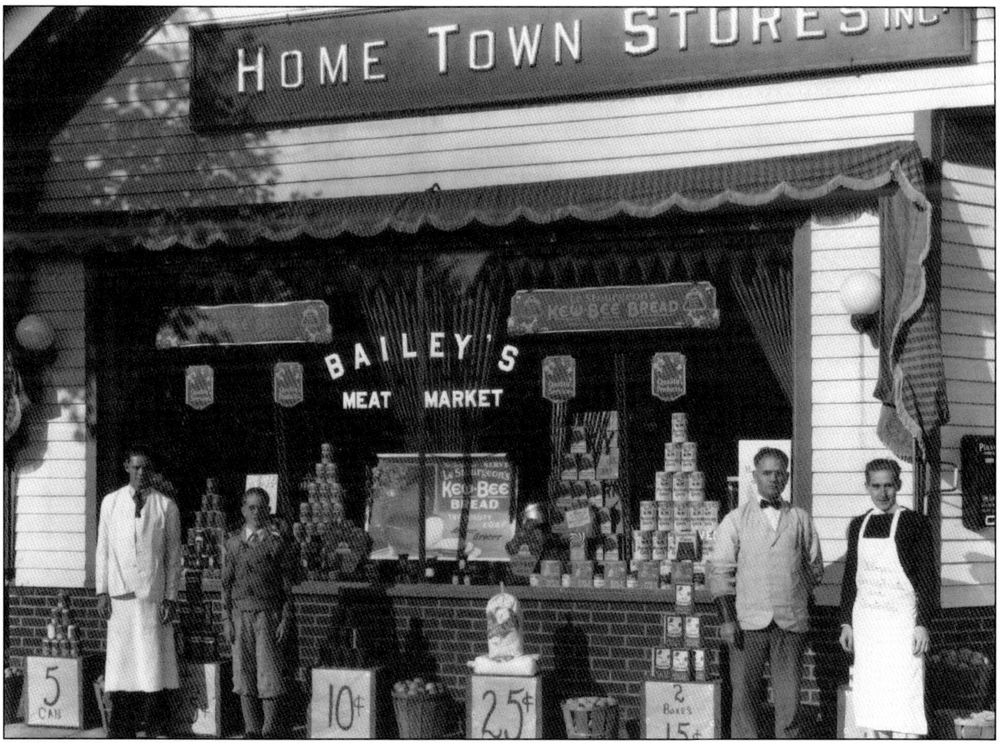

BAILEY'S HOME TOWN STORE. During the 1920s and 1930s, Merle Bailey operated grocery and meat stores on Church and Pearl Streets. In 1932, J.T. Roberts lined up the staff at one of them for a nice portrait. The stores, part of a cooperative chain, sold LeStourgeon's Kew-Bee bread.

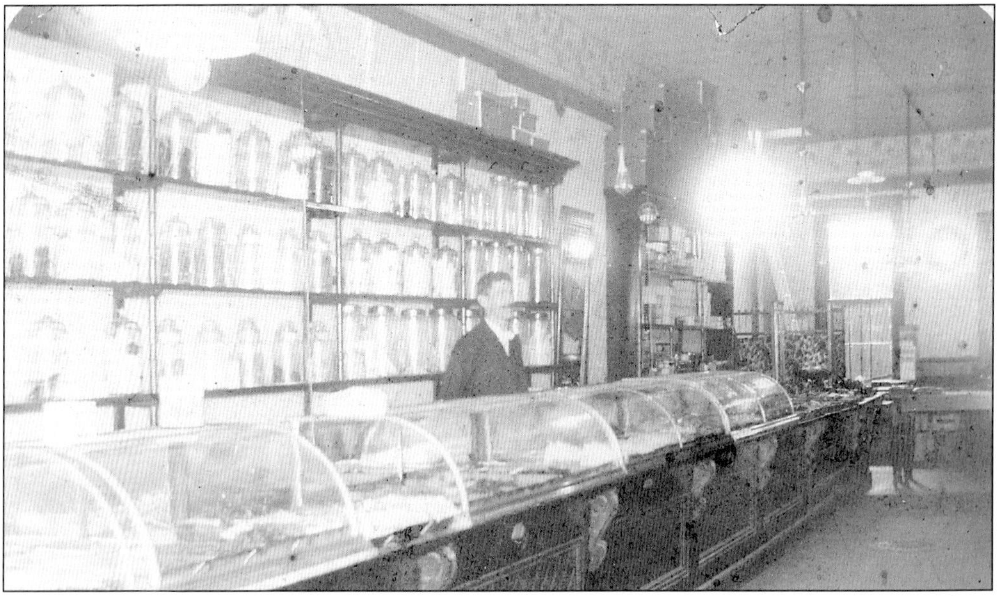

A BRIDGETON INSTITUTION. Still operating at the same site on South Laurel Street where it was established in 1888, Weber's Candy Store seems little changed since this photograph was taken near the turn of the century. Behind the counter is William Frederick Weber, the founder.

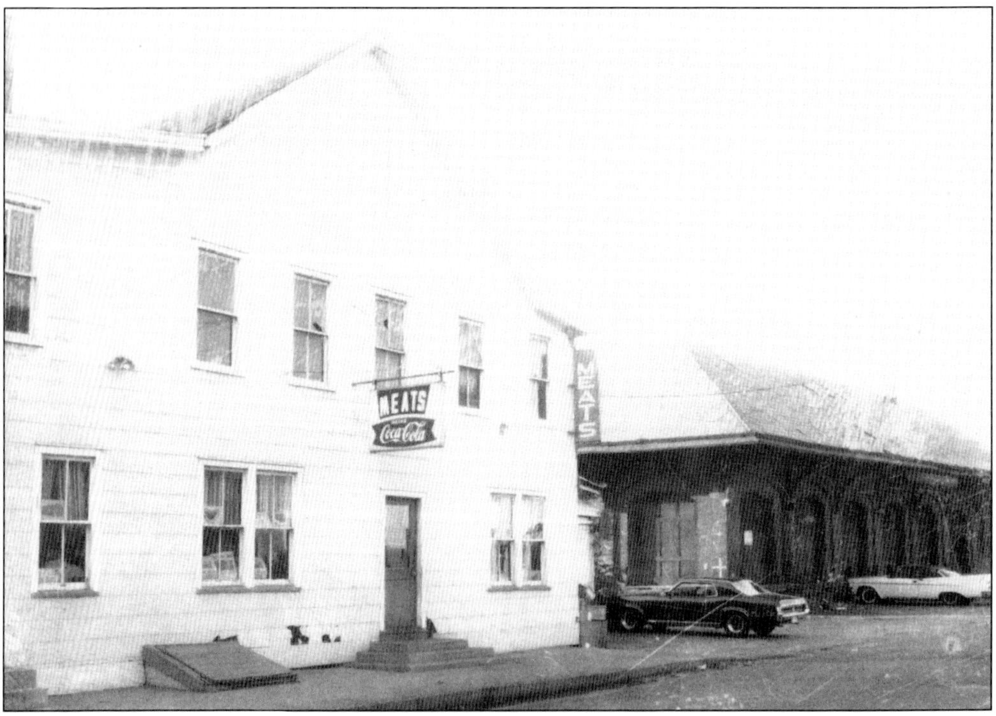

FISHER'S MEAT MARKET. Well into the 1960s, many Bridgeton area residents bought their meat at this shop on Cohansey Street adjacent to the old Central Railroad of New Jersey station, which burned in 1971. The firm, now known as Fisher's Food Center, relocated to Shiloh Pike.

Three

Memorable Moments

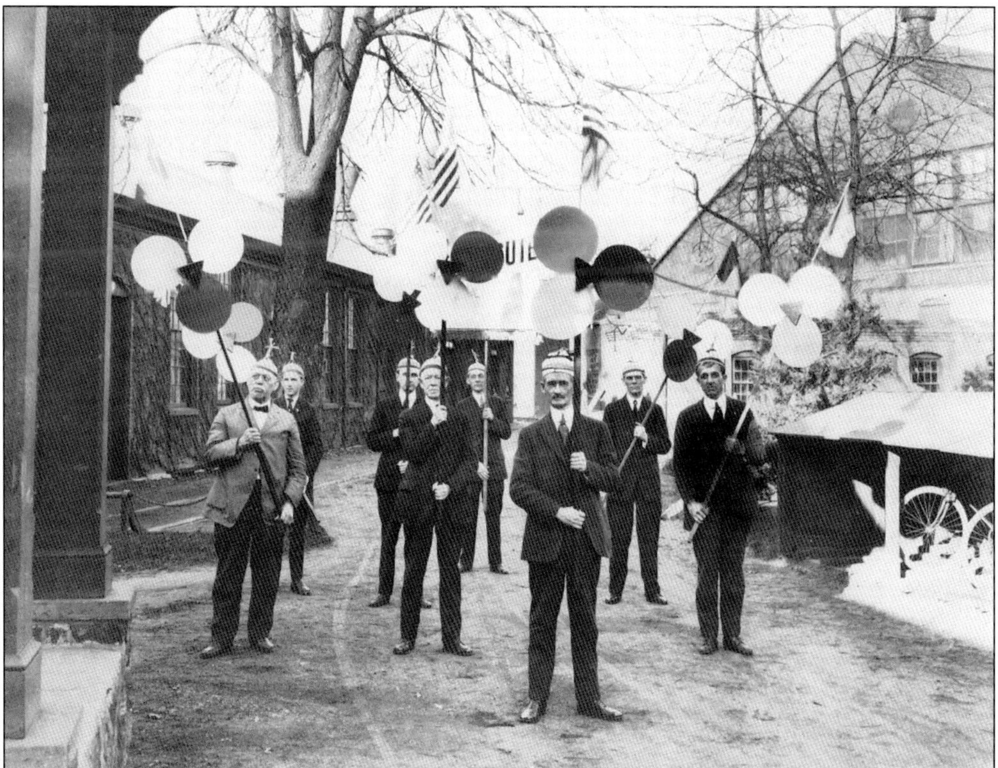

WHEN WORLD WAR I ENDED. In what has to be among the most peculiar photographs ever taken in Bridgeton, employees of the Ferracute Machine Company form a pinwheel unit for the Big Peace Parade on November 16, 1918. In the background is the plant.

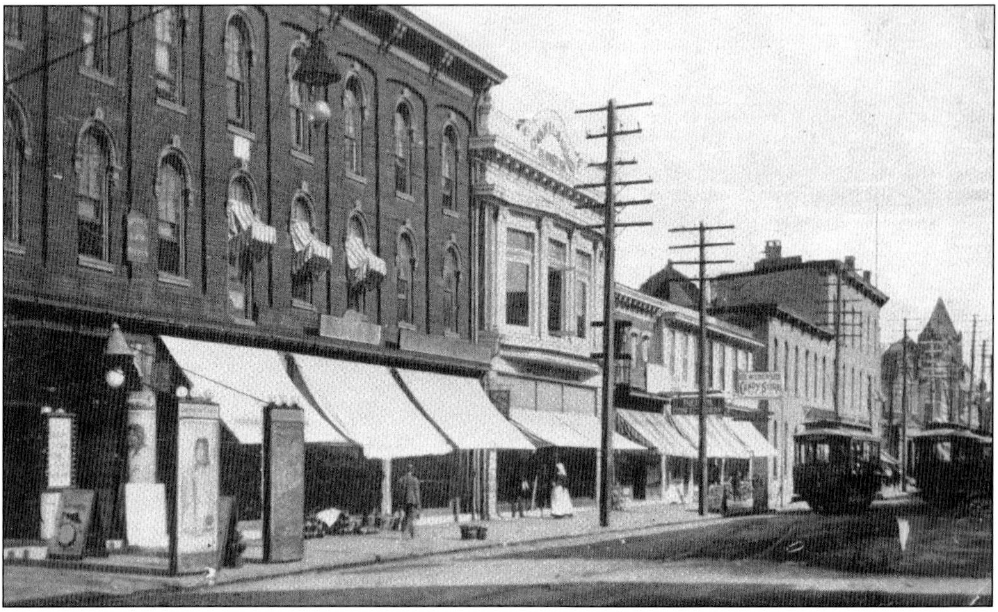

THE CRITERION THEATRE. Erected on South Laurel Street in 1880 as Moore's Opera House, this structure—shown at left in this c. 1906 postcard view—was renamed the Criterion Theatre in 1901. Among the prominent individuals who spoke here were Woodrow Wilson and Booker T. Washington.

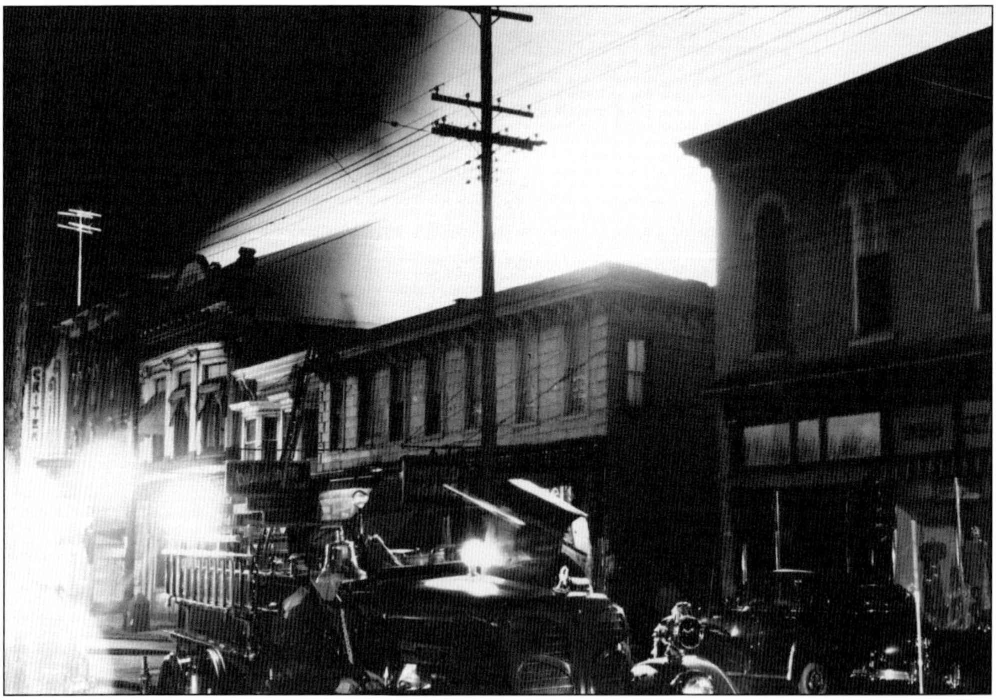

UP IN SMOKE. South Laurel Street was lit up by the burning Criterion Theatre building when the structure was consumed by flames in June 1949. Local amateur photographer Clem Lowe was on hand to take this photograph. Plans were soon made to erect another entertainment palace on the site.

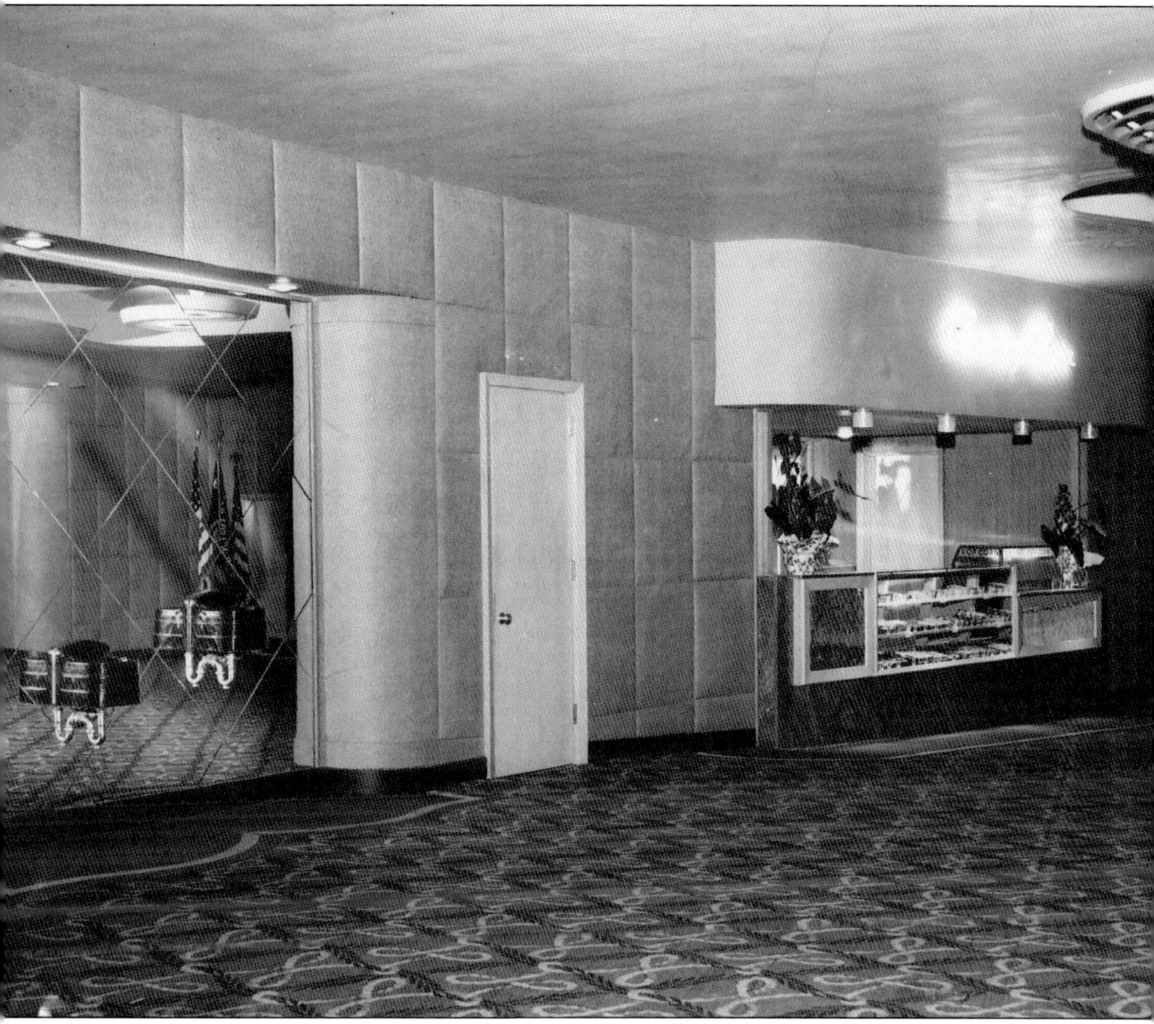

THE LAUREL THEATRE LOBBY. Opened in August 1950 on the site of the former Criterion Theatre, the Laurel Theatre offered every modern convenience of that era, including air-conditioning supported by water wells driven on the site. The modernistic lobby, seen here when new, featured deep, plush carpets, padded walls, and soft, indirect lighting. Manager Milton S. Marien was quoted at the time of the opening as saying, "We insisted on the best for this new theatre, and, even though it has meant waiting longer, we got it." The Laurel Theatre closed in 1979.

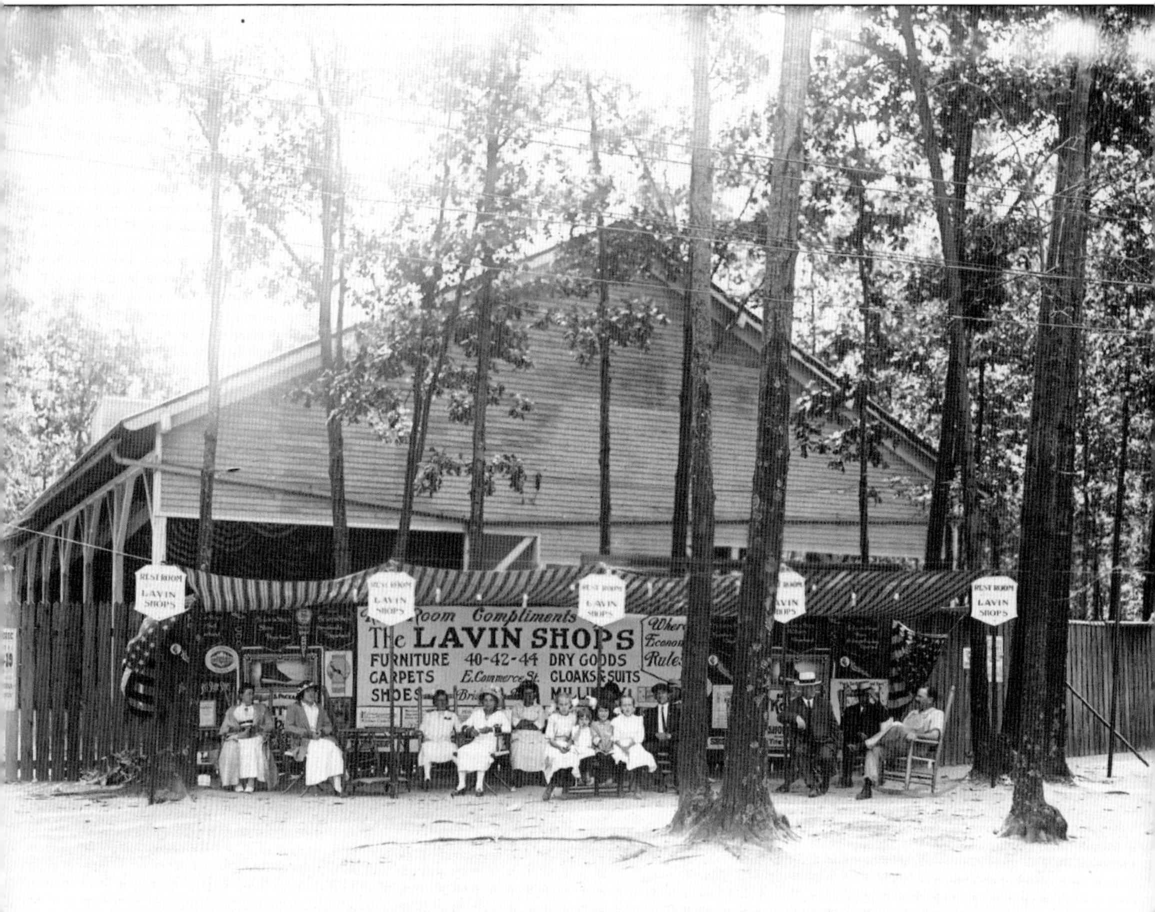

THE OPEN-AIR THEATRE AT TUMBLING DAM PARK. One of the most popular entertainment spots in old-time Bridgeton was Tumbling Dam Park on the east shore of Sunset Lake. On the bluff overlooking the site stood the Open-Air Theatre, sometimes called the Upper Pavilion, where acting troupes and musical groups often performed. In later years the structure was enclosed and became known as the Radio Barn. Local photographer Clayton McPherson captured this scene during the 1915 Cumberland County Fair when the Lavin Shops department store sponsored the rest spot.

GET IT AT GOLDBERG'S. During the 1915 county fair at Tumbling Dam Park, Bridgeton's I.W. Goldberg store at 31 South Laurel Street was hawking tires for automobiles, a transportation form then becoming increasingly popular. Also on sale were tire-patching kits, air pumps, and horns.

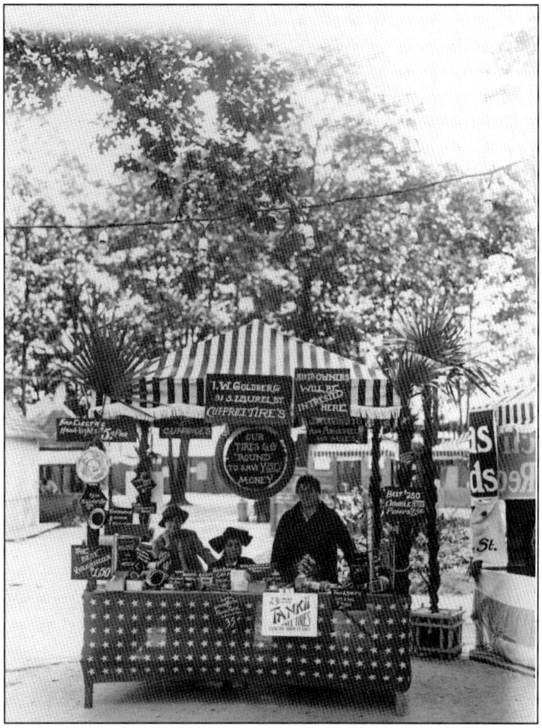

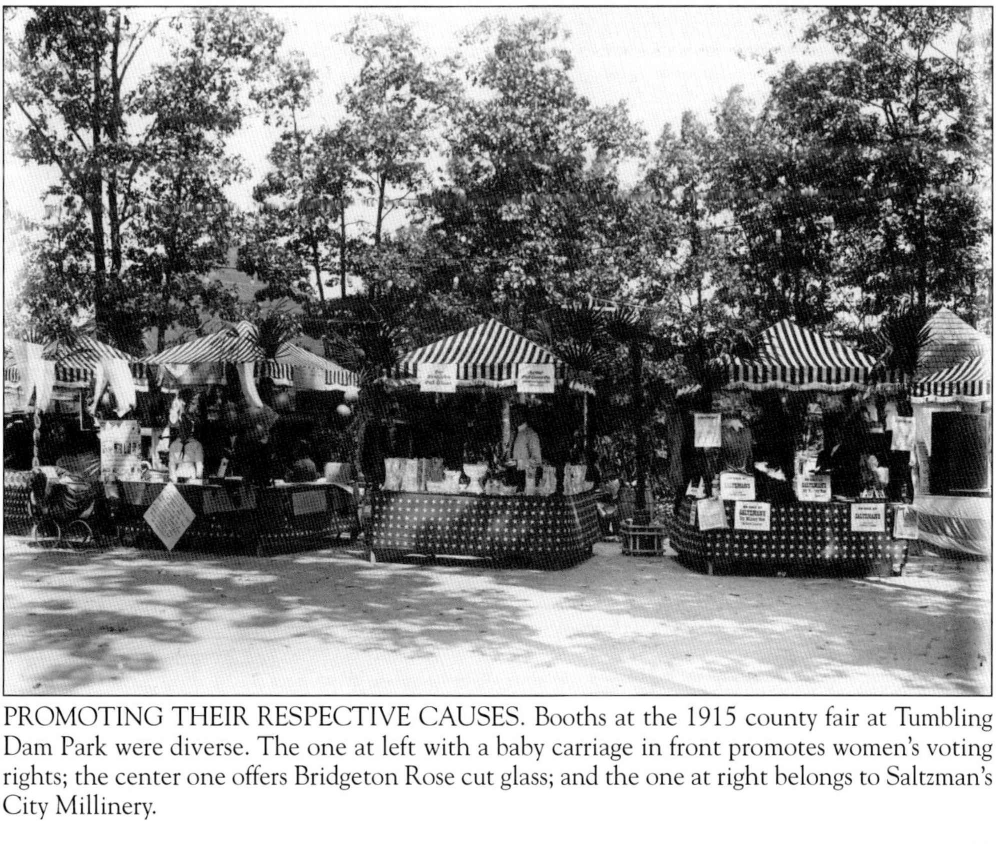

PROMOTING THEIR RESPECTIVE CAUSES. Booths at the 1915 county fair at Tumbling Dam Park were diverse. The one at left with a baby carriage in front promotes women's voting rights; the center one offers Bridgeton Rose cut glass; and the one at right belongs to Saltzman's City Millinery.

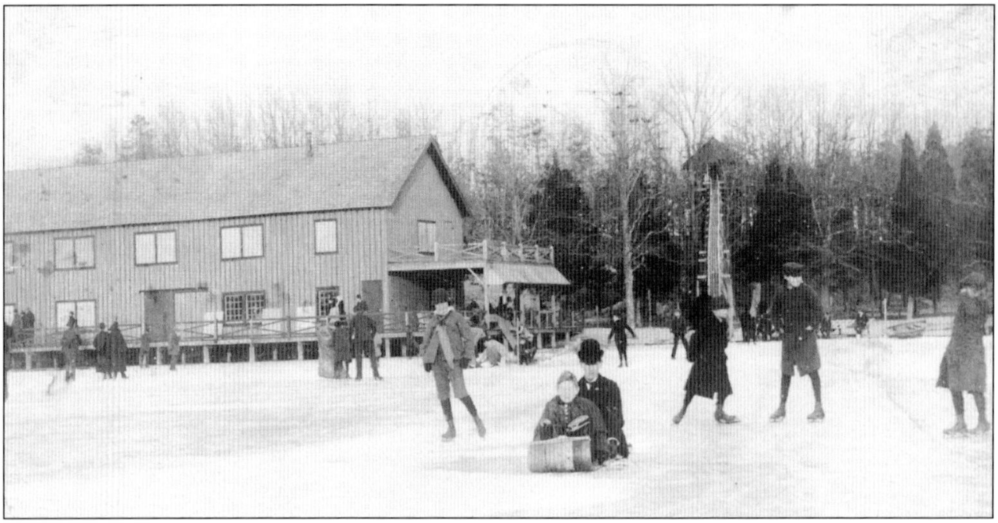

TUMBLING DAM PAVILION. Seen here in the winter months shortly after it was built in 1893, the lakefront pavilion at Tumbling Dam Park on Sunset Lake served until the early 1930s, when changing times dictated its removal to create more room for a swimming beach.

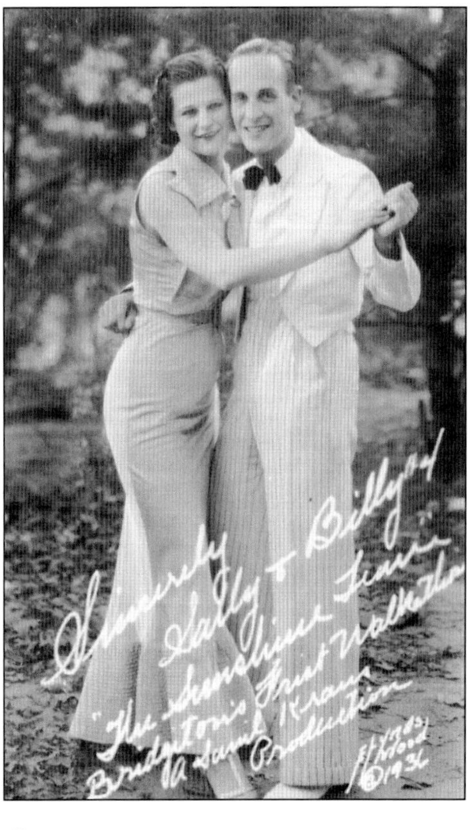

DEPRESSION-ERA ENTERTAINMENT. Signed "Sincerely, Sally & Billy, `The Sunshine Twins,' " this postcard from the Pedrick collection promoted Bridgeton's first walk-a-thon at Tumbling Dam Park in 1936. Local couples could pick up some extra money by outlasting their competitors.

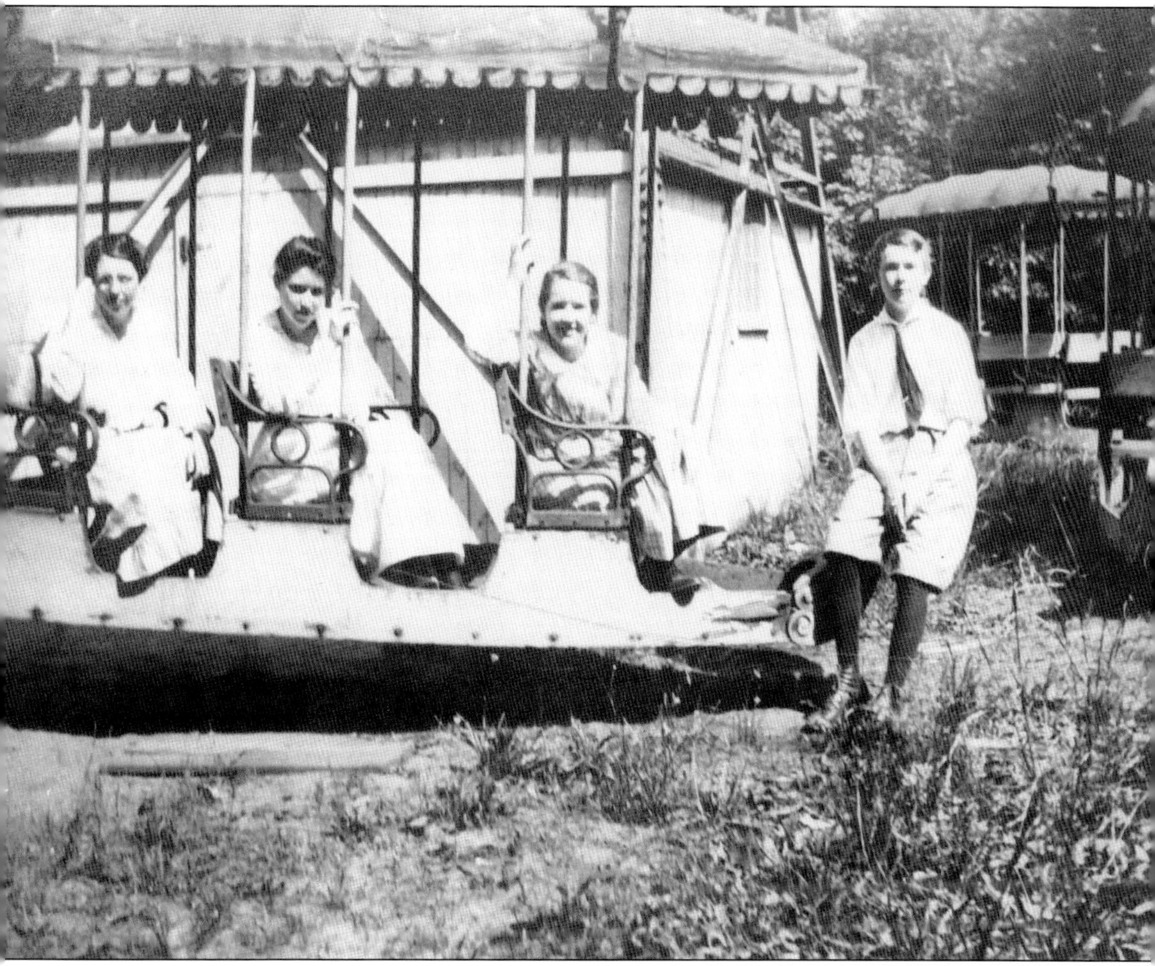

UP, UP, AND AWAY AT TUMBLING DAM PARK. At right, young Henry E. Jones sits on the bow of a gondola at the airship ride in the amusement park about 1914. At left is his sister Sarah, who is accompanied by her friends Sally and May. The ride, intended to mimic dirigibles when it first began operating at the site in 1910, was suspended from a 90-foot tower. In later years it was modified to incorporate a more daring swing. Henry E. Jones went on to become an employee of Owens-Illinois and one the earliest collectors of Bridgeton memorabilia.

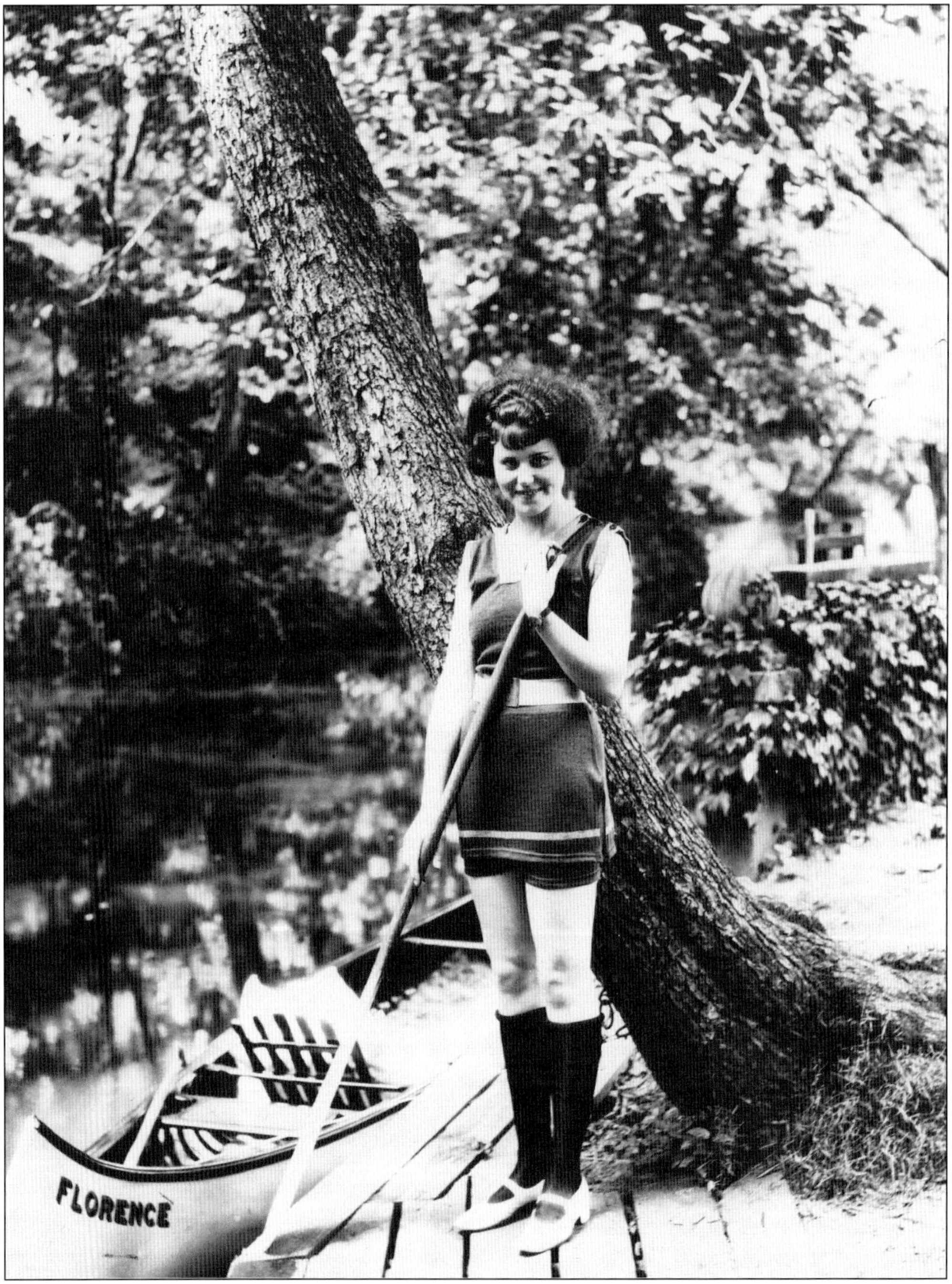

MISS BRIDGETON, 1921. The great Bridgeton photographer Harvey W. Porch took this beautiful portrait of Sara Bell along the Raceway in the Bridgeton City Park just prior to her competition in Atlantic City's Miss America Pageant in 1922. Sara graduated from Bridgeton High in 1920 and resided at 181 West Broad Street. Unlike today, during that era municipalities were allowed to enter contestants in the pageant. In the photograph, young Sara, who reportedly passed away in California in 1980, is sporting a permanent wave, a source of controversy in later pageants.

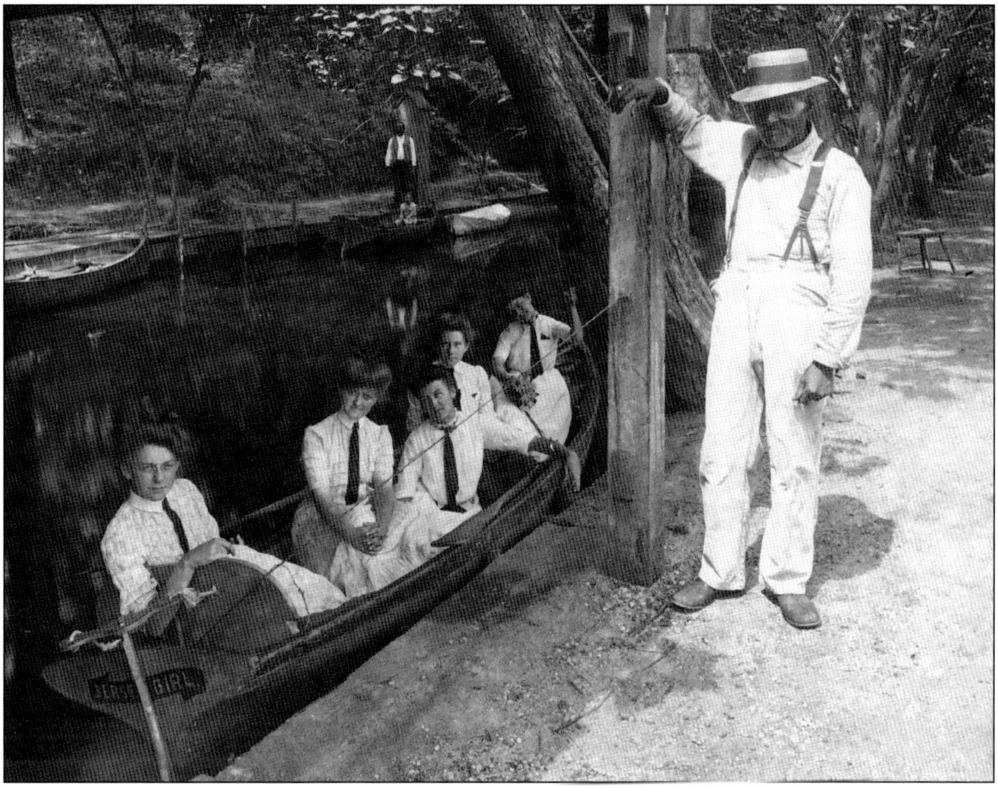

SUNDAY IN THE PARK. A group of young women, probably students at the Ivy Hall Seminary, await a push-off by the attendant in the appropriately named "Jersey Girl" Raceway boathouse about 1905. Once again, photographer Harvey W. Porch illustrates his talent with composition.

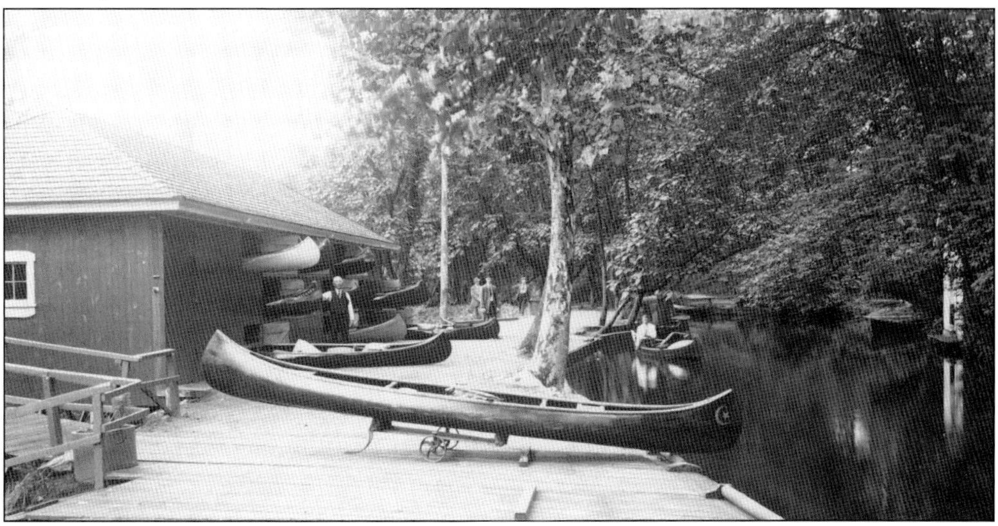

THE OLD RACEWAY CANOE HOUSE. About 1910, David C. and Jacob B. Jones operated the Bridgeton Pleasure Boat Company along the Raceway in the city park. The firm rented pleasure craft and also leased storage lockers to those who wished to keep privately owned canoes at the site.

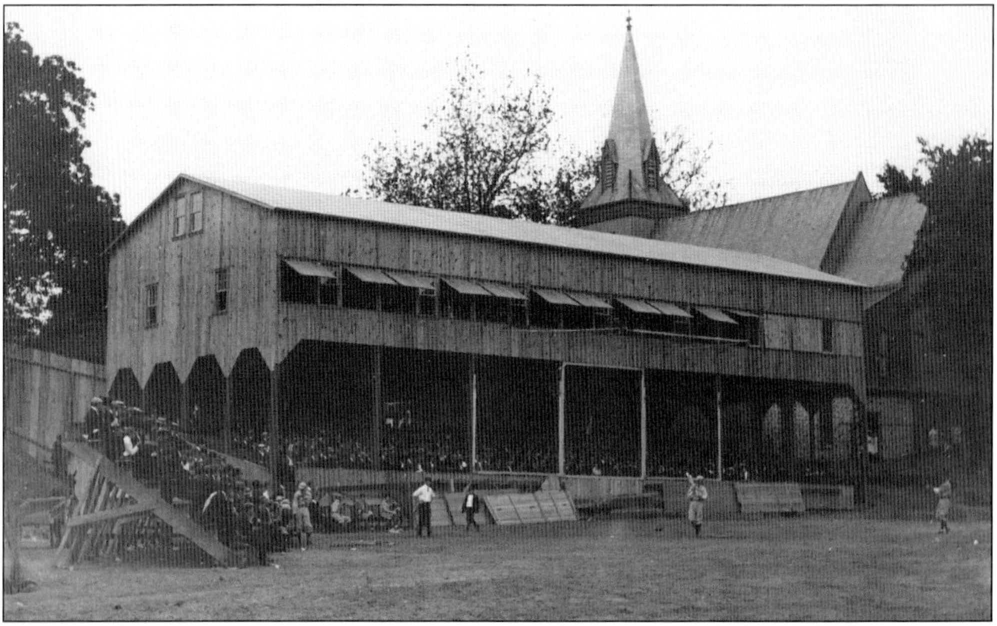

THE HIPPODROME, ERECTED 1909. Located on East Commerce Street where city hall would later rise, this rustic structure served as a grandstand for local baseball games and other events. It survived a relatively brief time and was demolished about 1916.

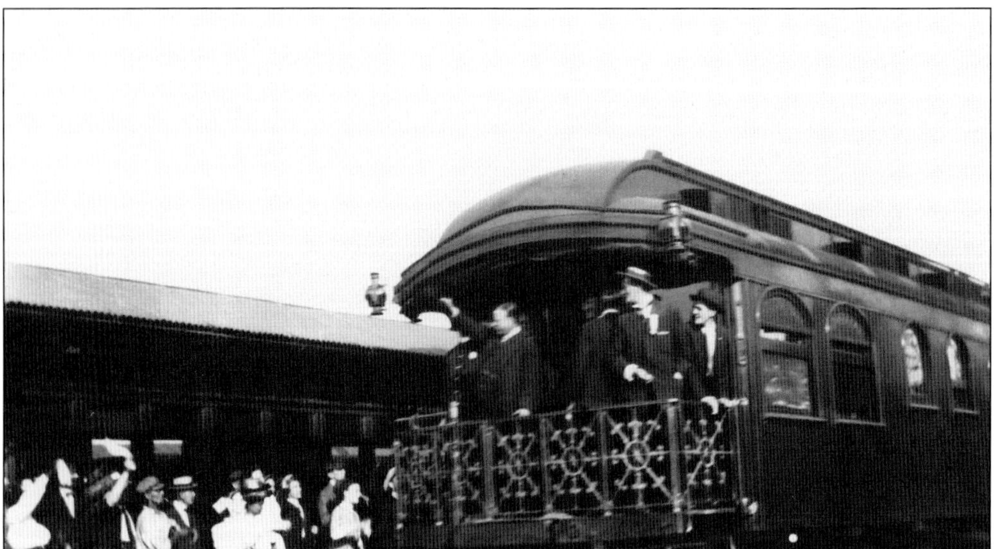

HAIL TO THE CHIEF. President William Taft arrives at the railroad station in Bridgeton on May 27, 1912, to campaign for office. Here he waves to the crowd from the back of an open observation car. Teddy Roosevelt also visited Bridgeton during the same campaign year.

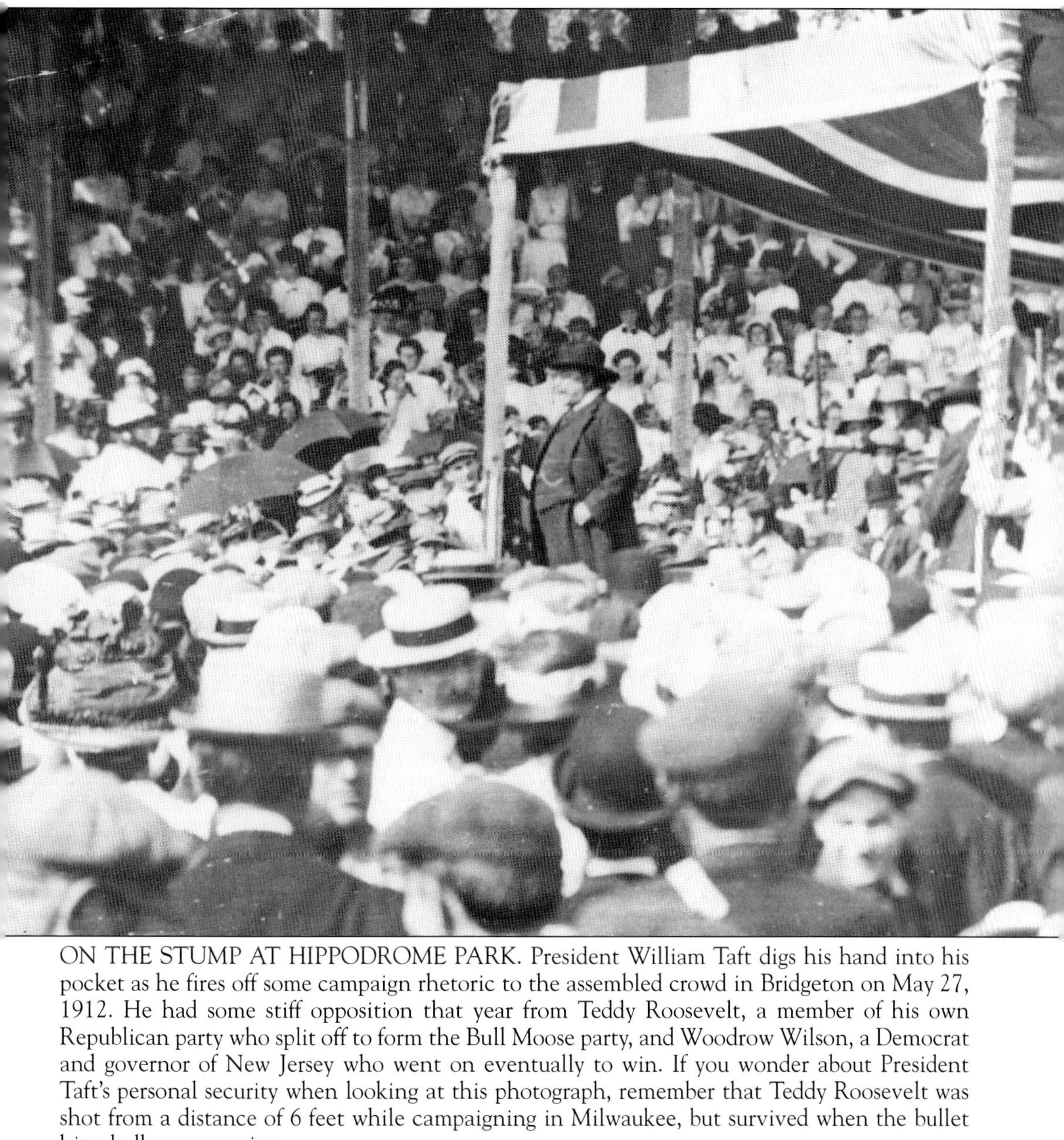

ON THE STUMP AT HIPPODROME PARK. President William Taft digs his hand into his pocket as he fires off some campaign rhetoric to the assembled crowd in Bridgeton on May 27, 1912. He had some stiff opposition that year from Teddy Roosevelt, a member of his own Republican party who split off to form the Bull Moose party, and Woodrow Wilson, a Democrat and governor of New Jersey who went on eventually to win. If you wonder about President Taft's personal security when looking at this photograph, remember that Teddy Roosevelt was shot from a distance of 6 feet while campaigning in Milwaukee, but survived when the bullet hit a bulky manuscript.

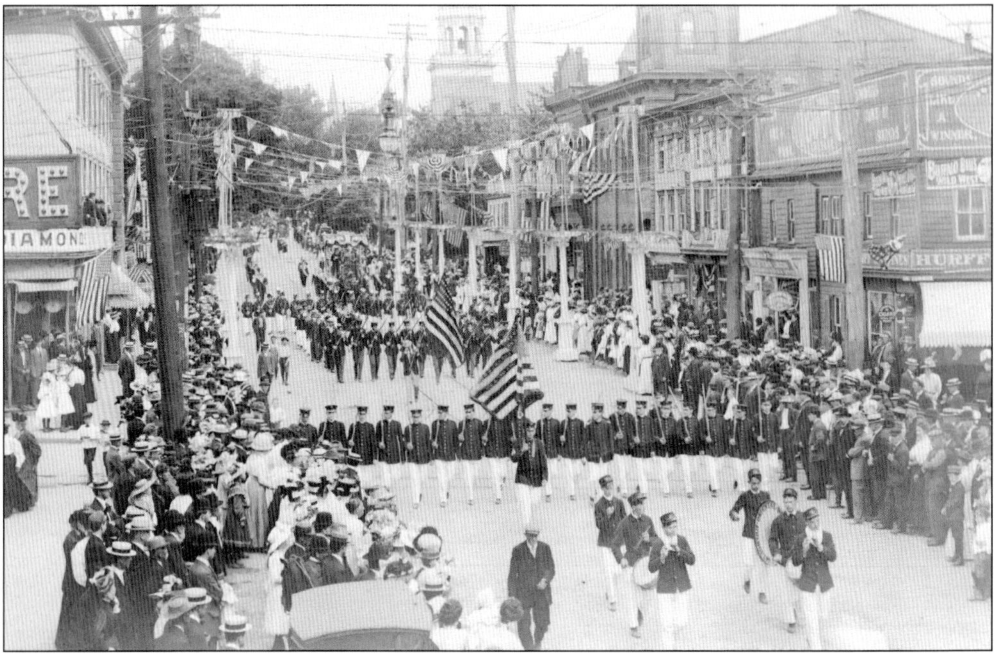

HERE COMES THE PARADE. In a scene dating about 1910, the Oriental Band marches through the intersection of Commerce and Laurel Streets. In the background lining the street can be seen the wooden columns erected on a temporary basis for events such as Memorial Day.

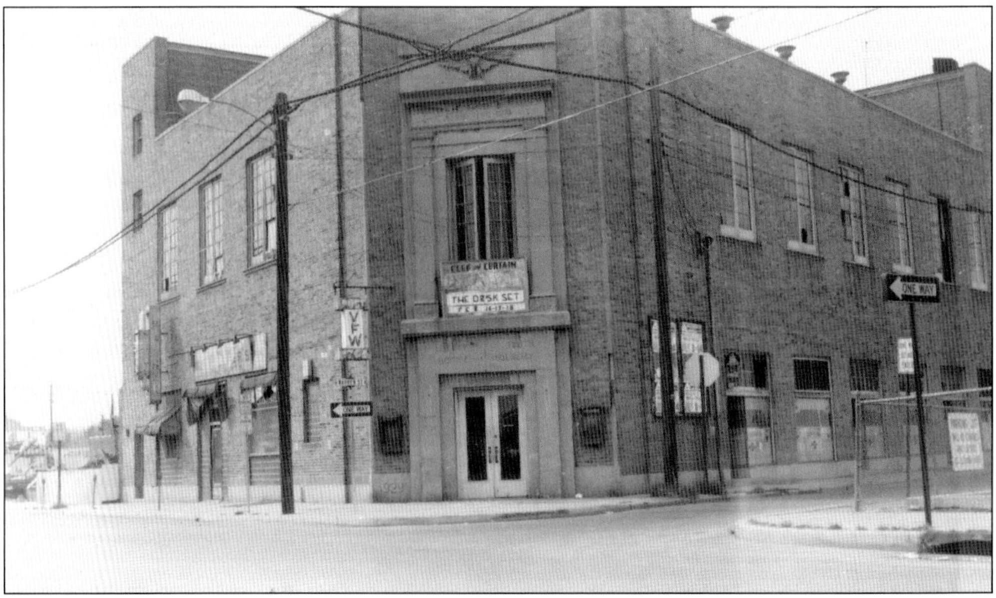

THE SOUTHWEST CORNER OF PEARL AND WARREN STREETS. Seen here just prior to its demolition about 1970, this structure housed the studio of radio station WSNJ during the World War II era. In 1945 it employed Bill Haley, who a decade later cut the first rock-and-roll record, "Rock Around the Clock."

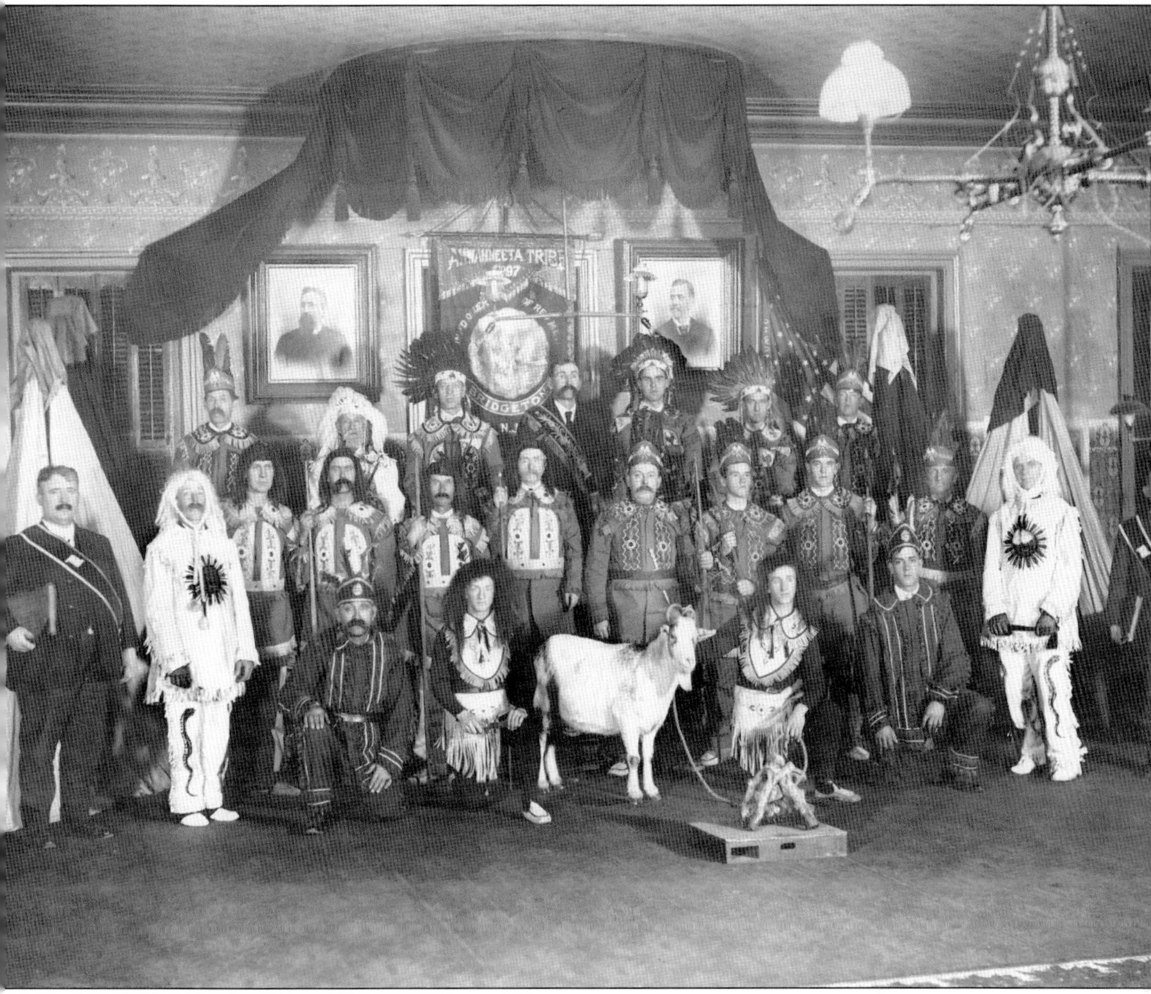

THE BRIDGETON RED MEN IN FULL REGALIA. Attired in their finest ceremonial garb, members of the Ahwahneeta Tribe of the Red Men's lodge and their mascot line up for a portrait by Daniel V. Ward about 1910. While these costumes might seem unusual for non-Native Americans, during the Victorian era and into the early twentieth century fraternal organizations often adopted unusual symbols and uniforms to exemplify role models. A little more than a decade before this picture was taken, the Red Men from Bridgeton were involved in one of the worst train wrecks in American history. The lives of forty-seven were lost near Atlantic City.

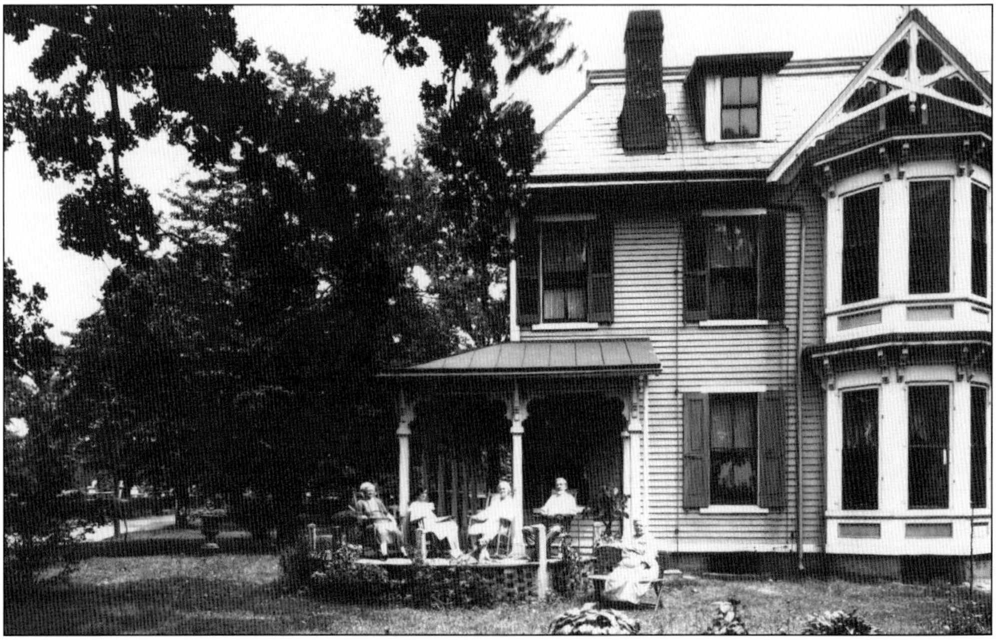

"SEVEN OAKS." Located at 440 East Commerce Street, this home gave its name to a women's club which remains active today. The club and member Elizabeth Reeves were instrumental in founding Bridgeton Hospital in 1898. J.T. Roberts caught the Whitaker family relaxing there in 1928.

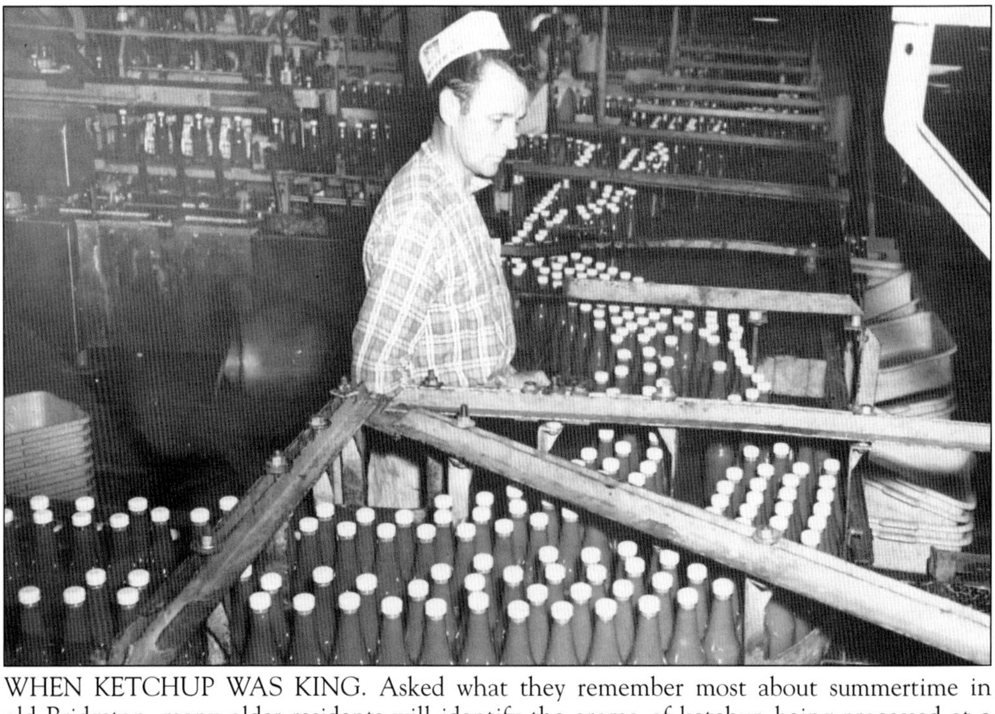

WHEN KETCHUP WAS KING. Asked what they remember most about summertime in old Bridgeton, many older residents will identify the aroma of ketchup being processed at a canhouse. Here a P.J. Ritter employee labors at the plant, which was a local mainstay from 1917 until 1976.

Four

Give Me That Ol' Time Religion

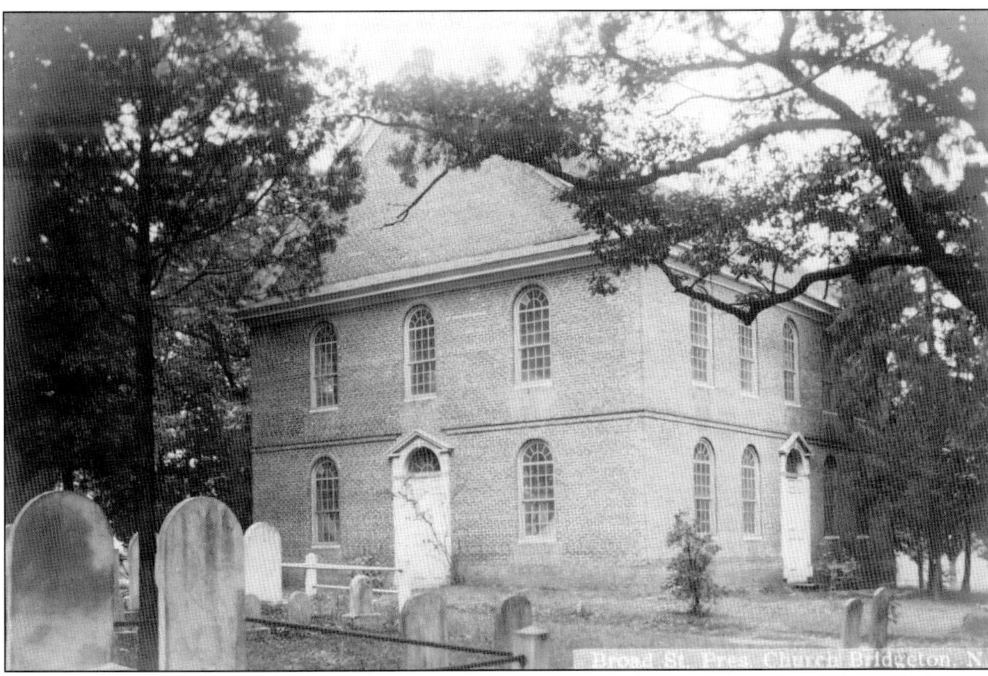

THE OLD BROAD STREET CHURCH. Erected between 1792 and 1795 and formally known as the Meeting House of the Congregation of Bridge Town, the Old Broad Street Presbyterian Church has changed little since this photograph from the Pedrick collection was taken about 1910.

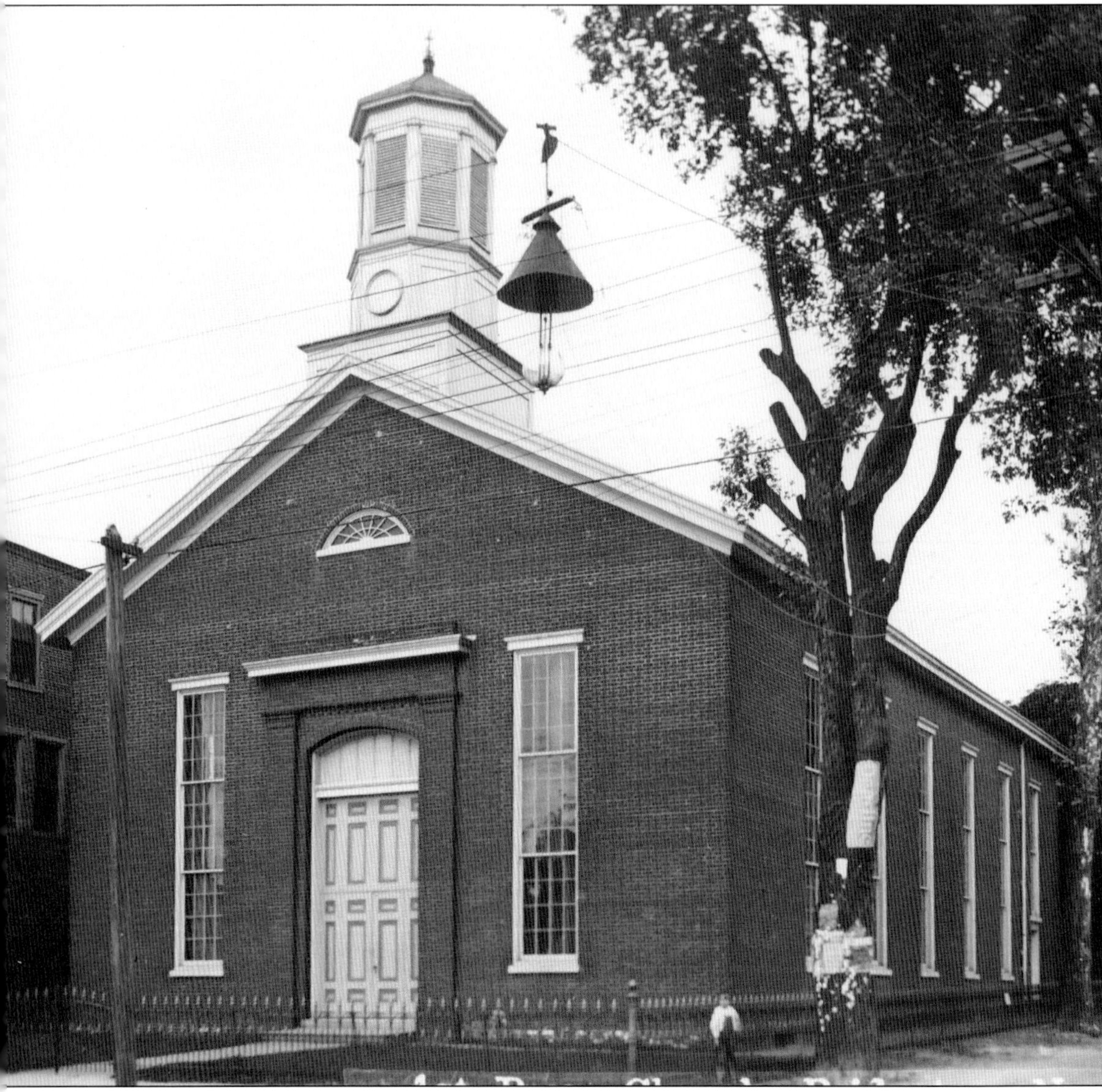

THE PRESBYTERIAN CHURCH, NORTH LAUREL STREET. When local Presbyterians decided that their Old Broad Street Church was too far out of town for convenience, they built this structure at North Laurel Street and Church Lane in downtown Bridgeton. The church was dedicated on March 31, 1836, and is seen here in a rare photograph about 1905. It continued to serve into the 1940s as a house of worship while the neighborhood around it became increasingly commercialized. In the post-World War II era, the structure became a drug store, a shoe store, and then burned in 1982.

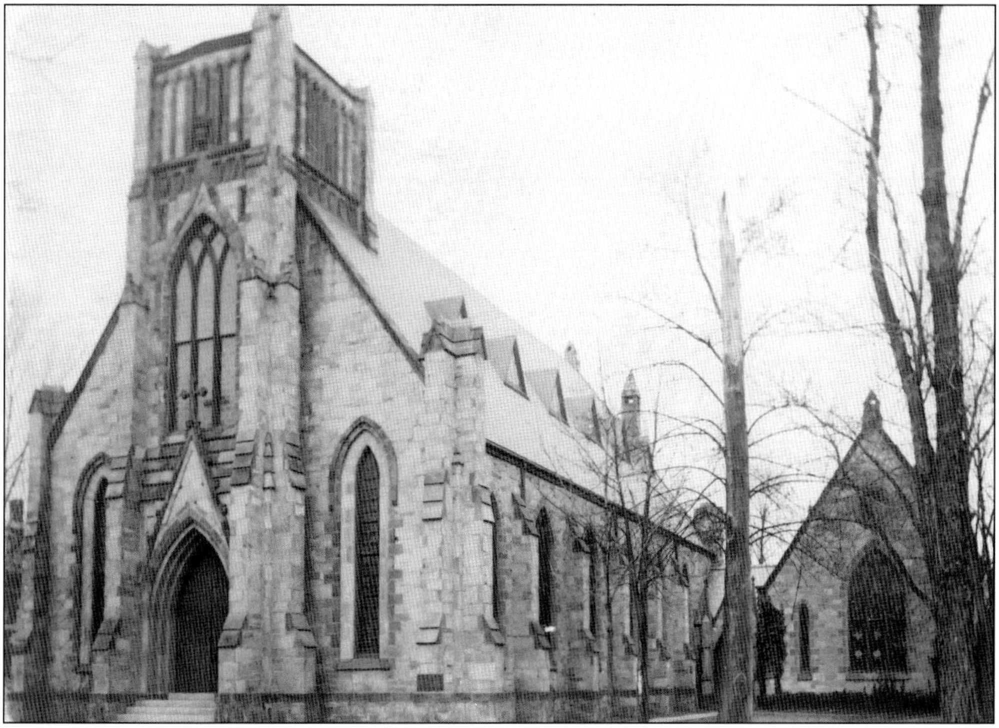

THE PRESBYTERIAN CHURCH, WEST COMMERCE AND GILES. Following the Civil War, local Presbyterians decided that once again there was need for a house of worship on the west side of the Cohansey. Constructed of Chester gneiss, the chapel was dedicated in 1869 and the adjacent church in 1878.

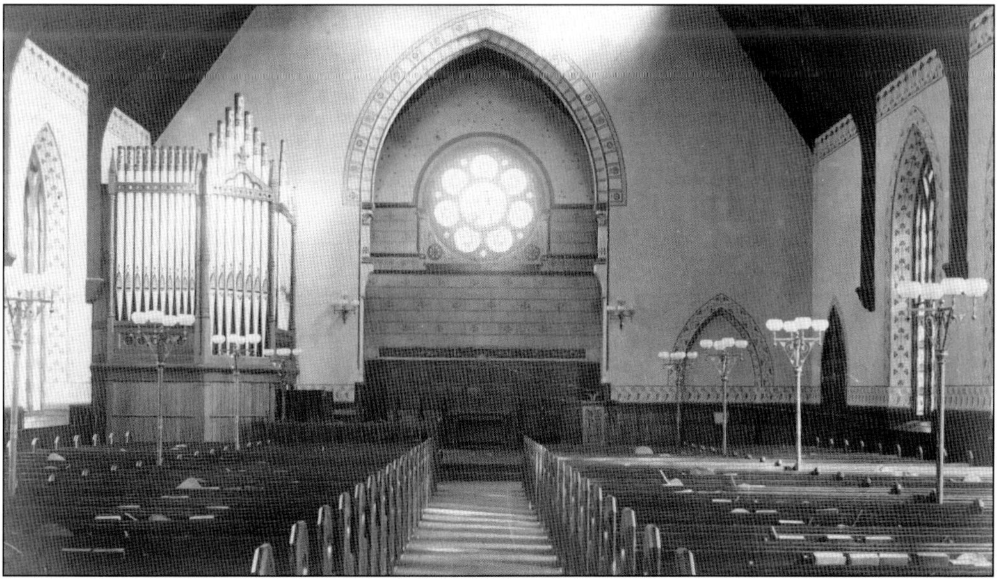

THE WEST COMMERCE STREET PRESBYTERIAN CHURCH INTERIOR. The style of the church, seen here about 1910 with its early fixtures, was evidently influenced by the Victorian Gothic, exemplified in the pointed arches. Originally designed by famous Philadelphia architect Samuel Sloan, it was completed by architect James P. Sims.

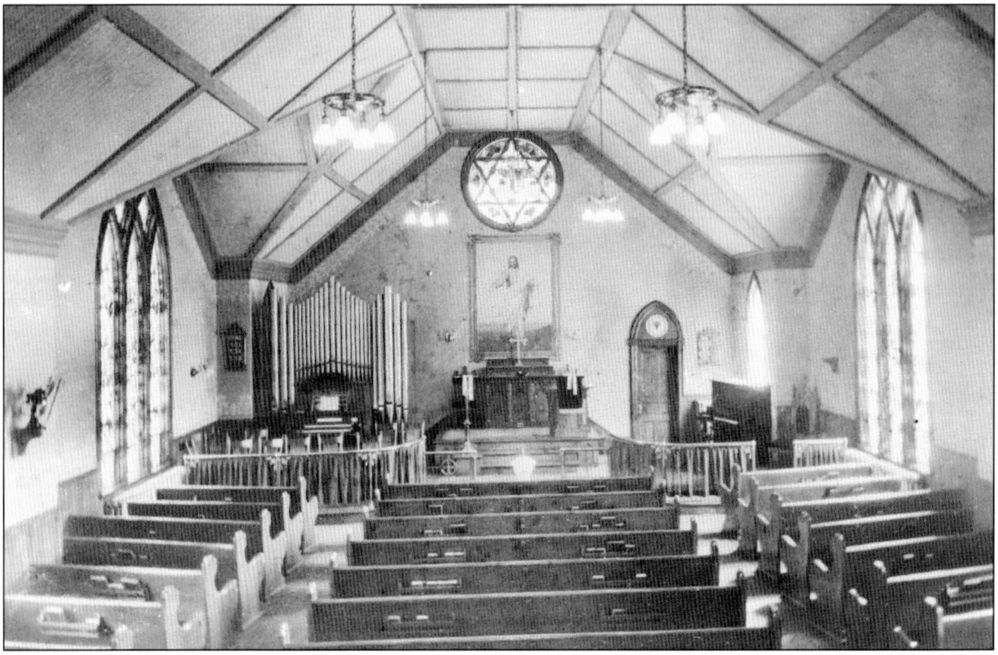

CHRIST'S ENGLISH LUTHERAN CHURCH. Many of Bridgeton's earliest Lutherans were of the German-speaking tradition. But times changed and English-speaking Lutherans erected this sanctuary on Bank Street designed by builder Charles Woodnut in 1892.

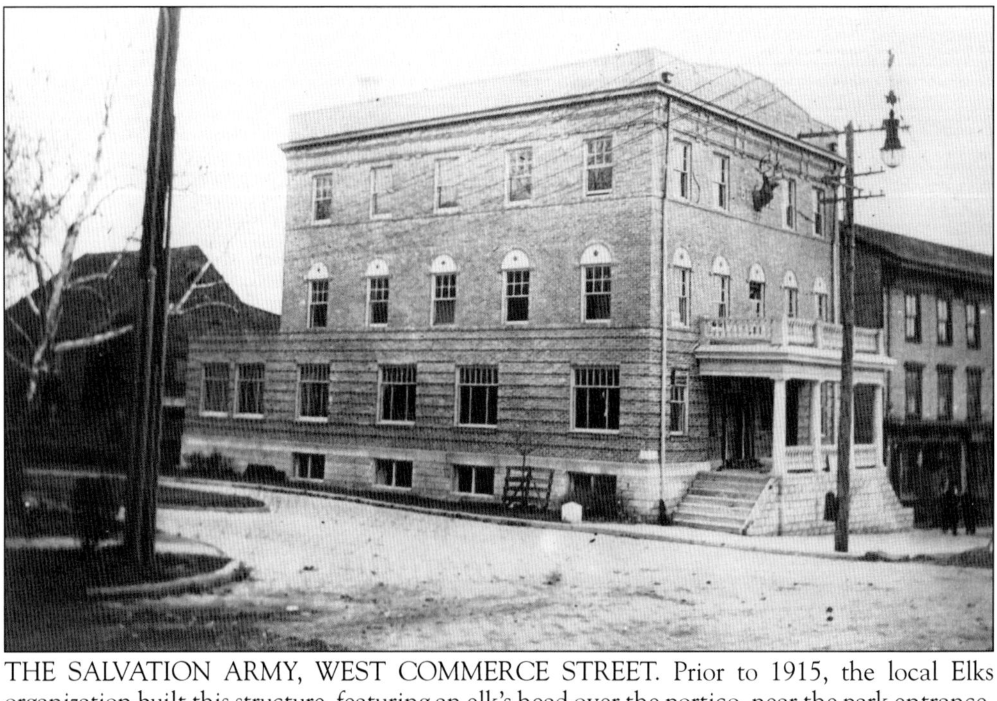

THE SALVATION ARMY, WEST COMMERCE STREET. Prior to 1915, the local Elks organization built this structure, featuring an elk's head over the portico, near the park entrance. By the time World War II came along, it became home to the Salvation Army and served as such until its demolition in 1974.

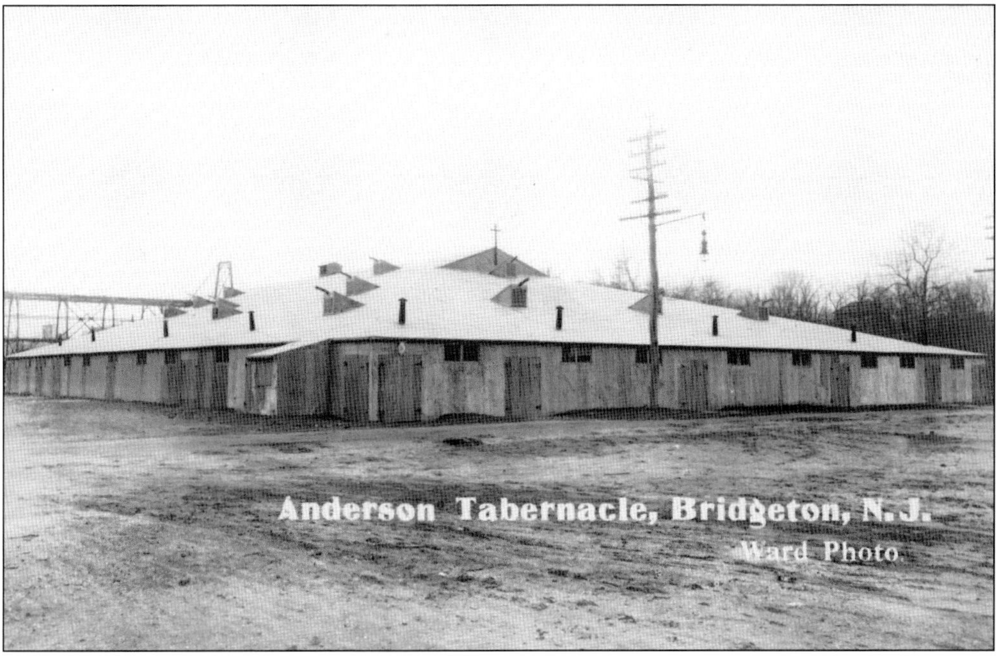

THE ANDERSON TABERNACLE. What appears to be a hastily constructed glass works or cannery is actually the revival chapel, dubbed the "Glory Shed," of Pastor George Wood Anderson. It stood on the south side of Washington Street near the Cohansey River in 1916.

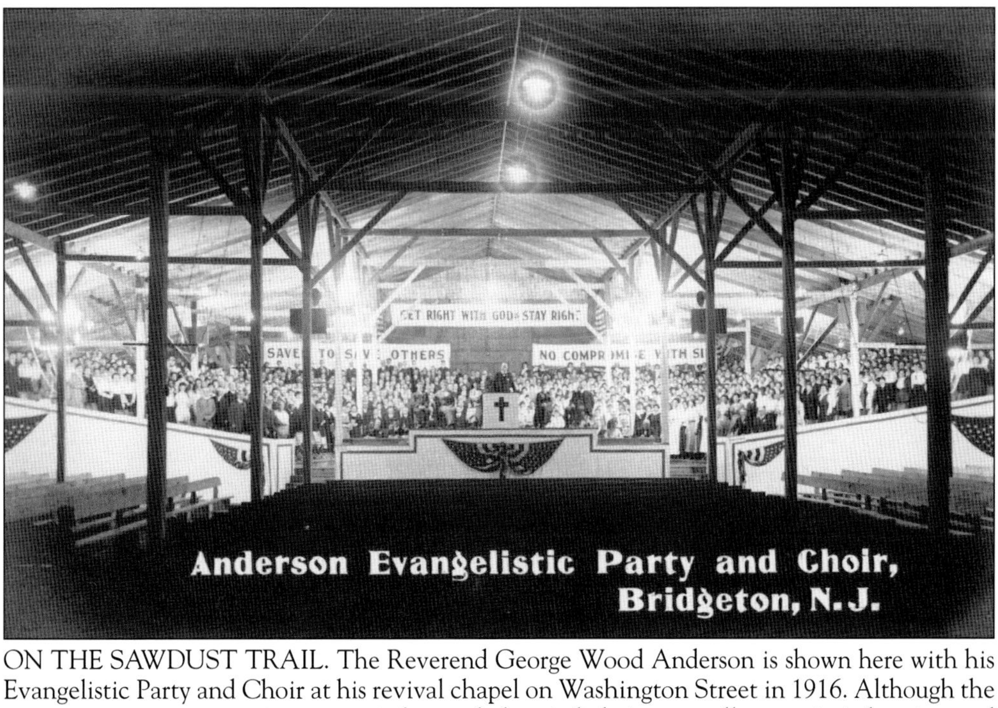

ON THE SAWDUST TRAIL. The Reverend George Wood Anderson is shown here with his Evangelistic Party and Choir at his revival chapel on Washington Street in 1916. Although the structure was temporary in nature, it featured electric lighting as well as patriotic bunting and religious banners.

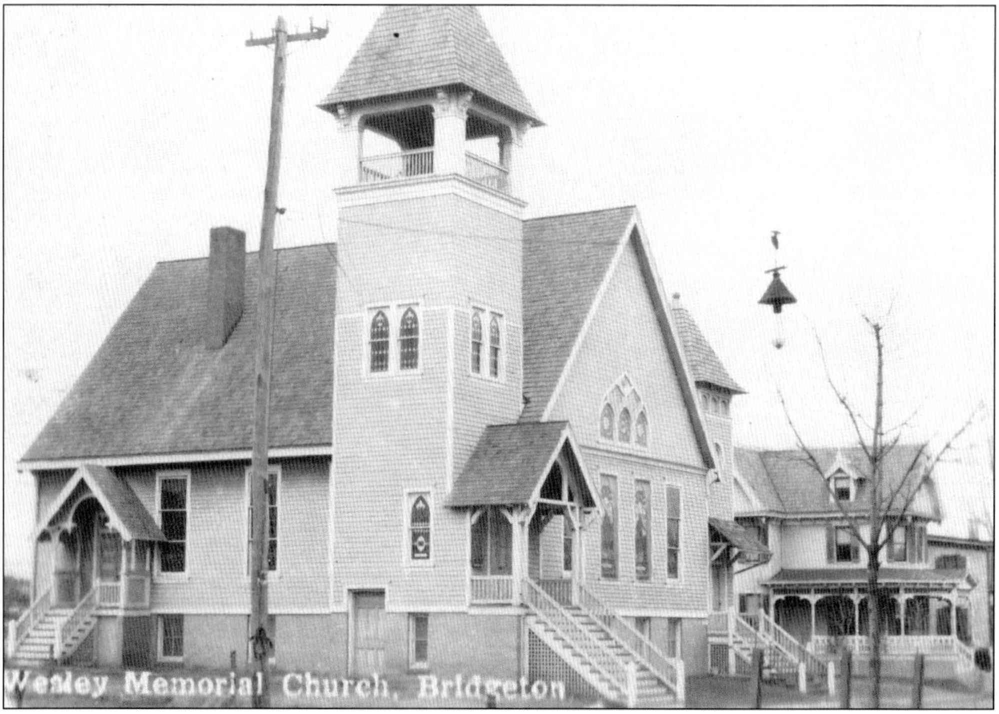

THE WESLEY MEMORIAL METHODIST EPISCOPAL CHURCH. Under the patronage of glass magnate Clement W. Shoemaker, Methodists in Bridgeton first erected a church on North Pearl Street in 1892 and steadily improved upon it. This is how it appeared by about 1906.

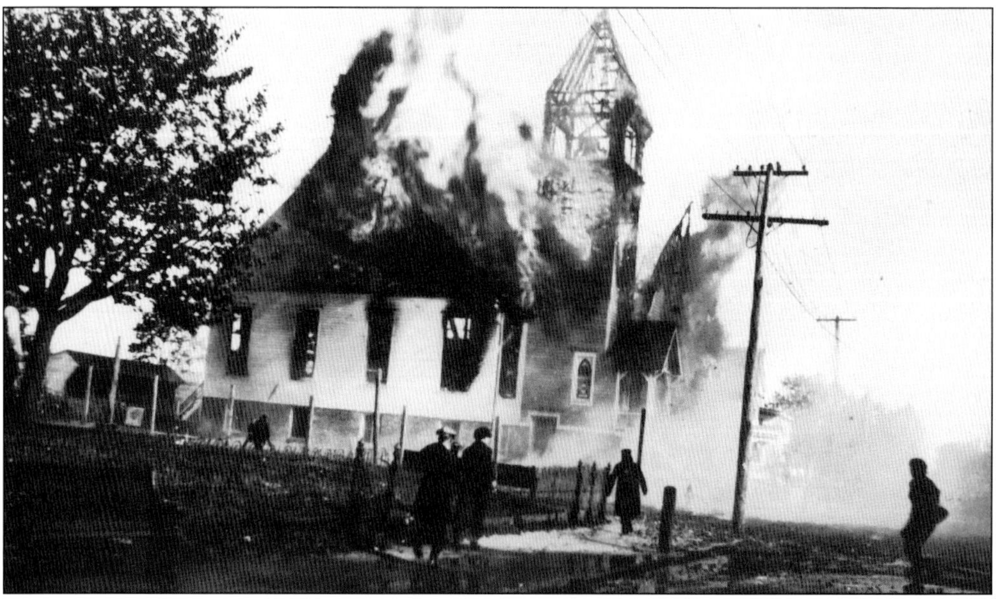

UP IN SMOKE. On Sunday, October 24, 1915, the congregation of the Wesley Memorial Methodist Episcopal Church at North Pearl and Morton Streets was shocked to see its house of worship go up in flames. In this scene, the church's belfry has already been consumed and the roof is fully engulfed.

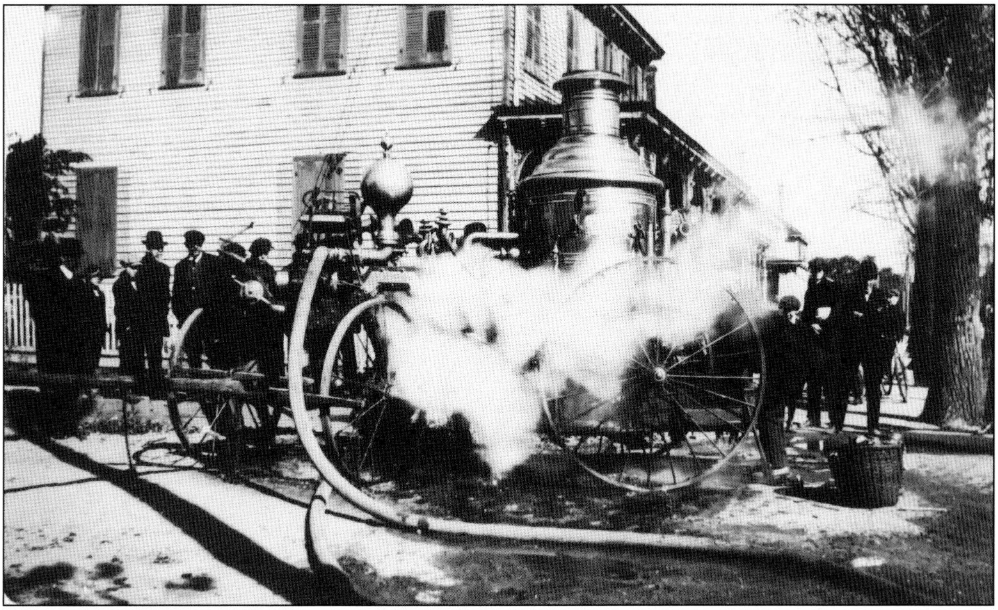

A SILSBY STEAMER IN ACTION. On a crisp autumn day in 1915, steam envelops the Bridgeton Fire Department's horse-drawn, steam-powered Silsby engine as it helps to battle the Wesley Memorial Methodist Episcopal Church fire on North Pearl Street. This proved to be the last fire for the venerable apparatus.

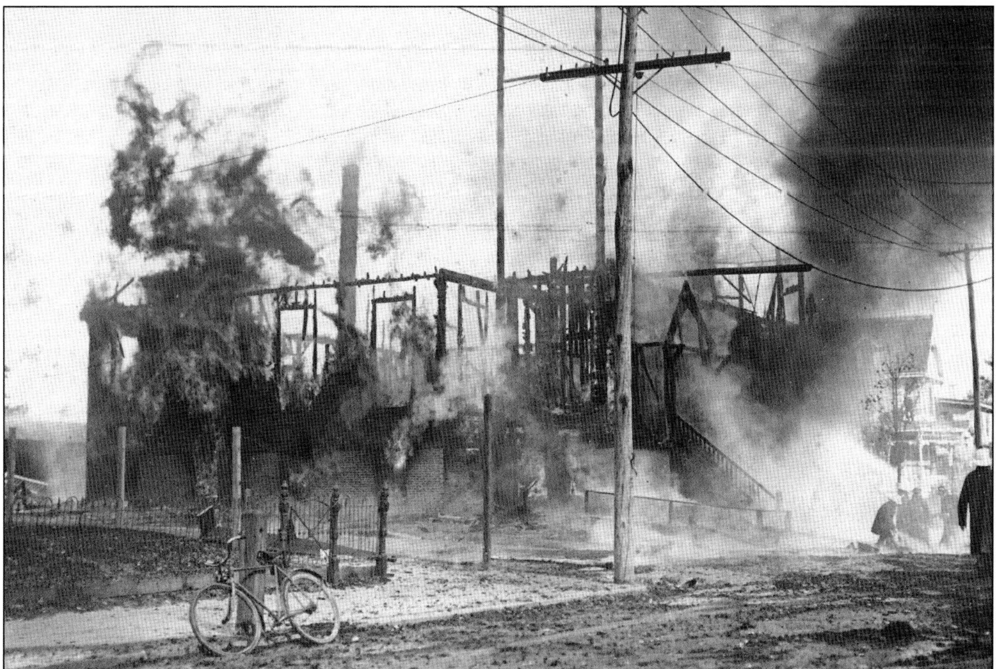

THE DREADFUL AFTERMATH. Although firemen battled bravely to save the structure, little remained of the Wesley Memorial Methodist Episcopal Church except its charred frame. The congregation vowed to rebuild and soon erected a beautiful and enduring edifice made of stone.

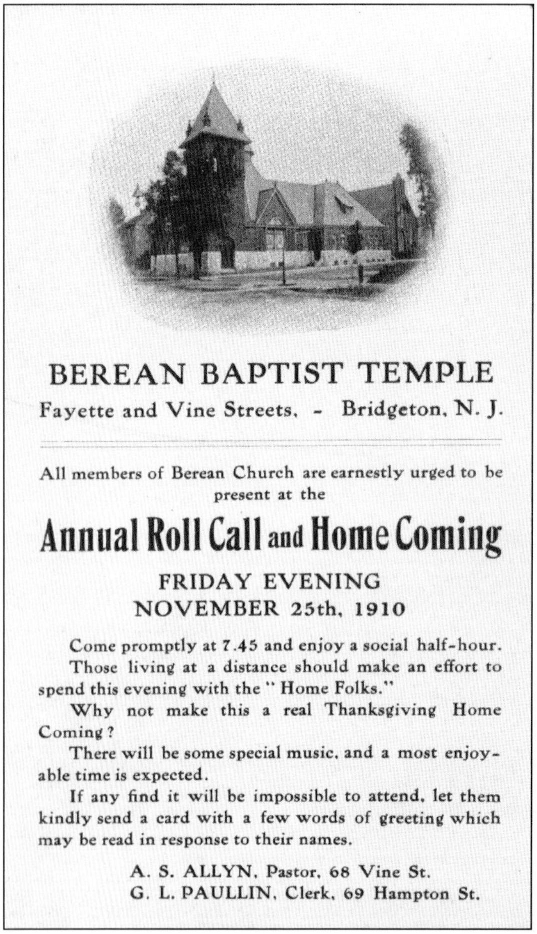

BERFAN BAPTIST TEMPLE
Fayette and Vine Streets, - Bridgeton, N. J.

All members of Berean Church are earnestly urged to be present at the

Annual Roll Call and Home Coming

FRIDAY EVENING
NOVEMBER 25th, 1910

Come promptly at 7.45 and enjoy a social half-hour.

Those living at a distance should make an effort to spend this evening with the " Home Folks."

Why not make this a real Thanksgiving Home Coming?

There will be some special music, and a most enjoyable time is expected.

If any find it will be impossible to attend, let them kindly send a card with a few words of greeting which may be read in response to their names.

A. S. ALLYN, Pastor, 68 Vine St.
G. L. PAULLIN, Clerk, 69 Hampton St.

AT FAYETTE AND VINE STREETS. The congregation of the Berean Baptist Temple published this promotional card to welcome members in 1910 when the Reverend A.S. Allyn was pastor. The Richardsonian Romanesque structure, designed by Frank Watson, dates from 1894.

FOR WHOM THE BELL TOLLS. Two members of the Central Methodist Church at East Commerce and Bank Streets inspect an enormous bell, one of ten, donated by Cumberland Glass Company magnate Joseph A. Clark in 1909. Architects Hazlehurst and Huckel designed the main church in 1891.

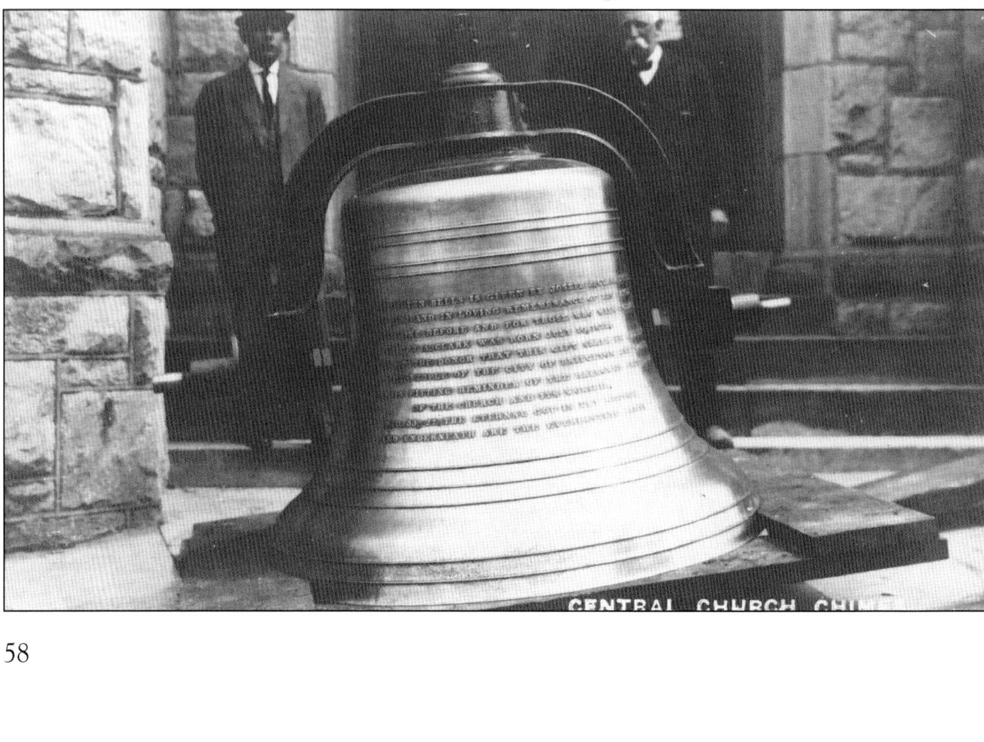

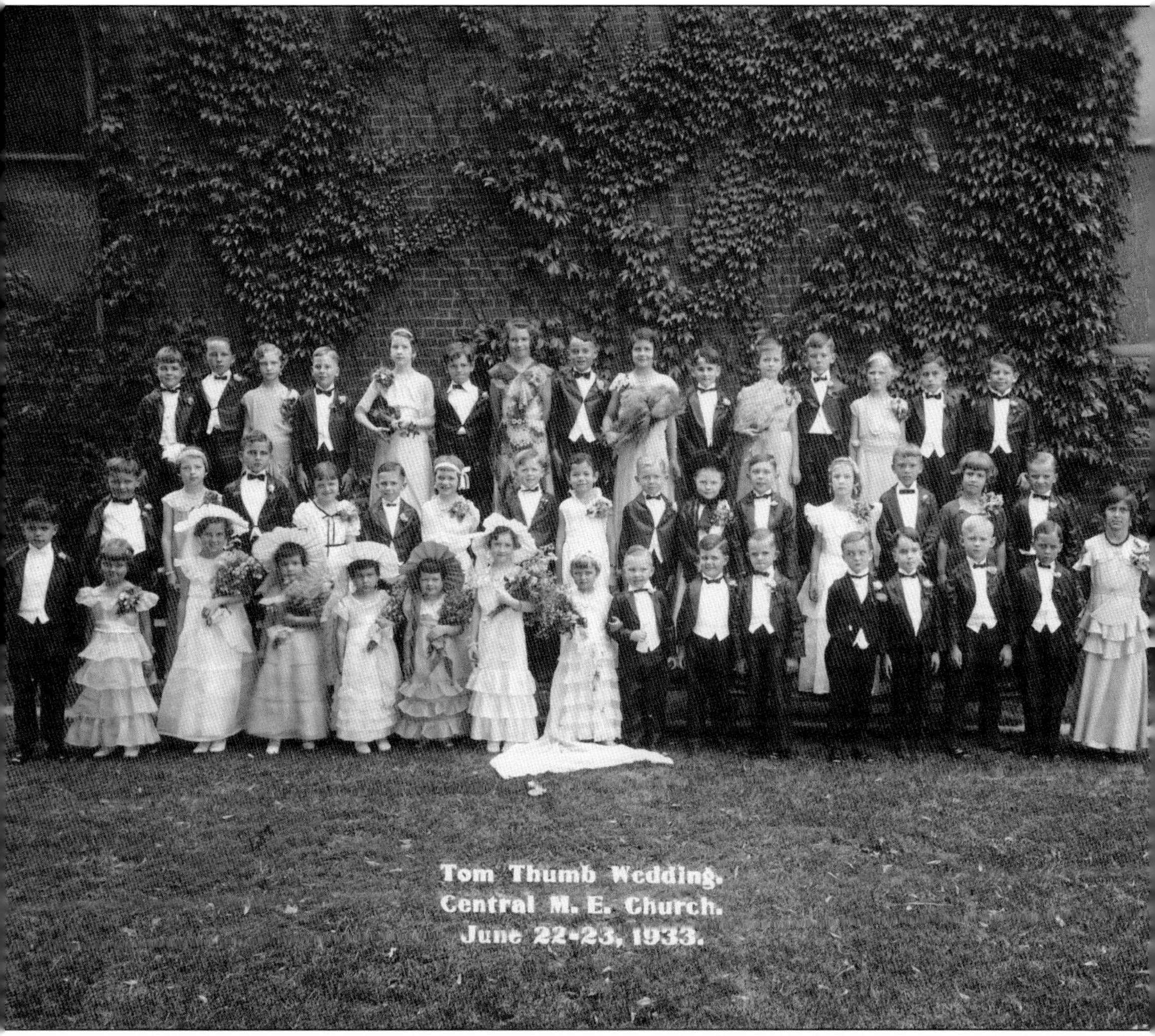

A TOM THUMB WEDDING, JUNE 22–23, 1933. Members of the Central Methodist Episcopal Church organized this event intended to mimic the wedding of P.T. Barnum's famous personality General Tom Thumb and his bride, the former Lavinia Warren. It was photographed by the Laurel Studio. Although the congregation may have been unaware of it, General Tom Thumb and his wife actually did visit Bridgeton in February 1879 when they made a personal appearance at Grosscup's Hall at Commerce and Laurel Streets. They were billed as "The Celebrated Lilliputians."

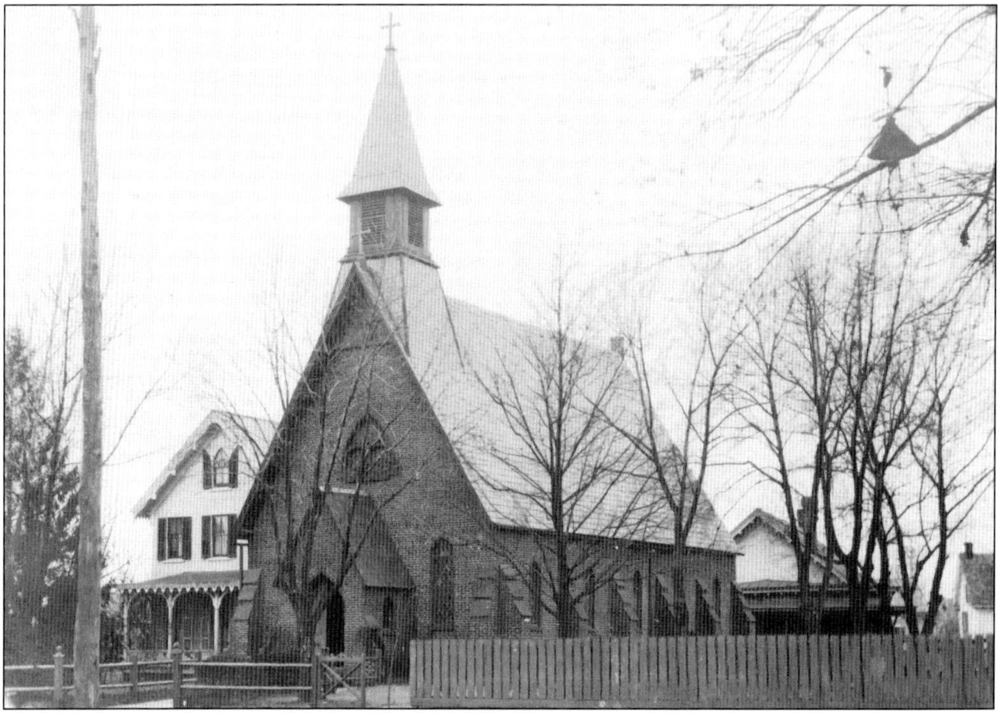

OLD SAINT MARY'S CHURCH. The Roman Catholics of the Bridgeton area constructed this church at North Pearl and North Streets in 1866 during the tenure of Father Martin Gessner. At the time of its dedication in June 1867, the site was surrounded by corn fields.

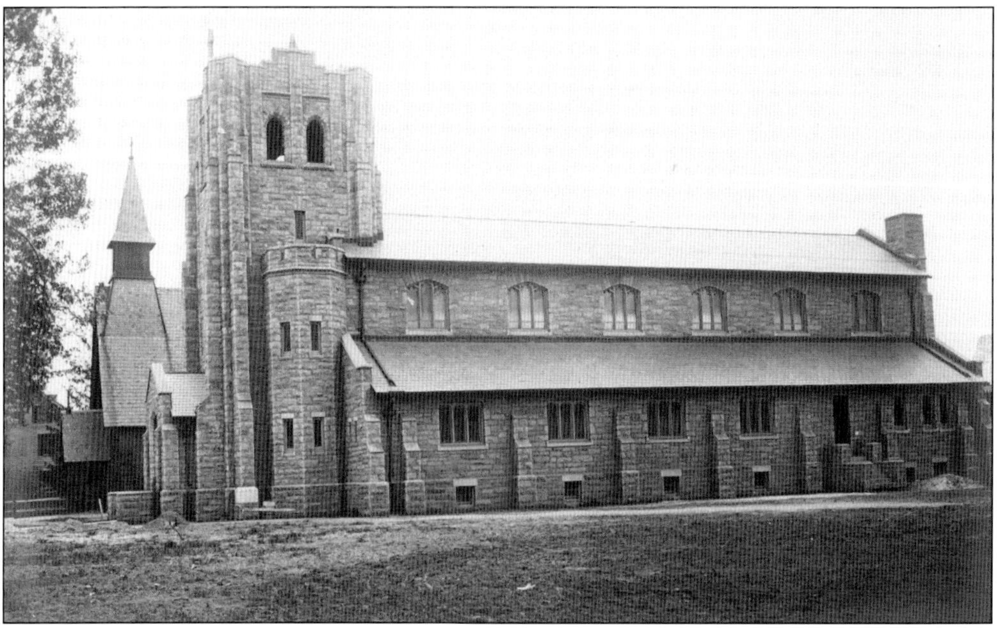

THE OLD AND THE NEW. By 1913, Bridgeton's Roman Catholic parish had outgrown its original church, which can be seen still standing in the background. In June 1913 the cornerstone was laid for the new Church of the Immaculate Conception, seen in a view from the Pedrick collection.

MOUNT CARMEL DAY IN BRIDGETON. Between 1915 and 1953, Bridgeton's Roman Catholics who traced their ancestry to Southern Italy celebrated the Feast of Our Lady of Mount Carmel on July 16 with a massive procession up Pearl Street. This card was printed to announce the event.

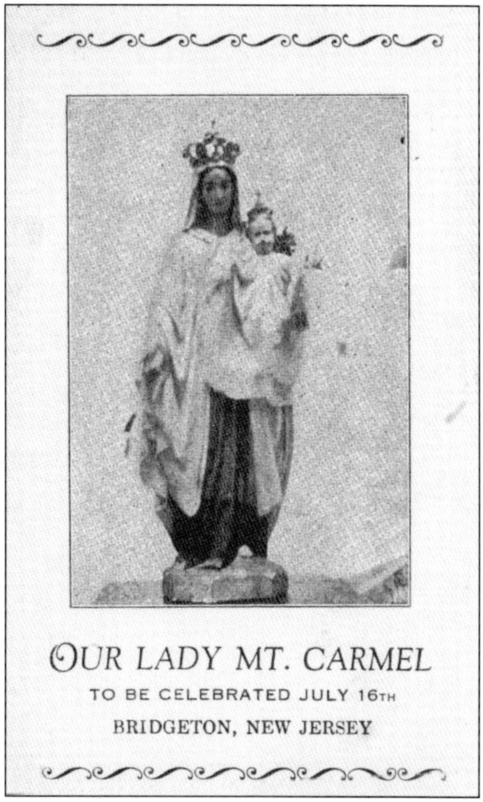

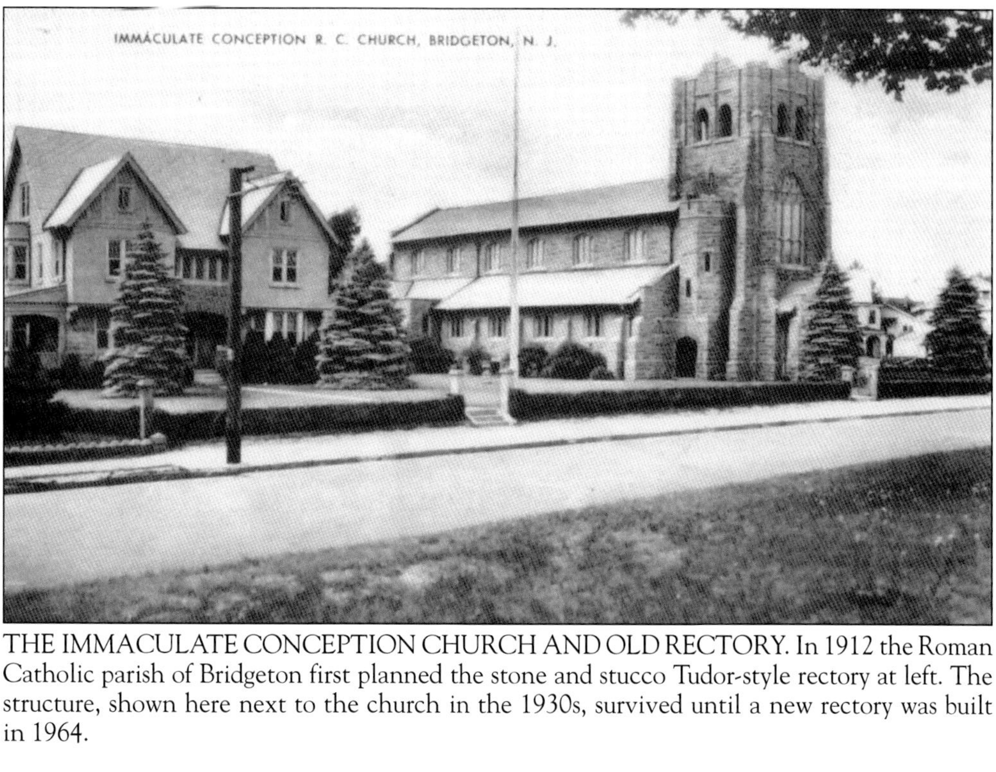

THE IMMACULATE CONCEPTION CHURCH AND OLD RECTORY. In 1912 the Roman Catholic parish of Bridgeton first planned the stone and stucco Tudor-style rectory at left. The structure, shown here next to the church in the 1930s, survived until a new rectory was built in 1964.

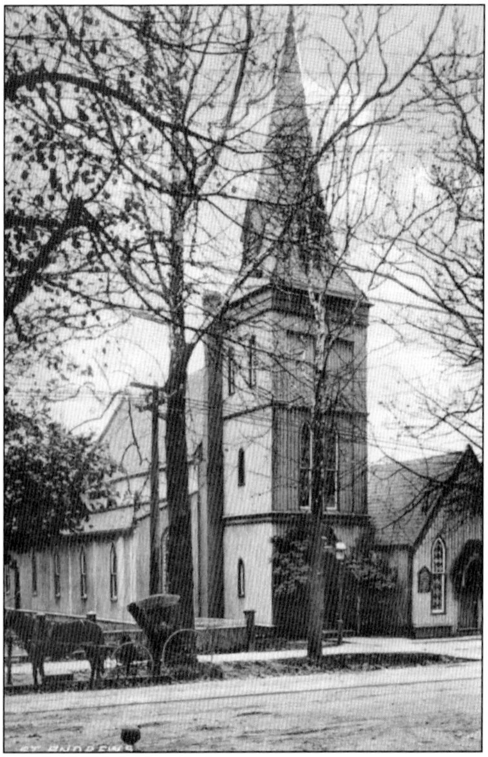

SAINT ANDREW'S EPISCOPAL CHURCH. Depicted here in 1911 with its original board and batten siding, this structure was erected by the congregation on East Commerce Street during the Civil War and was first occupied on July 31, 1864. The structure at right, now gone, was the choir's robing room.

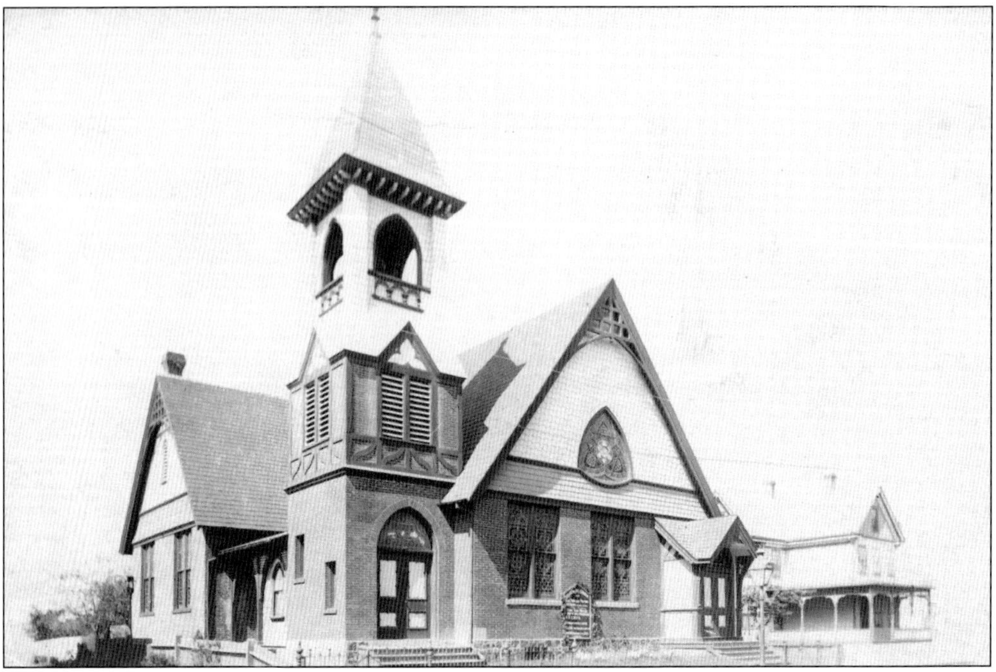

THE FOURTH METHODIST EPISCOPAL CHURCH. This Queen Anne-style house of worship with interesting Stick and Shingle-style elements was built on South Avenue north of River Street in 1888 at a cost of $7,000. In more recent years, the structure became a Pentecostal church.

THE SECOND PRESBYTERIAN CHURCH. Seen about 1910 with its original steeple, this stone church on North Pearl Street was dedicated in 1840 under the pastorate of the Reverend J.L. Bartlett. During its formative years, it was supported by members of Bridgeton's Brewster family, of *Mayflower* fame.

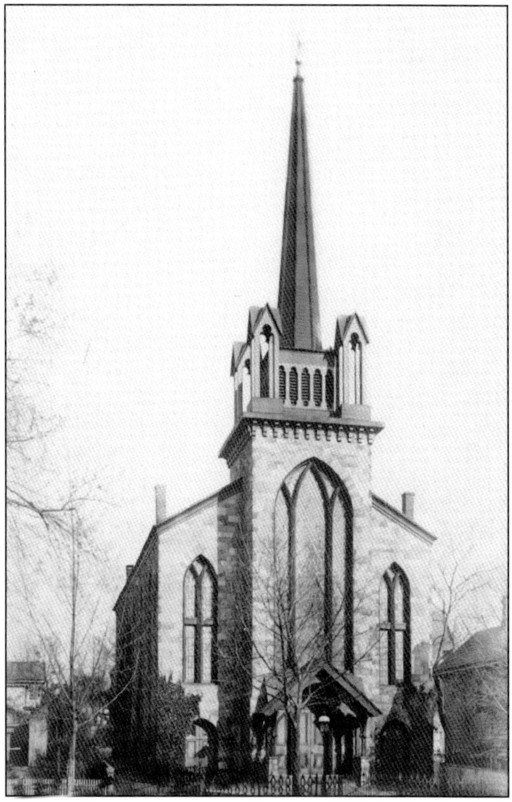

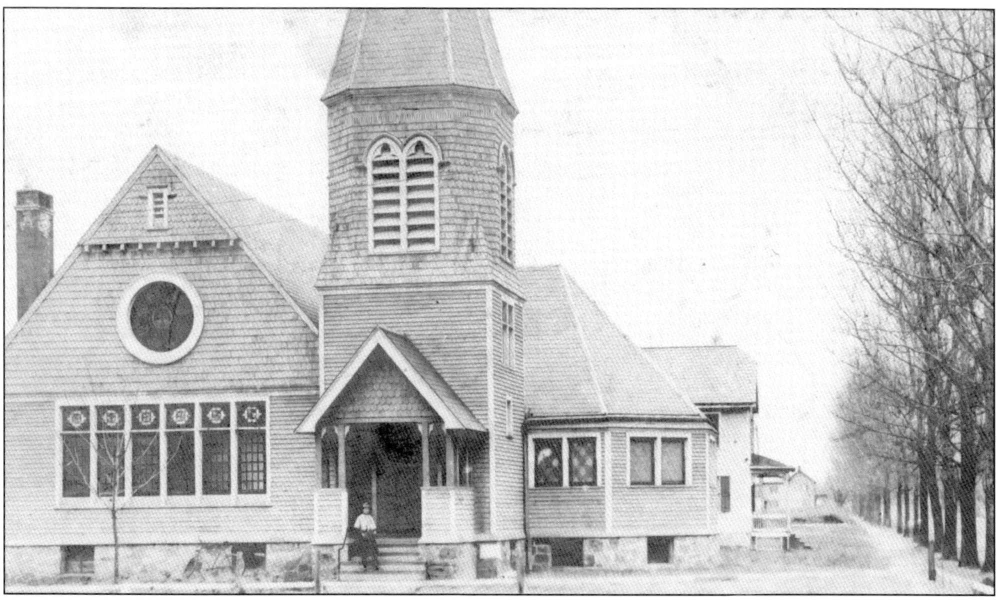

THE IRVING AVENUE PRESBYTERIAN CHURCH. Adherents of the Presbyterian faith in east Bridgeton laid the cornerstone for this structure on the northeast corner of Irving and Manheim Avenues on September 30, 1893. This view dates from 1925. The church survived through the 1950s and was then demolished.

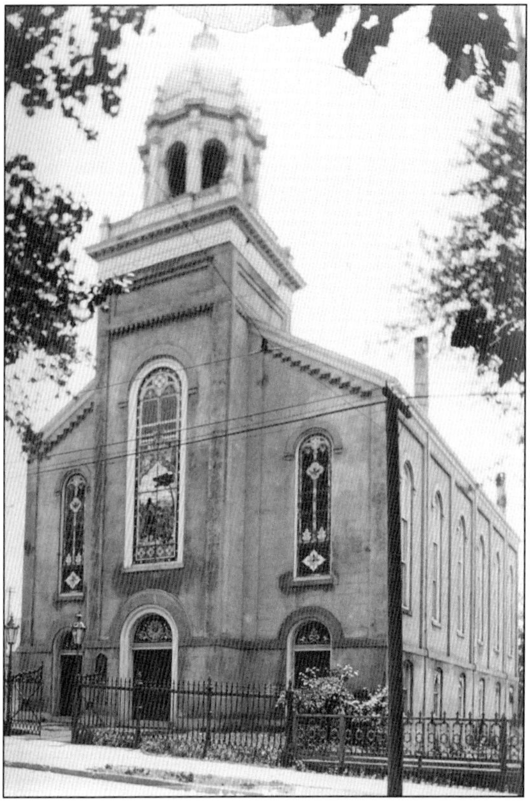

THE FIRST BAPTIST CHURCH. Located on East Commerce Street, this edifice was completed by 1854 and may have been designed by Thomas U. Walter, a devout Baptist who was architect of the Capitol. The Baroque cupola was added about 1900, shortly before this photograph was made.

A HEBREW SCHOOL CLASS. Congregation Beth Abraham dedicated its synagogue on the North Laurel Street hill not far from downtown Bridgeton in 1916. Standing on the steps of the synagogue about 1947 are members of the Hebrew school class, most of whom went on to become professionals and business people.

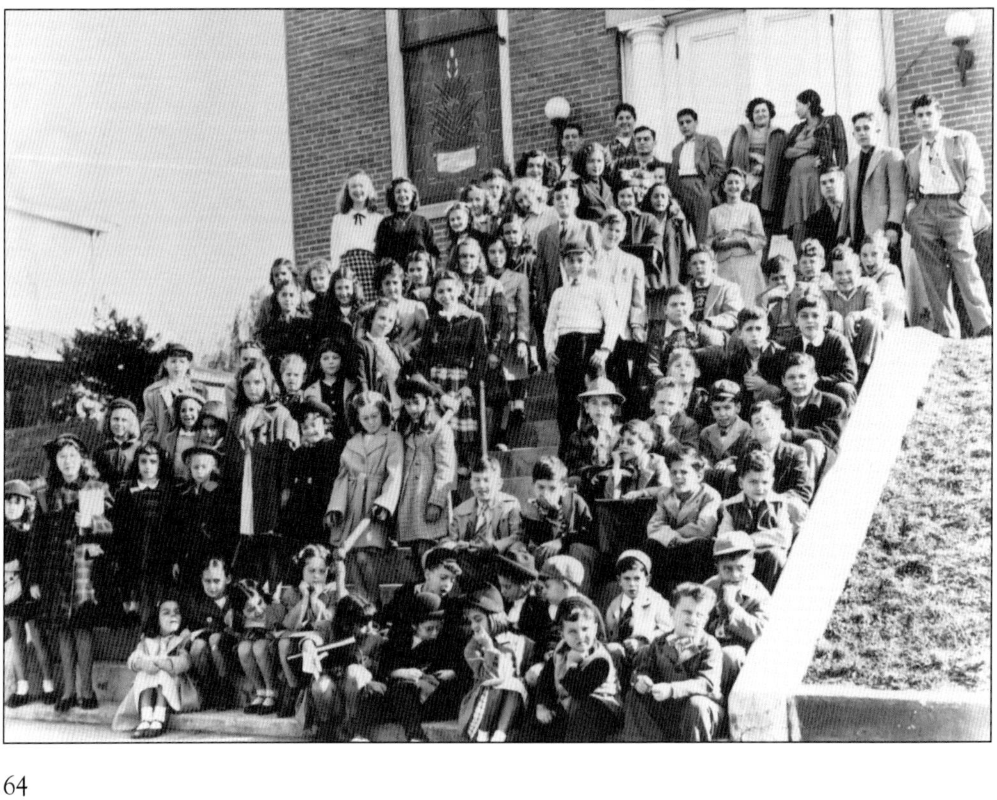

Five

Classic Halls of Learning

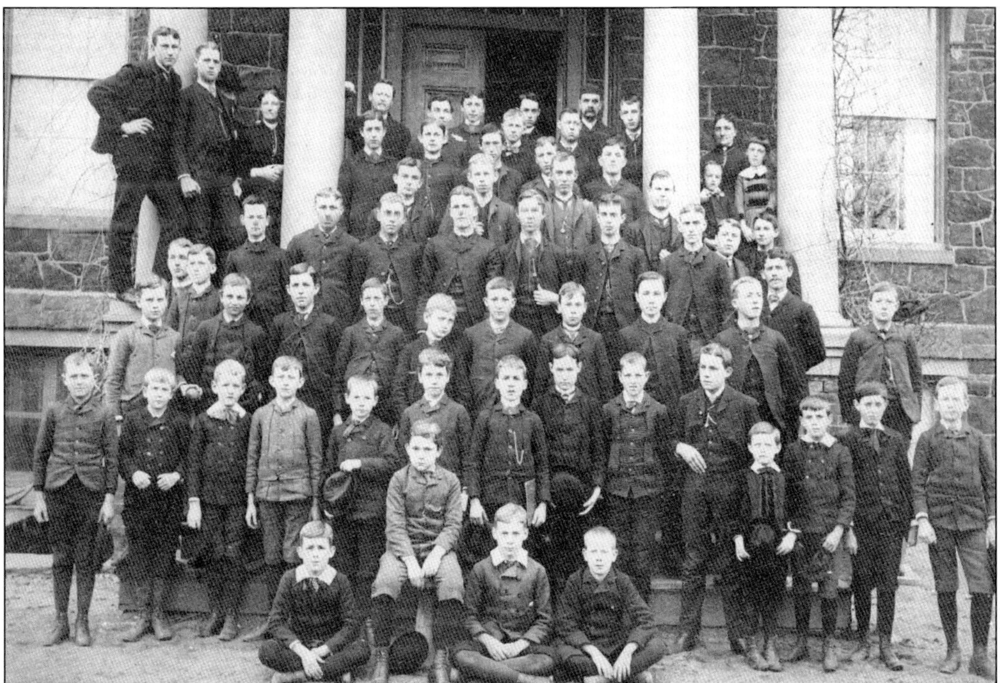

WEST JERSEY ACADEMY STUDENTS, 1885. Blue-blood families of Bridgeton and neighboring areas sent their sons to the West Jersey Academy military school on Broad Street at West Avenue. Here a group of these students, along with some faculty members, assemble on the front steps of the structure.

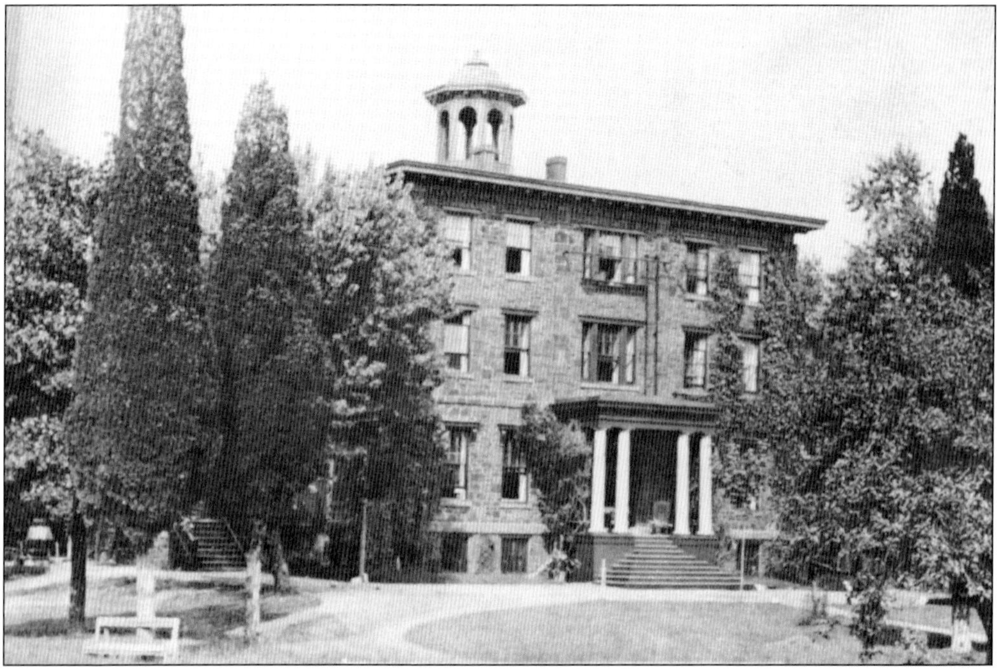

ON ACADEMY HILL. The West Jersey Academy was first proposed by Presbyterian clergyman Dr. Samuel Beach Jones in 1850, and its cornerstone was laid on August 9, 1852. The expressed intention of the school was to meet the need for "the education of boys on a moral and Christian basis."

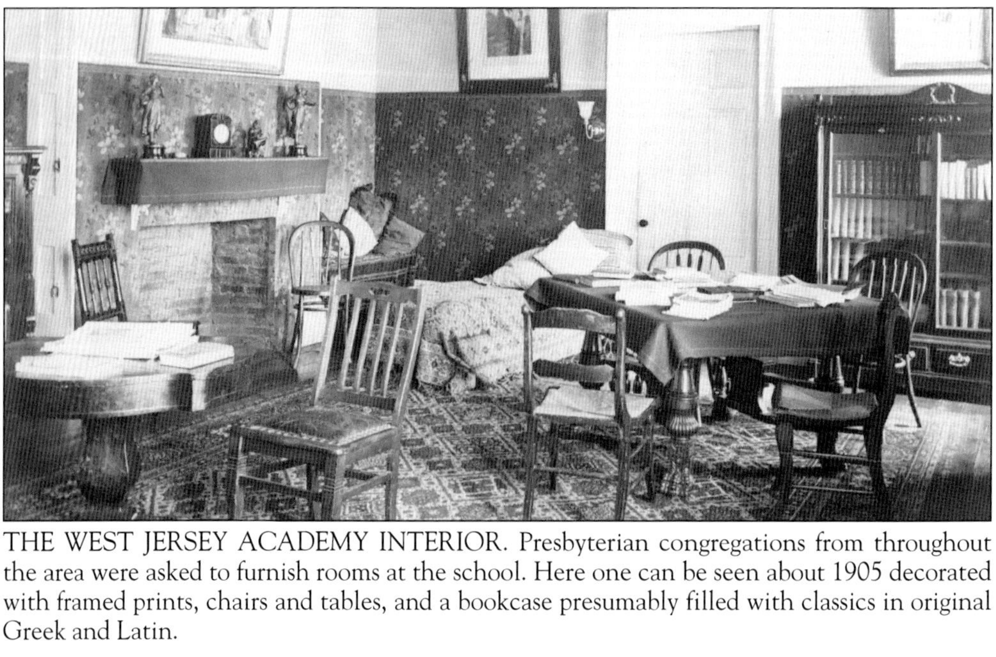

THE WEST JERSEY ACADEMY INTERIOR. Presbyterian congregations from throughout the area were asked to furnish rooms at the school. Here one can be seen about 1905 decorated with framed prints, chairs and tables, and a bookcase presumably filled with classics in original Greek and Latin.

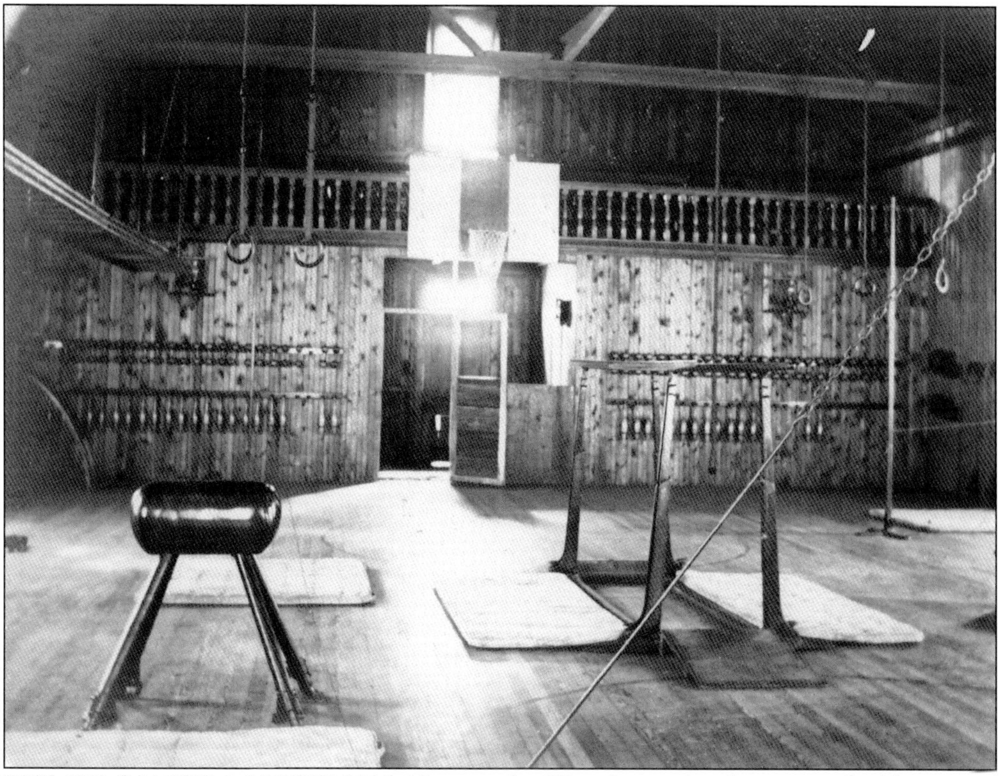

THE GYMNASIUM ABOUT 1905. Next to the West Jersey Academy main building stood a small Carpenter Gothic-style gymnasium which was filled with equipment to train young cadets. Visible are Indian clubs, rings, a vaulting horse, parallel bars, and a basketball net and backboard.

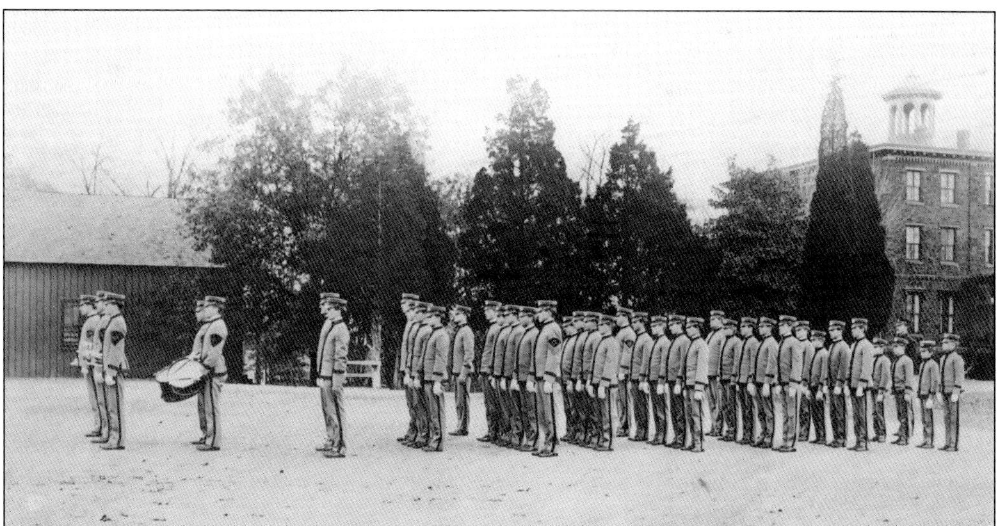

ON THE PARADE GROUND. West Jersey Academy cadets were expected to dress in military uniforms and learn how to drill. Shown here lined up with a drum and bugle unit about 1900, the cadets are ready for inspection. At right can be seen the academy building and, at left, the frame gymnasium.

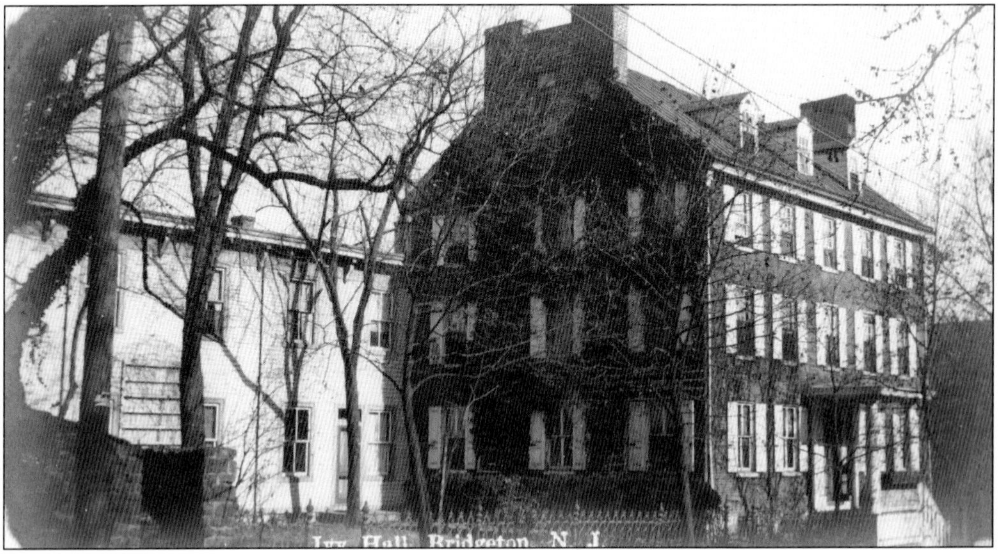

THE IVY HALL GIRLS' SEMINARY. Originally built on West Commerce Street as the home of David Sheppard in 1792, by 1861 this structure had been converted into a girls school which took its name from the vines then climbing the walls of the ancient structure.

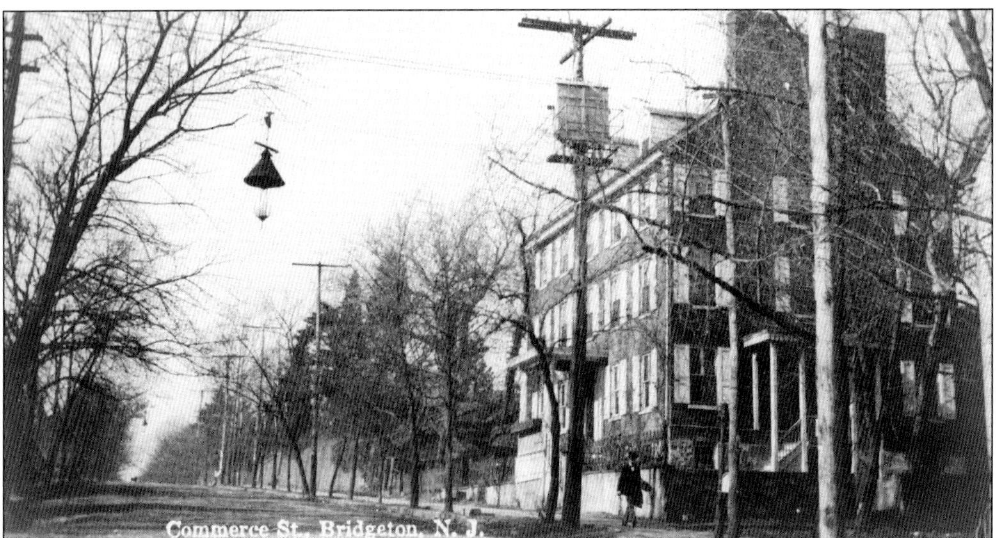

THE WEST COMMERCE STREET HILL. Dominating the northwest corner at the park entrance in this 1905 view from the Pedrick collection is Ivy Hall. During the Civil War era, young women perched in its windows to witness parades of soldiers returning to their hometown.

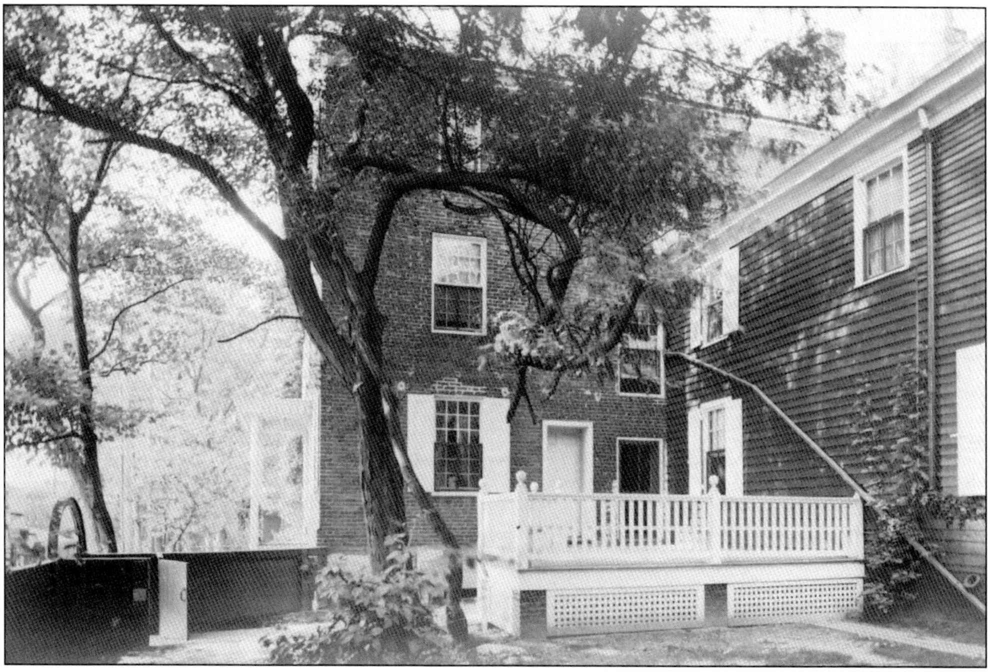

THE NORTH SIDE OF IVY HALL. When Margaretta C. Sheppard founded her school in 1861, she encouraged her young female charges to enjoy the outdoor life, take in the air on this porch, and walk the nearby Raceway banks. The rear section of the building was demolished in 1995.

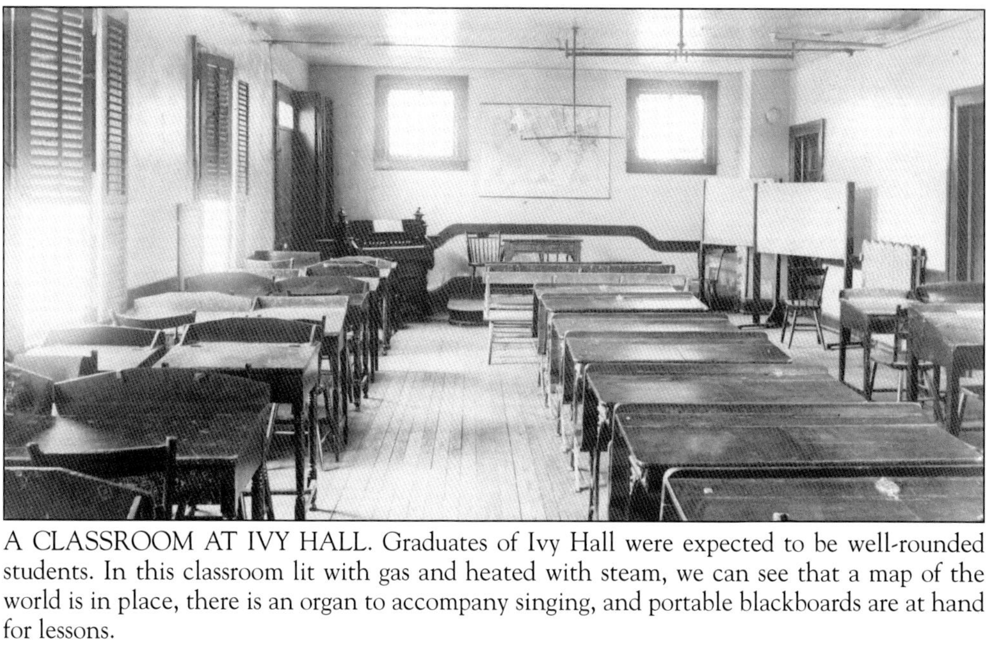

A CLASSROOM AT IVY HALL. Graduates of Ivy Hall were expected to be well-rounded students. In this classroom lit with gas and heated with steam, we can see that a map of the world is in place, there is an organ to accompany singing, and portable blackboards are at hand for lessons.

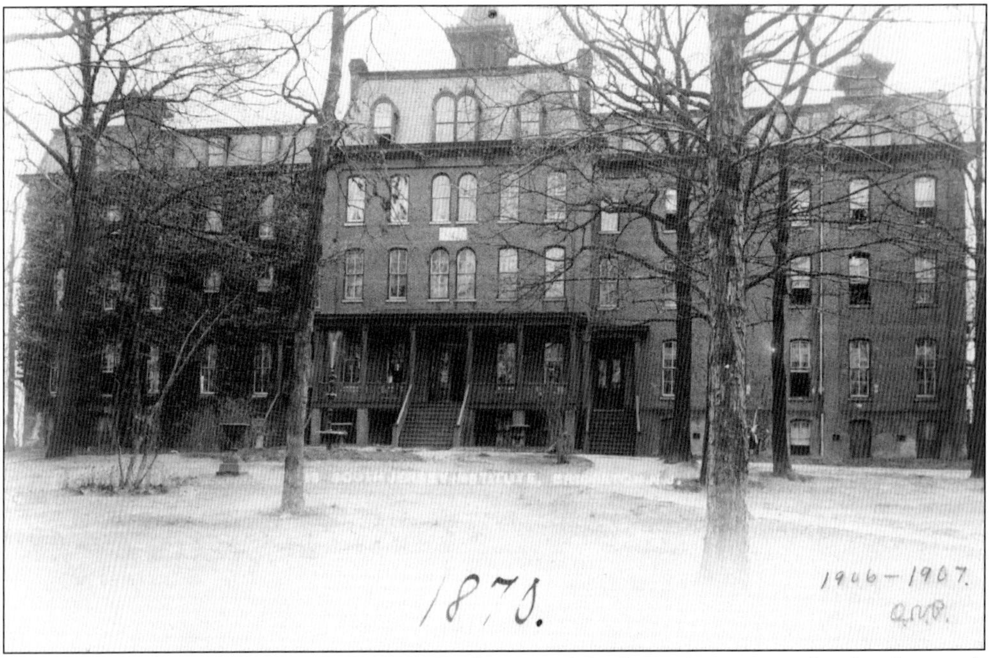

THE SOUTH JERSEY INSTITUTE. The largest of Bridgeton's private schools, the coed, Baptist-affiliated South Jersey Institute off Atlantic Street first opened on October 5, 1870, and continued to serve students until 1907, when this picture was taken. It was demolished in 1923.

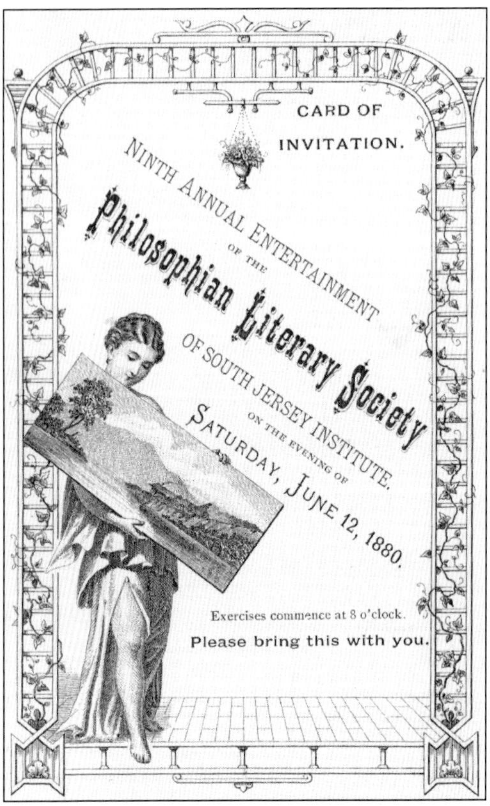

YOU'RE INVITED. The Philosophian Literary Society sent this invitation to guests to attend exercises on the evening of June 12, 1880. The event included an oration, piano and vocal presentations, essay readings, and a debate on the influence of women.

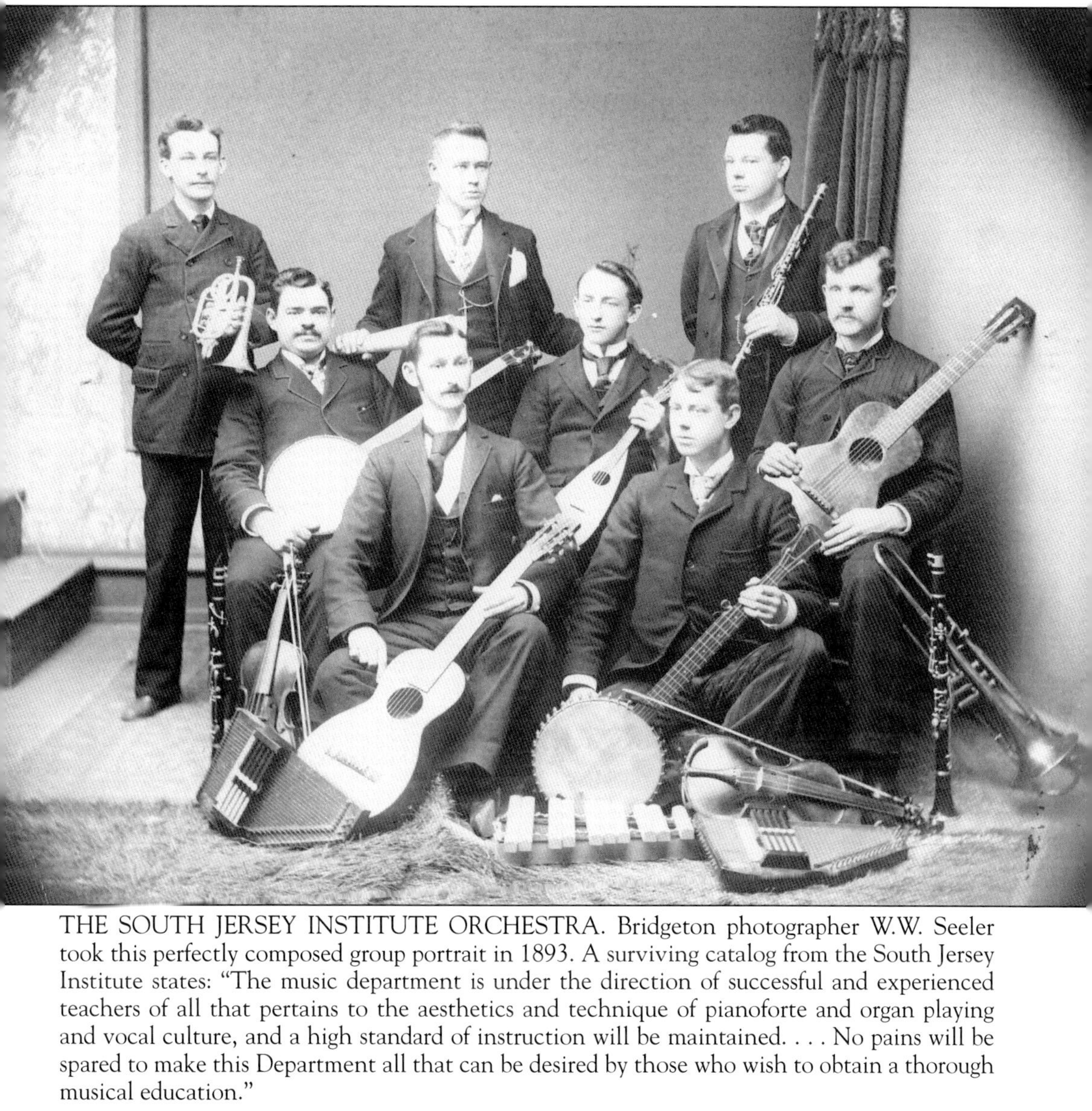

THE SOUTH JERSEY INSTITUTE ORCHESTRA. Bridgeton photographer W.W. Seeler took this perfectly composed group portrait in 1893. A surviving catalog from the South Jersey Institute states: "The music department is under the direction of successful and experienced teachers of all that pertains to the aesthetics and technique of pianoforte and organ playing and vocal culture, and a high standard of instruction will be maintained. . . . No pains will be spared to make this Department all that can be desired by those who wish to obtain a thorough musical education."

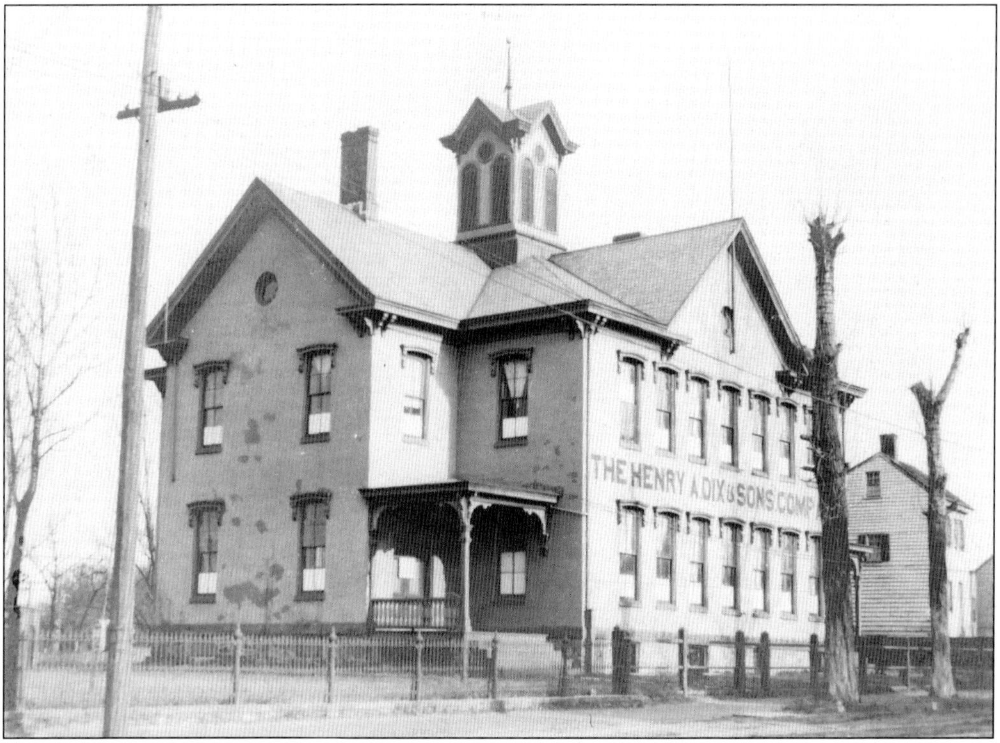

THE SECOND WARD PUBLIC SCHOOL. Constructed in 1873 at South Avenue and Willow Street, this is the oldest surviving public school building in Bridgeton, although it has not been utilized for educational purposes since the turn of the century. When photographed about 1905, it was a garment factory.

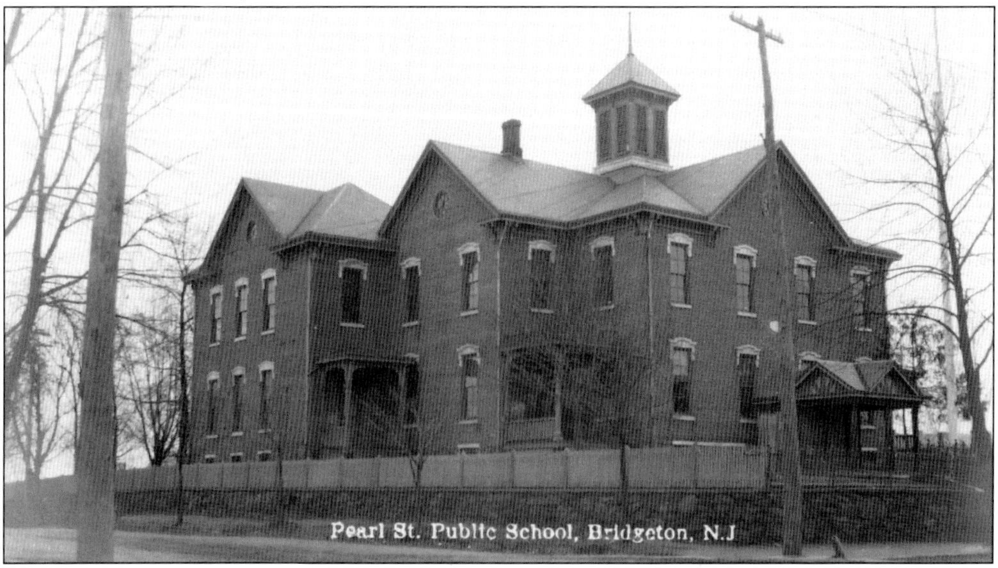

THE PEARL STREET PUBLIC SCHOOL. Although often referred to as a twin of the Second Ward Public School, the Pearl Street School was in fact different in several ways from the building it was modeled upon. Originally constructed in 1884 and pictured here about 1910, this building underwent many changes over the years.

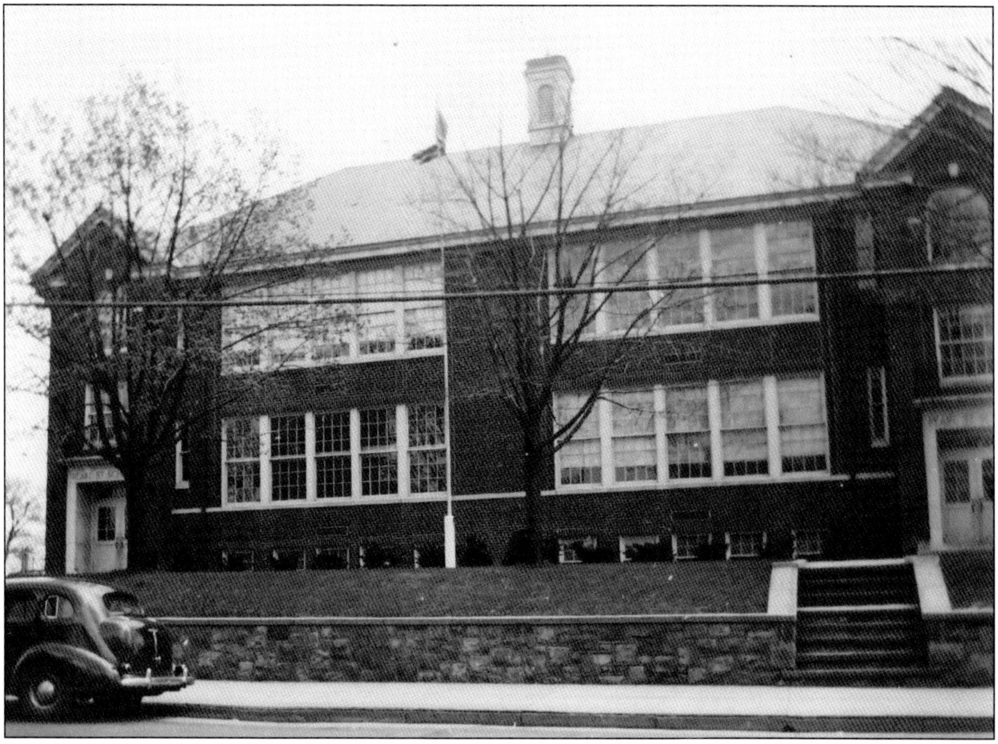

THE PEARL STREET SCHOOL, ABOUT 1940. Following additions and renovations in 1928, it is likely that little remained of the original Victorian-era structure. When the Bridgeton Middle School opened in 1982, this school ceased operating; it burned in 1992.

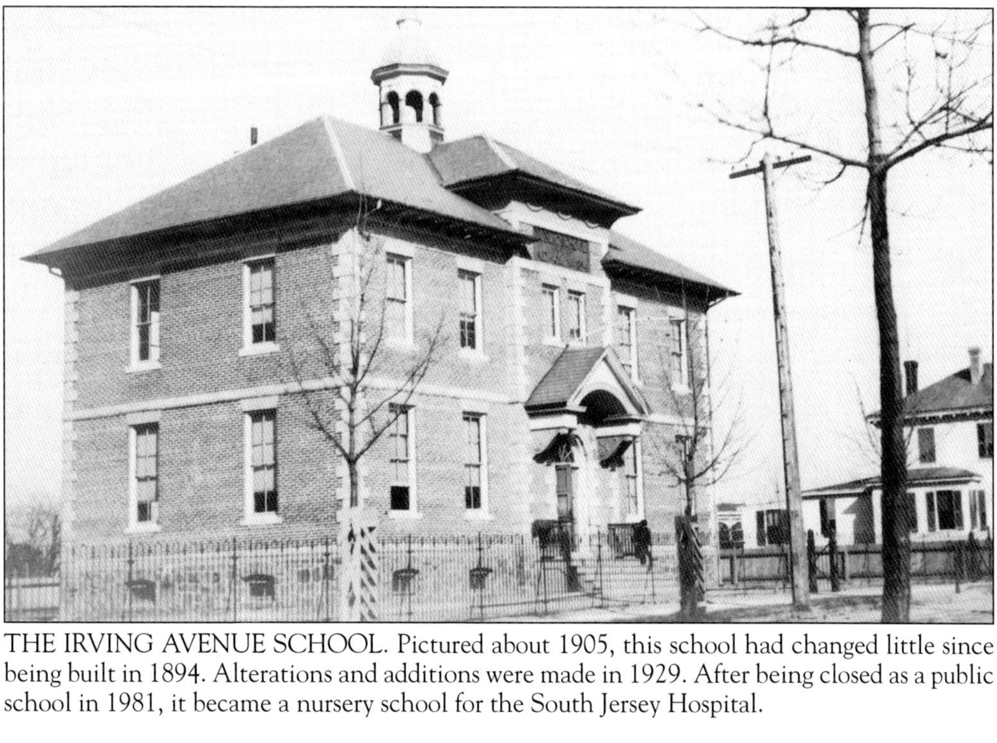

THE IRVING AVENUE SCHOOL. Pictured about 1905, this school had changed little since being built in 1894. Alterations and additions were made in 1929. After being closed as a public school in 1981, it became a nursery school for the South Jersey Hospital.

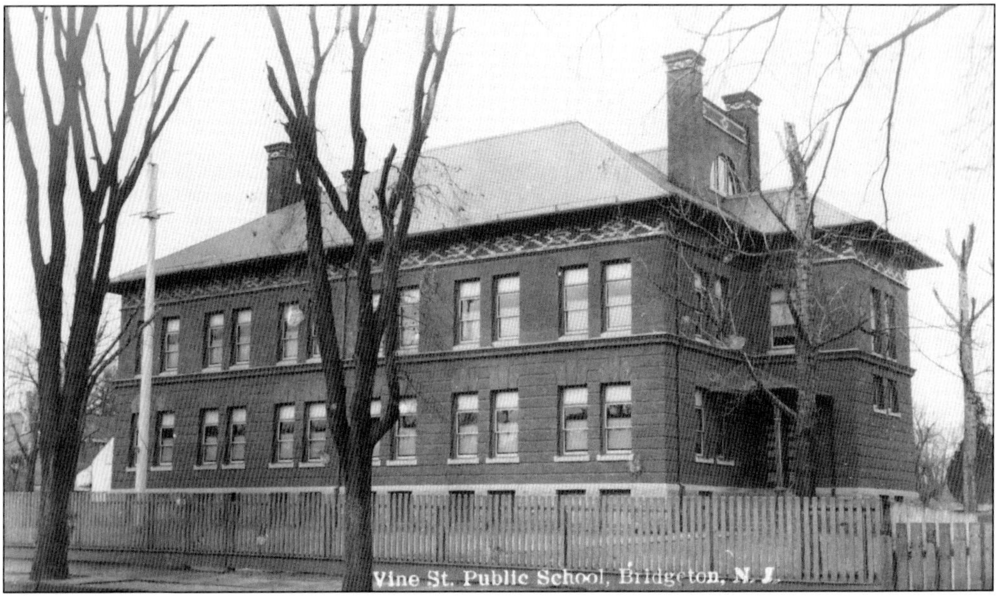

THE VINE STREET SCHOOL. Among the most beautiful of Bridgeton's public elementary schools when built in 1898, the Vine Street School featured graceful chimneys and brickwork laid in elaborate patterns as revealed in this photograph dating about 1910. The school last housed students in 1981.

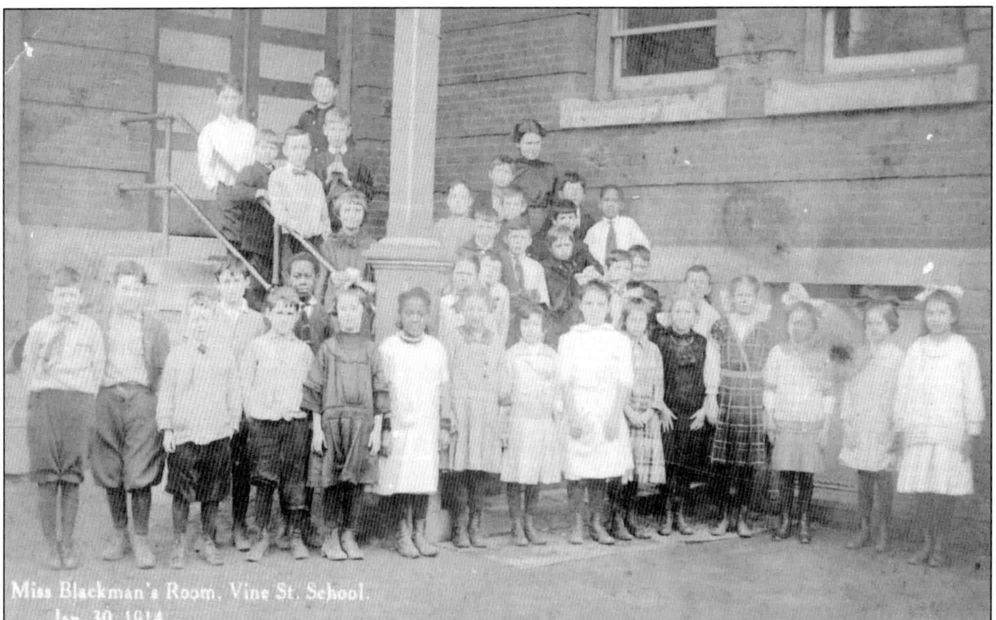

OUR GANG, BRIDGETON STYLE. The multicultural nature of Miss Blackburn's students at the Vine Street School is revealed in this *c.* 1914 photograph by Daniel Ward, now in the Pedrick collection. The neighborhood school served blue-collar, white-collar, and aristocratic families.

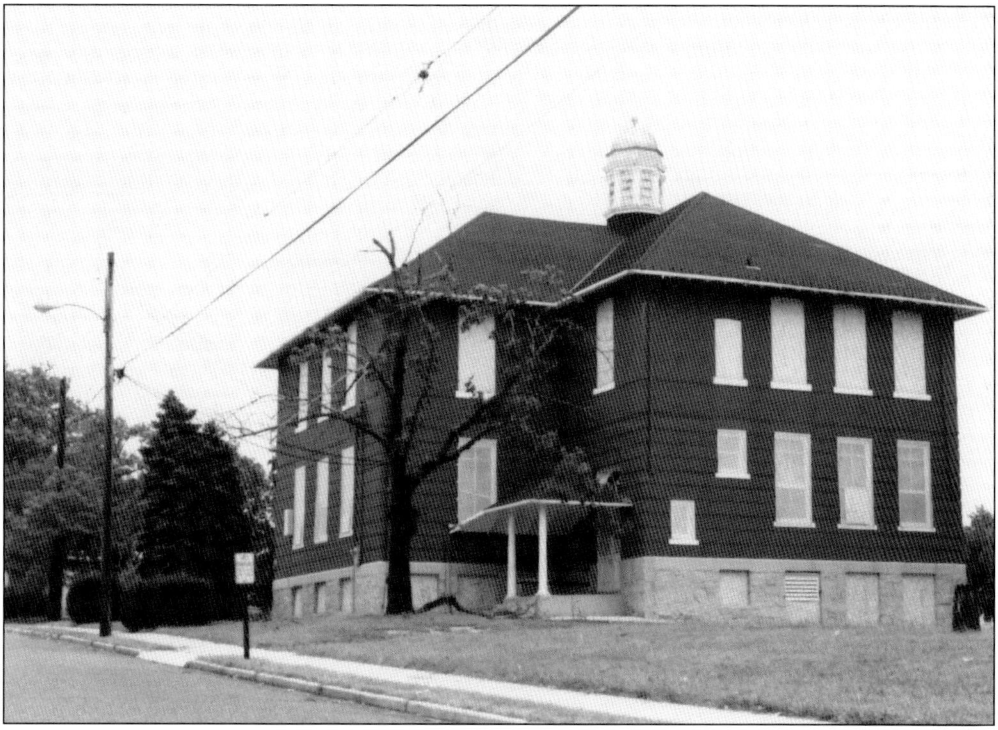

THE MONROE STREET SCHOOL. Reflecting the attitudes of the era in which it was built, the 1899 Monroe Street School in north Bridgeton included separate entrances for boys and girls. The structure was razed in 1994, much to the lament of former students.

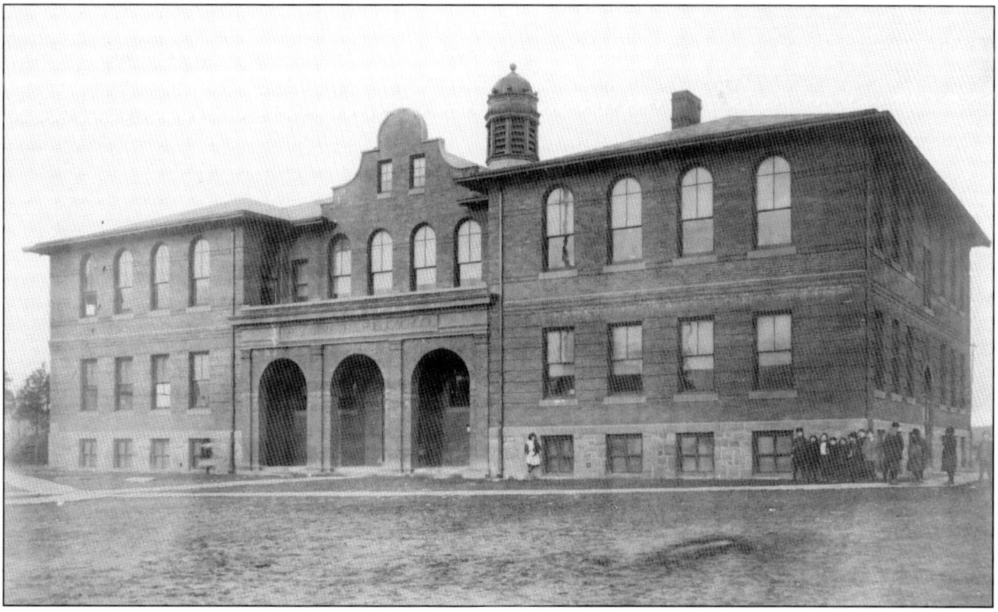

THE SOUTH AVENUE PUBLIC SCHOOL. Although its symmetrical facade reflects Neoclassical influence, the building's architectural details, particularly the ogee parapeted gable, are evocative of the Queen Anne style. This structure was built in 1903, and burned in 1975 when in use as a health clinic.

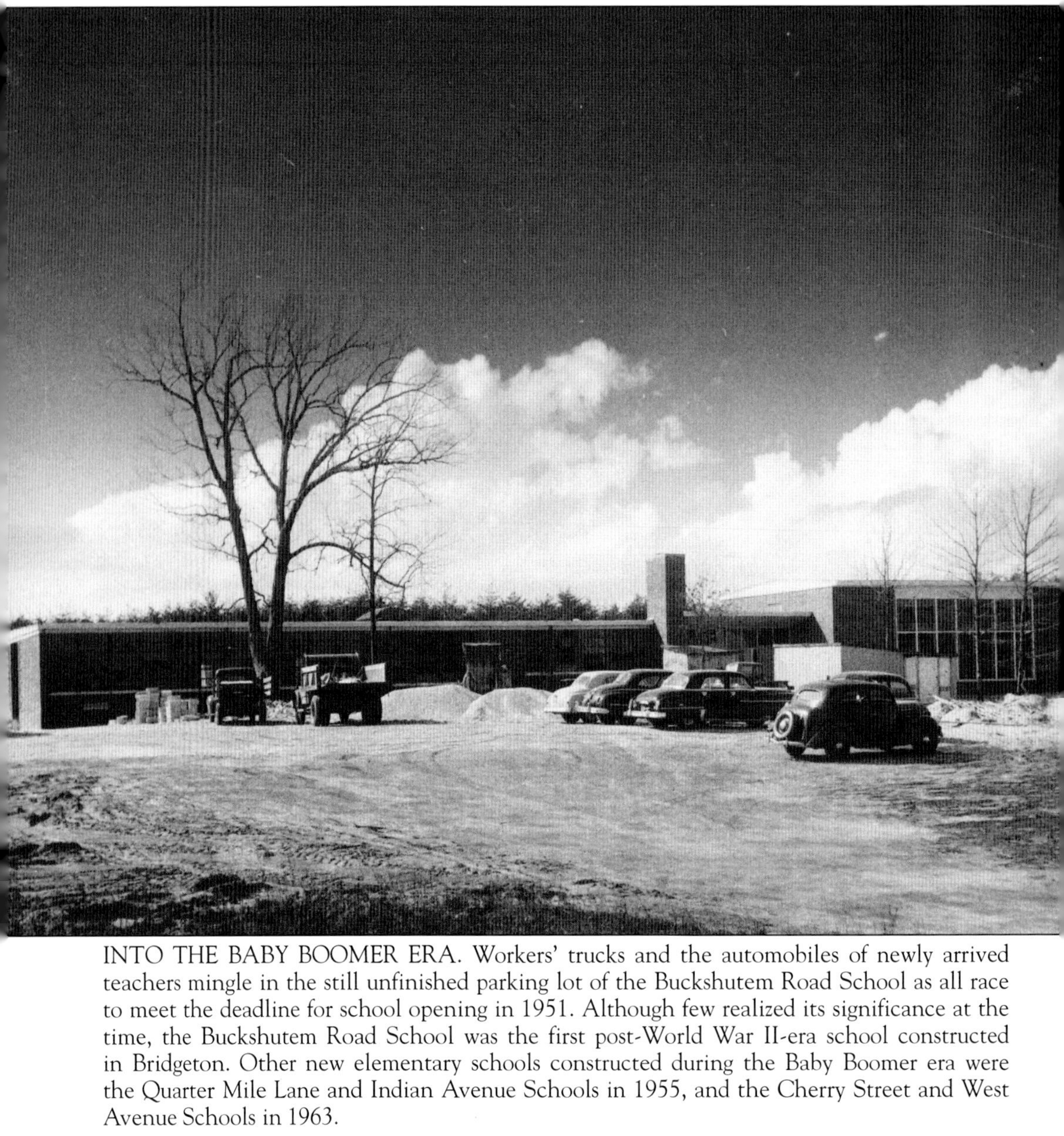

INTO THE BABY BOOMER ERA. Workers' trucks and the automobiles of newly arrived teachers mingle in the still unfinished parking lot of the Buckshutem Road School as all race to meet the deadline for school opening in 1951. Although few realized its significance at the time, the Buckshutem Road School was the first post-World War II-era school constructed in Bridgeton. Other new elementary schools constructed during the Baby Boomer era were the Quarter Mile Lane and Indian Avenue Schools in 1955, and the Cherry Street and West Avenue Schools in 1963.

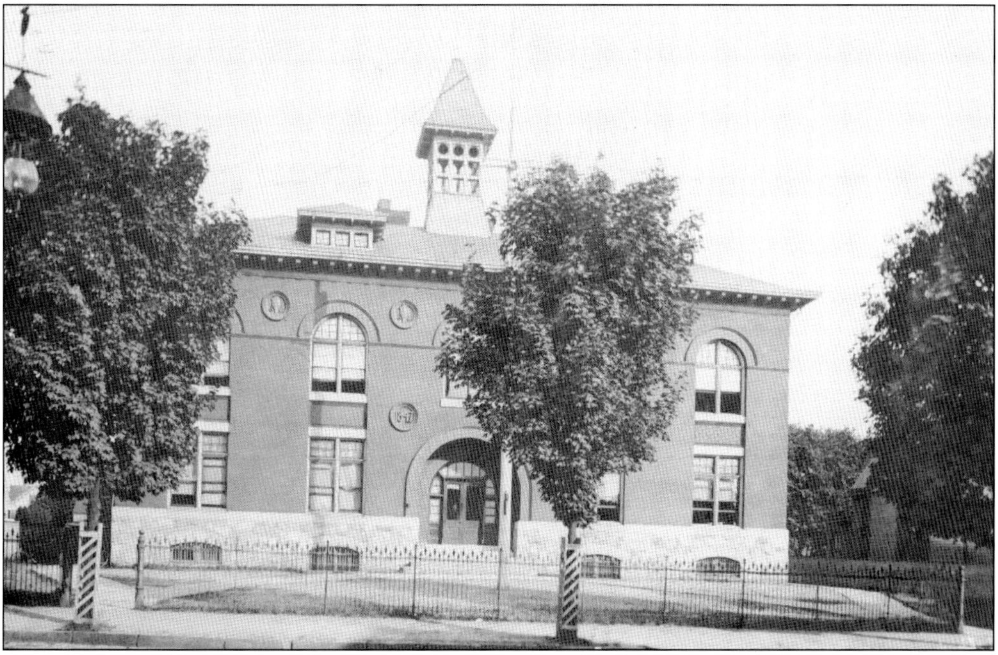

BRIDGETON HIGH SCHOOL, BANK STREET CAMPUS. Designed in the Richardsonian Romanesque style, this building was begun in 1892 on the former site of an 1847 frame school—hence the dual date bosses that flank its entrance. The first class graduated in 1894.

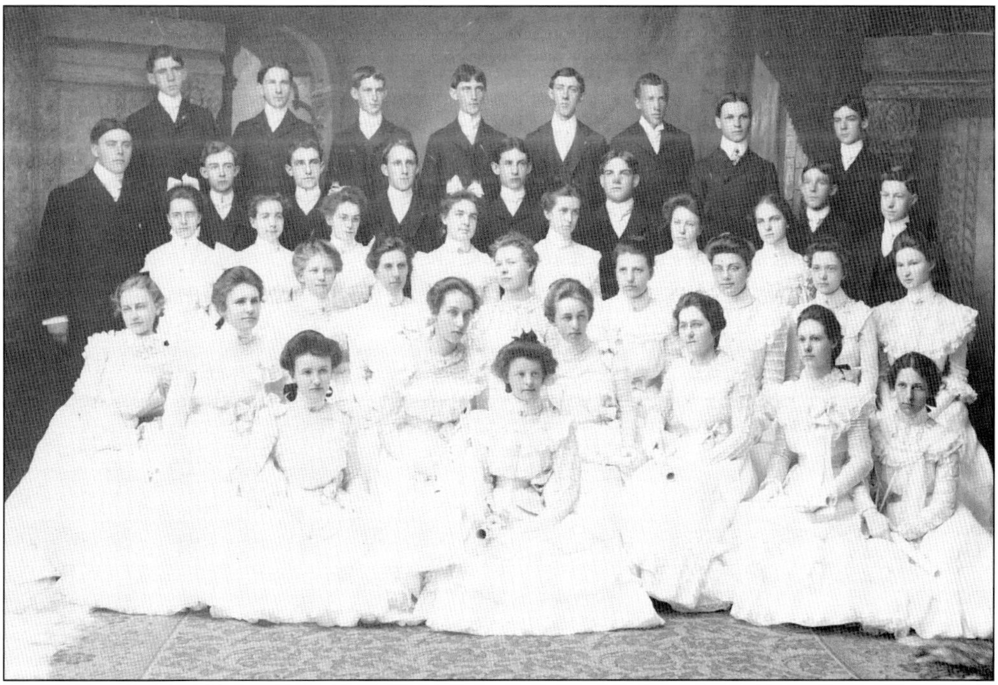

THE BRIDGETON HIGH CLASS OF 1900. Confidently facing a new century, members of this class donned their finest for a portrait taken by William E. Service. When Bridgeton High was located on Bank Street, commencements were held at Moore's Opera House, later the Criterion Theatre.

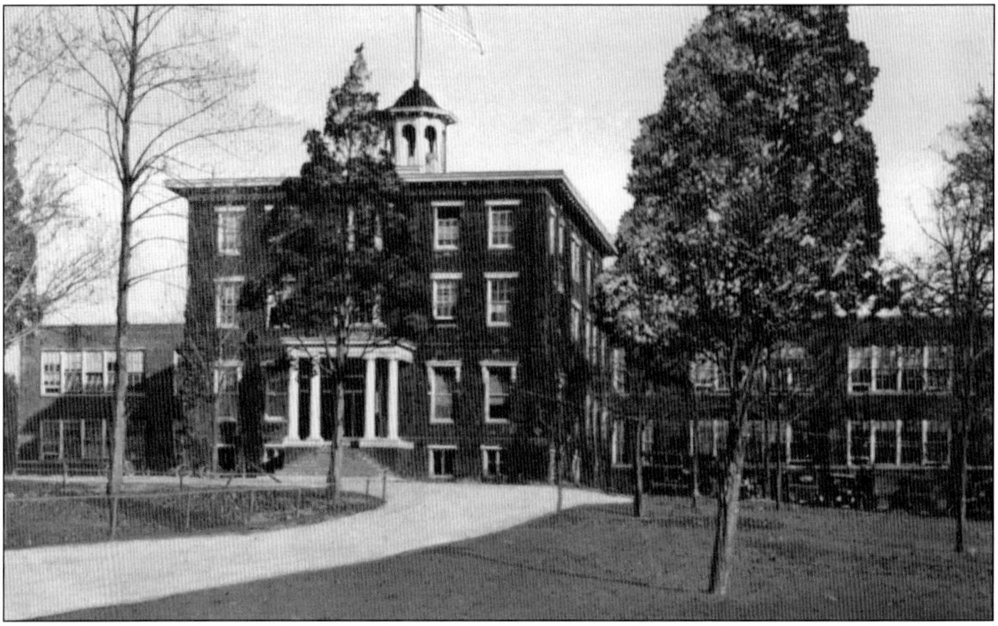

BRIDGETON HIGH SCHOOL, BROAD STREET CAMPUS. After the school outgrew its Bank Street campus, between 1923 and 1929 Bridgeton High students attended the renovated and expanded former West Jersey Academy on Broad Street. When the high school was expanded again in 1929–30, the academy wing was razed.

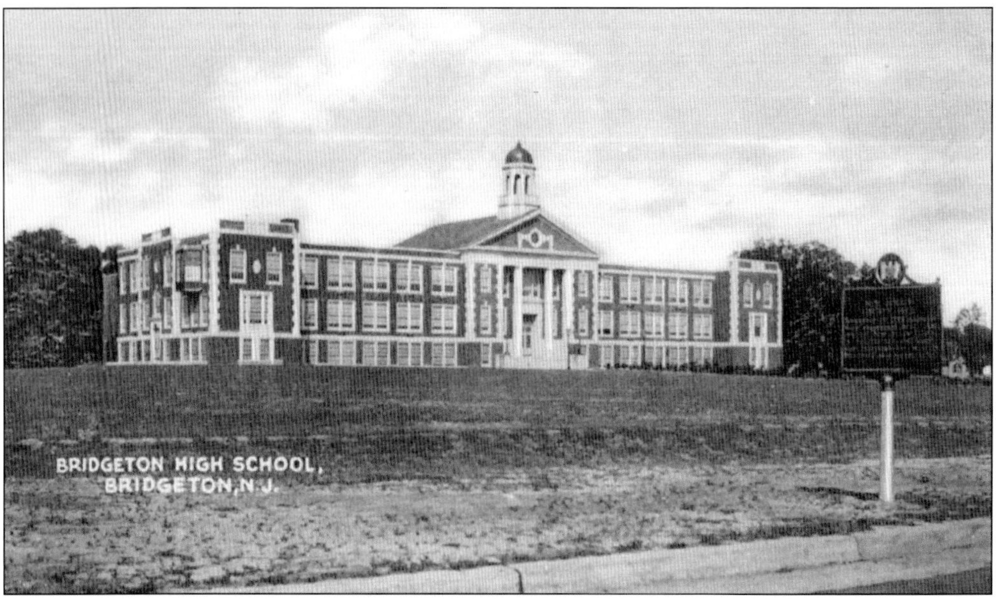

A NEOCLASSICAL GEM. When completed in 1930, the south facade of Bridgeton High School became a favorite landmark. Designed by Walter Custer of Edwards & Green, the brick structure is trimmed in Indiana limestone. It became the junior high, and then in 1981, the middle school.

A FAVORITE HANGOUT. Reinhard's Store on the Lawrence Street side of the Bridgeton High School campus was a meeting place for students in the 1950s. Engineer boots and loafers were "in" for guys, as were rolled-up cuffs. The young lady favors a mid-calf length skirt and blazer.

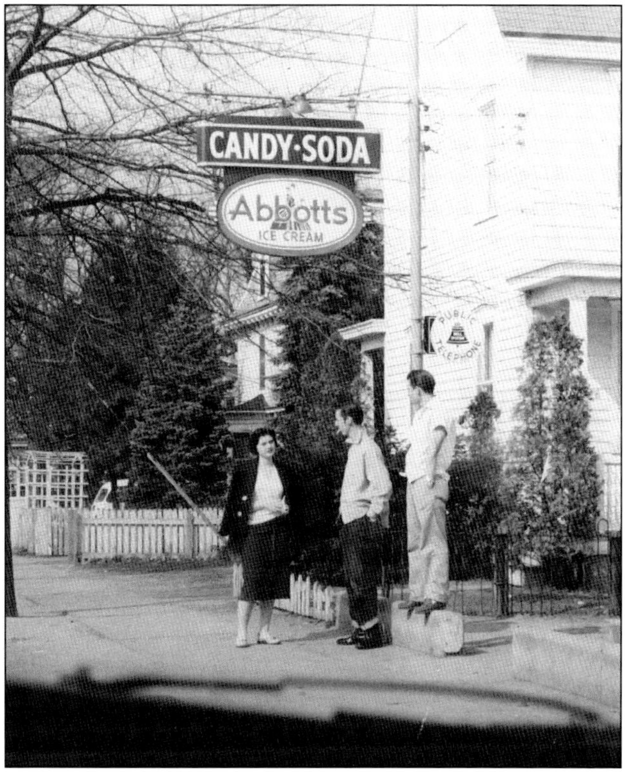

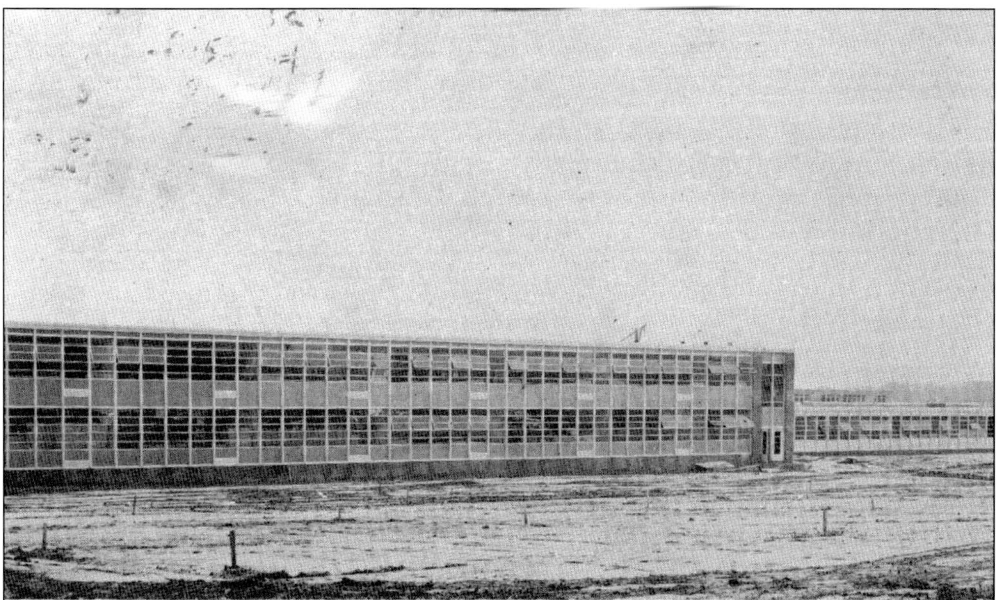

BRIDGETON HIGH SCHOOL – ON JUNE 28, 1958

WELCOME TO THE NEW BRIDGETON HIGH. Students who would be attending the newly constructed Bridgeton High School on West Avenue received this postcard announcement in August 1958. It was sent by Pete's Men's Store in the Laurel Theatre building to remind students of the store's back-to-school sale.

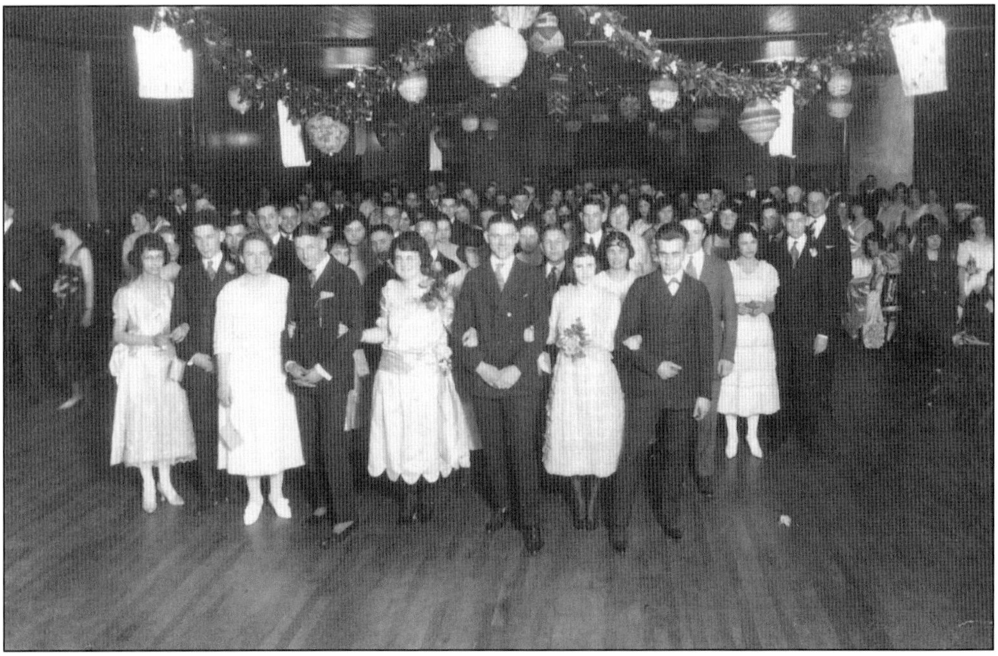

PROM NIGHT, 1921. Members of the junior and senior classes of Bridgeton High gathered in the Chinese lantern-festooned third floor of the Moose Hall on South Laurel Street on February 18, 1921, to hold their reception. Class officers and their dates lead the formal promenade.

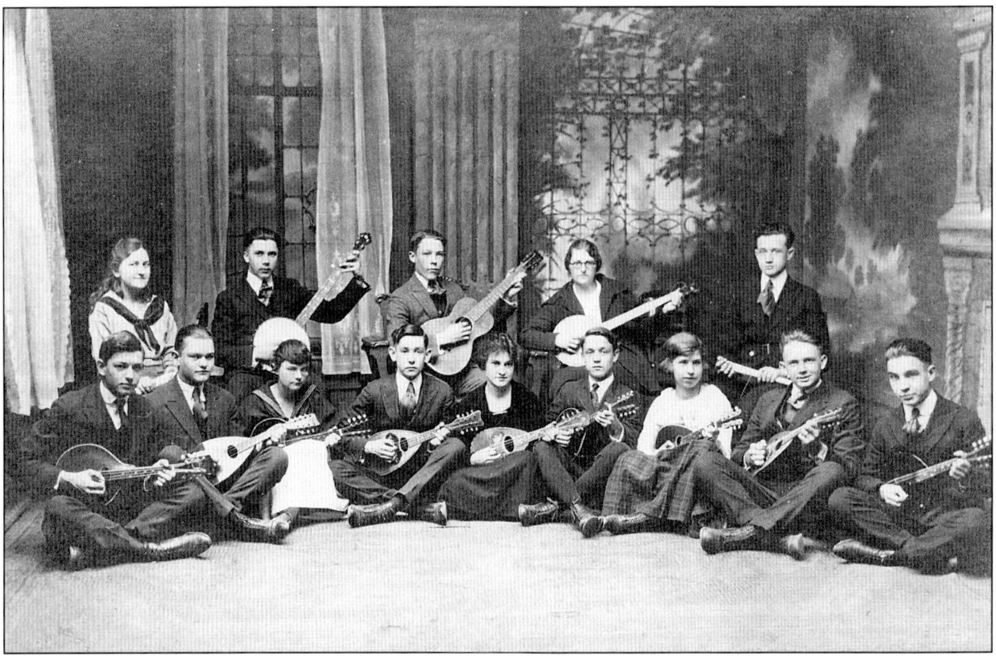

THE BHS STRING ENSEMBLE OF 1921. Students included in this photograph are as follows: (front row) G. Hampton, E. Mulford, S. Shoemaker, P. Dare, M. Westcott, E. Meyers, D. Parker, N. Rodman, and H. Loder; (back row) F. Stratton, A. Lang, D. Patchell, B. Eisenhower, and G. Stanger.

Six

The Flood of '34

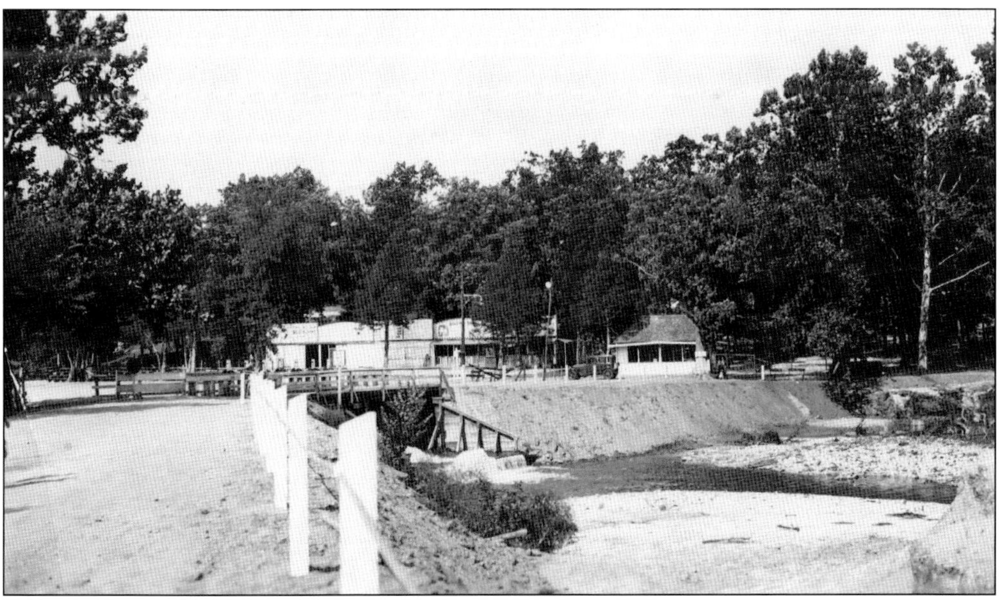

TUMBLING DAM PARK—BEFORE. A photographer standing on the dam embankment at Sunset Lake looking northeast captured this scene in 1931, three years prior to the big flood. The gates are visible, and behind them one can see, from left to right, the bath house, the game area, and the refreshment stand.

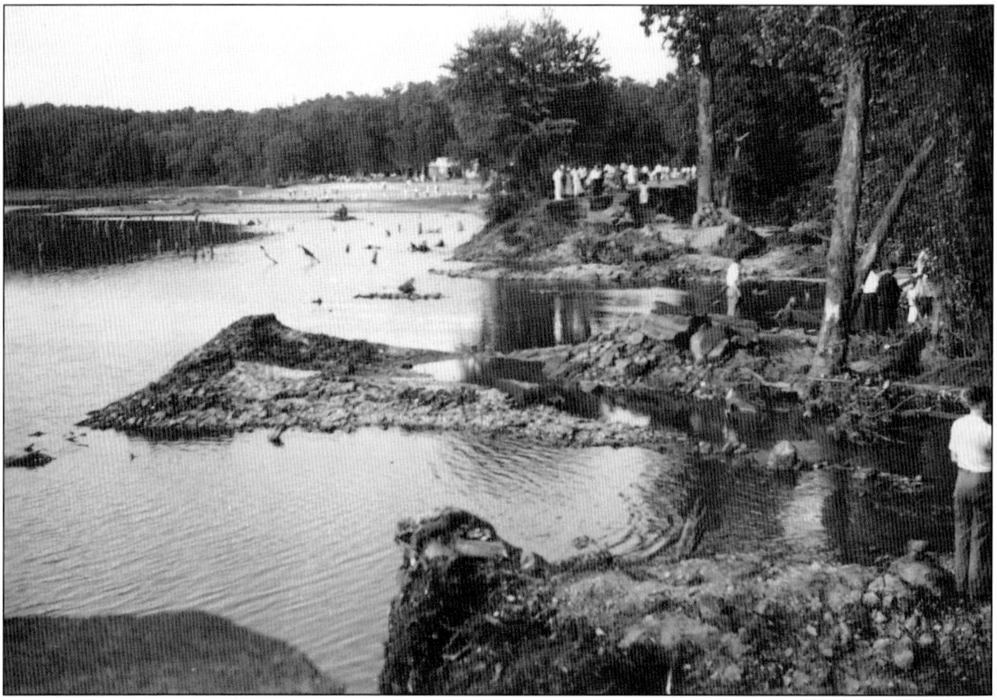

TUMBLING DAM—AFTER. When a tremendous rainstorm hit the Bridgeton area on August 2 and 3, 1934, waters cascaded down the Cohansey River. A series of dams was destroyed, and a wall of water made its way into downtown Bridgeton and caused havoc.

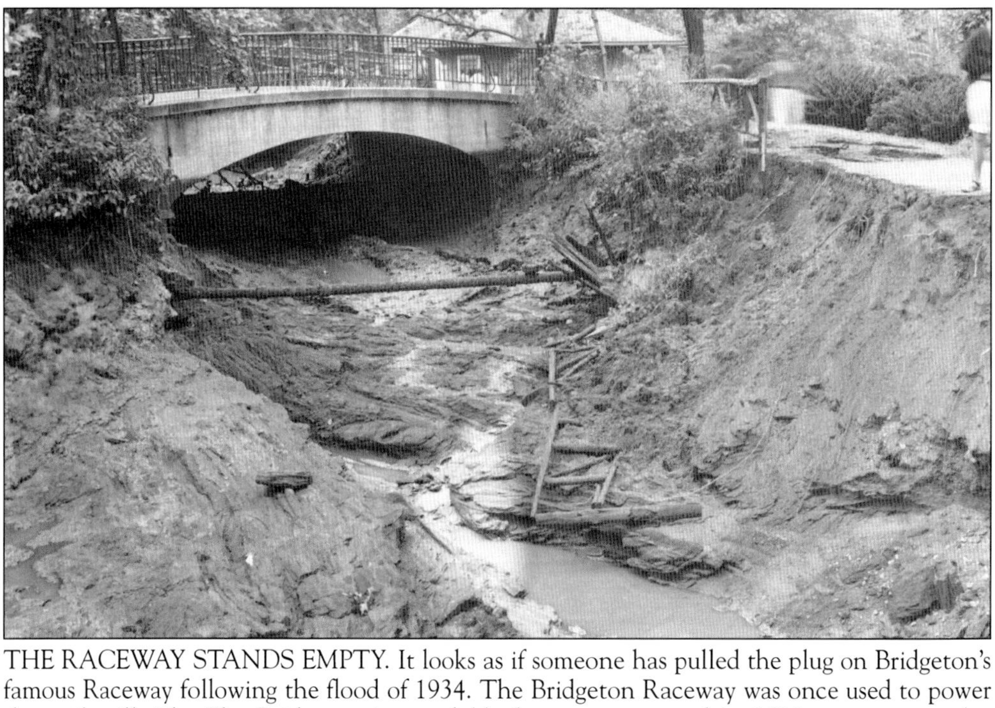

THE RACEWAY STANDS EMPTY. It looks as if someone has pulled the plug on Bridgeton's famous Raceway following the flood of 1934. The Bridgeton Raceway was once used to power the nail mill. The Flat Bridge, as it was dubbed, was constructed in 1912 near present-day Mayor Aitken Drive and Washington Street.

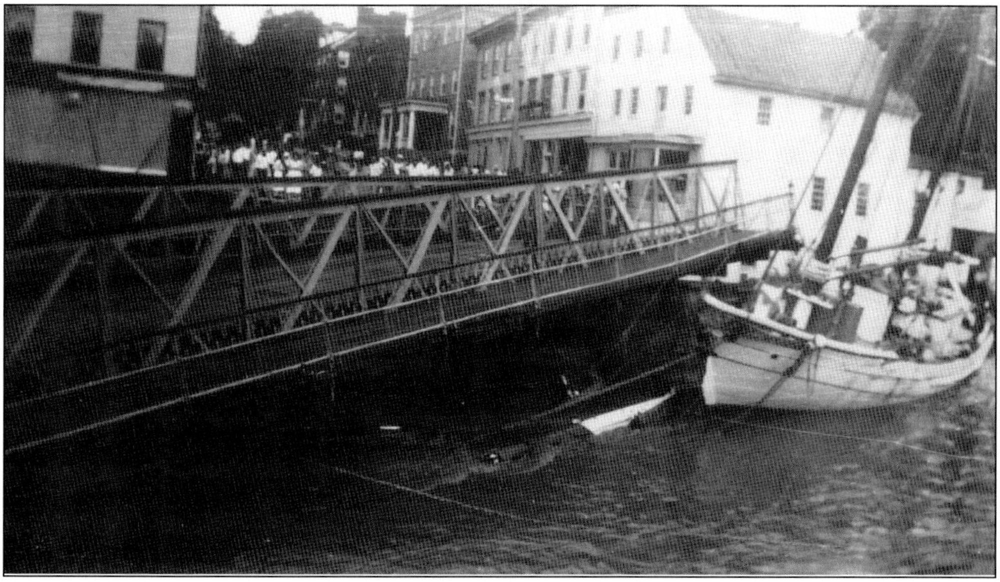

TOSSED ABOUT LIKE TOYS. Following the breaking of dams upstream, a wall of water picked up the oyster schooner *C.J. Peterson* and slammed it into the Commerce Street bridge, completely disabling the span. This photograph is from the river's east bank looking toward West Commerce Street.

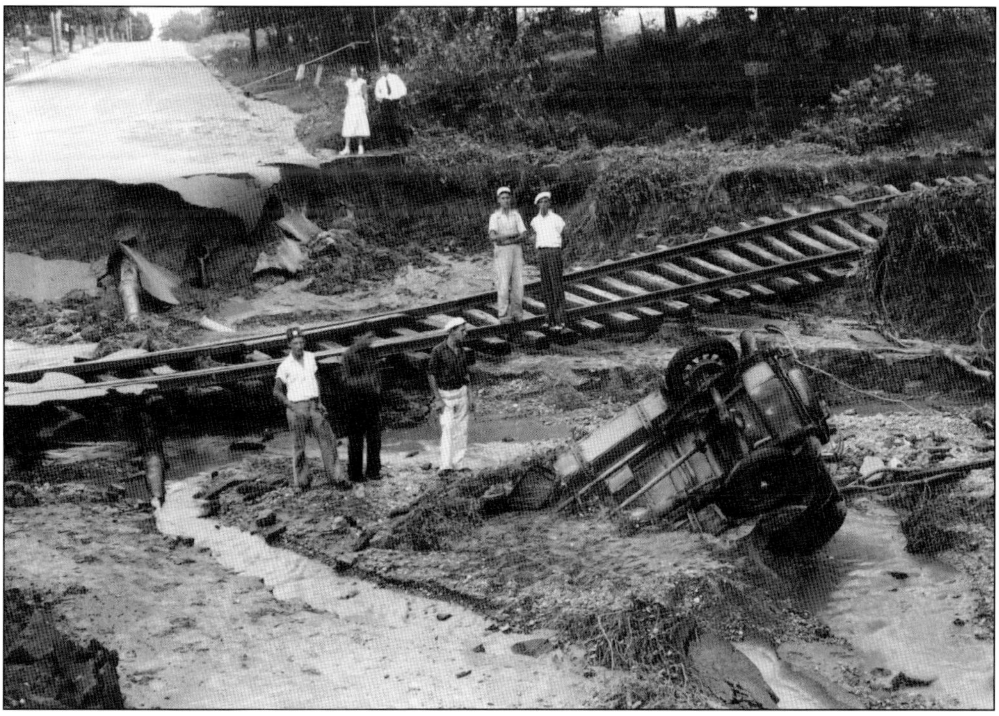

WEST AVENUE WAS ALSO AFFECTED. Looking north along West Avenue at the Central Railroad of New Jersey crossing, the damage in the vicinity of aptly named Muddy Run can be seen. The railroad tracks were undermined and one unlucky motorist lost his vehicle to the rushing waters.

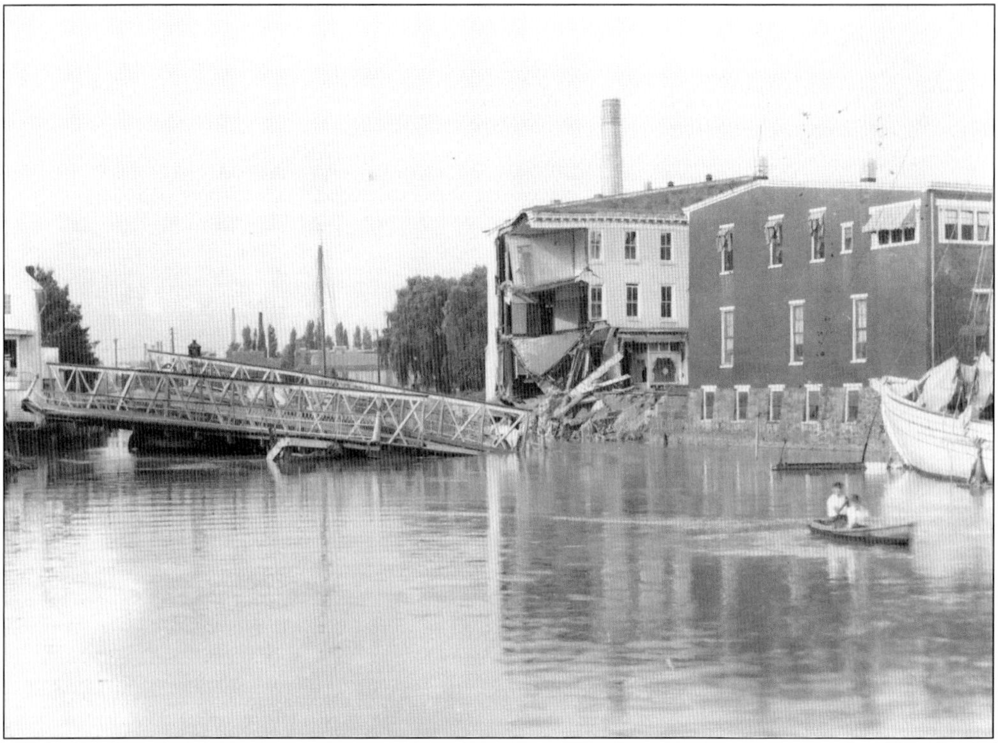

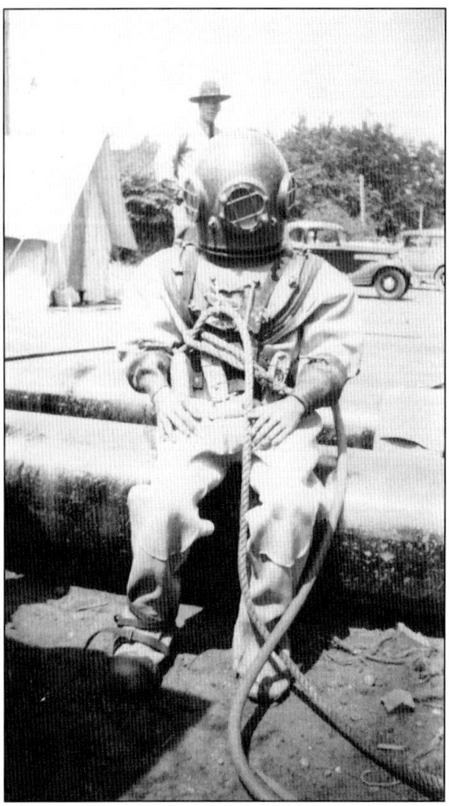

LOOKING NORTH. In this photograph by the Laurel Studio, the Commerce Street bridge is in shambles and the barber shop at its east end is open following the flood, but not for business. The building location is today the site of Bridgeton's Fountain Plaza and the Art McKee Memorial.

READY TO DIVE. In an attempt to clear wreckage from the Cohansey River in 1934, a team of hard-hat divers was brought to the scene. This is how famed Bridgeton native and treasure diver Art McKee got his start; while working as an assistant in this operation, McKee "borrowed" the equipment one evening.

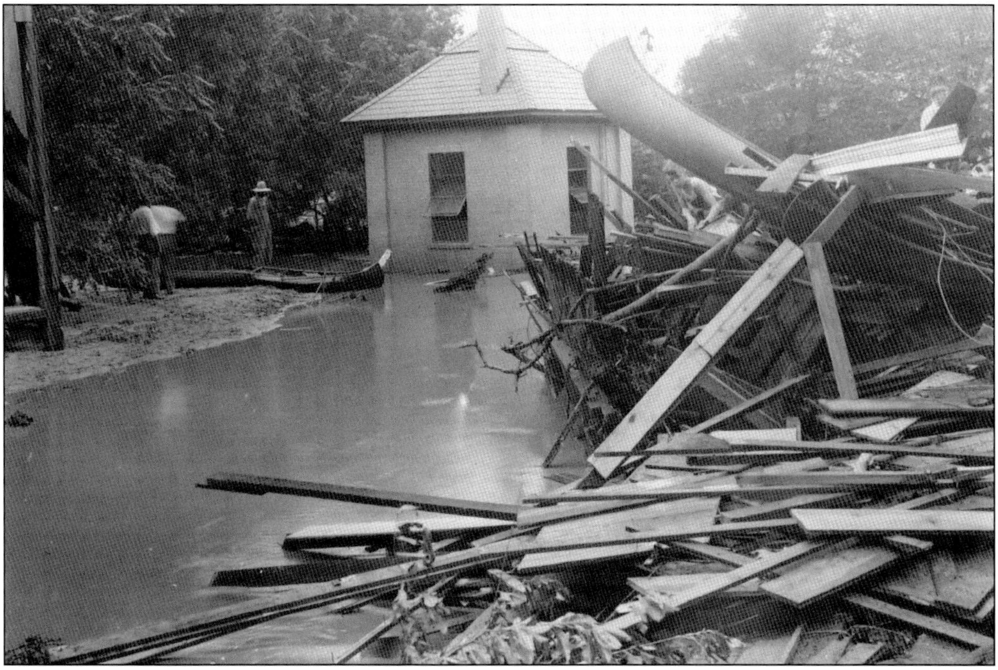

REDUCED TO SCRAP WOOD. The tremendous force of water from the flood can be appreciated after seeing the wreckage of the Raceway canoe house and the craft it housed. The brick building was a pump house for the city's water system, which also was disabled.

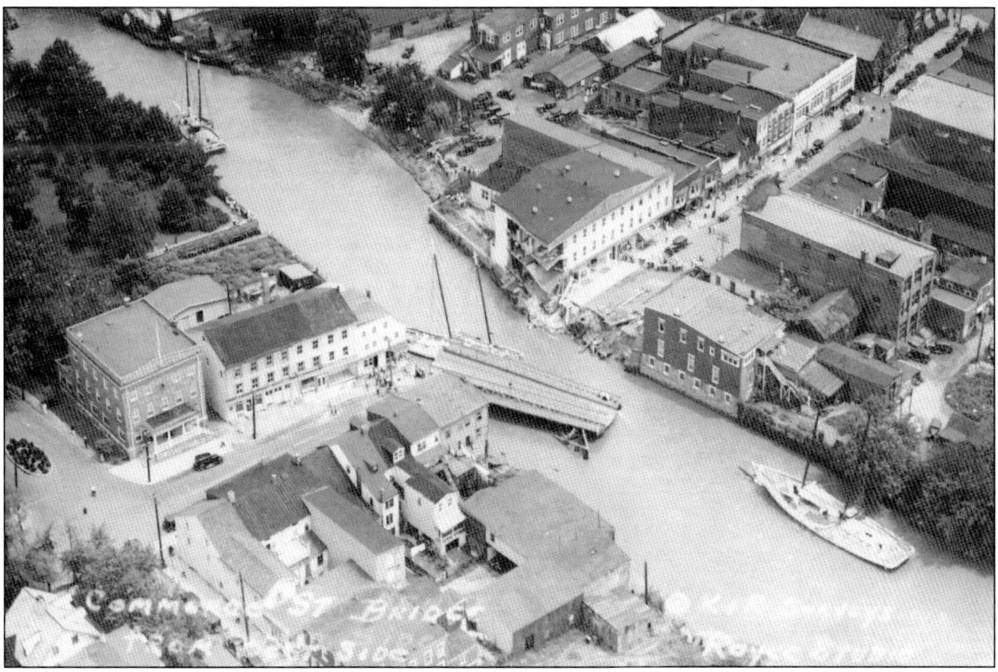

LOOKING NORTHEAST FROM THE AIR. A photographer from Royce Studio took to the air for this view of the Commerce Street bridge in the wake of the flood. At least three of the vessels involved in this calamity, which also involved bridges at Washington and Broad Streets, can be seen here.

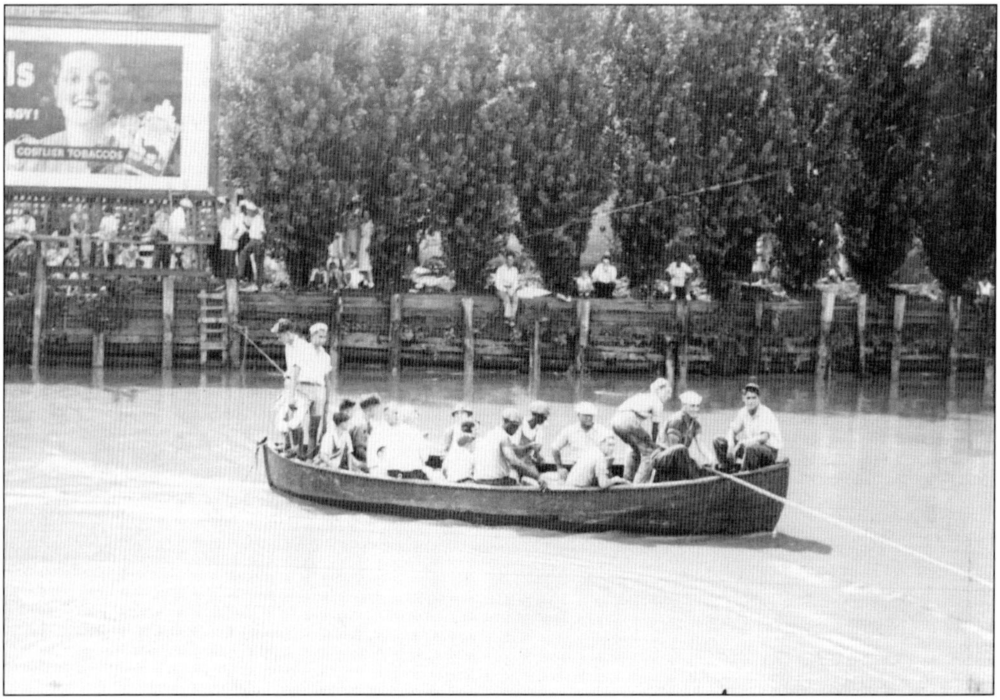

"BE PREPARED." A team of Sea Scouts man their lifeboat, dubbed the *S.S. Ferry*, to transport local residents across the Cohansey River after Bridgeton was left without a bridge. The nickel fare saved 4,800 people a 21-mile detour by means of the nearest upstream route.

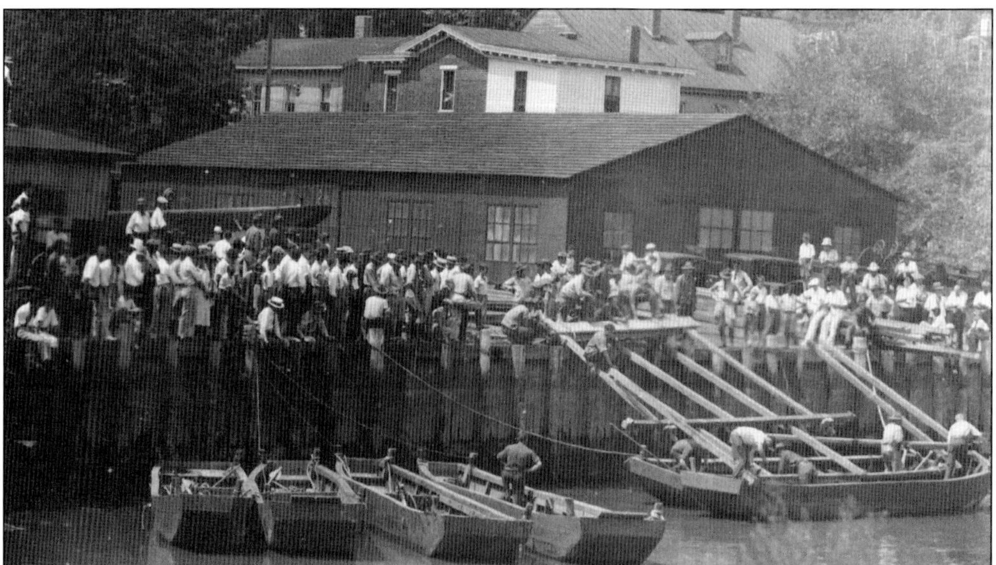

ARMY ENGINEERS TO THE RESCUE. Realizing the severe nature of the crisis in Bridgeton, a unit from the Army Corps of Engineers arrives on the scene to place a pontoon bridge over the Cohansey midway between the damaged bridges at Broad and Commerce Streets.

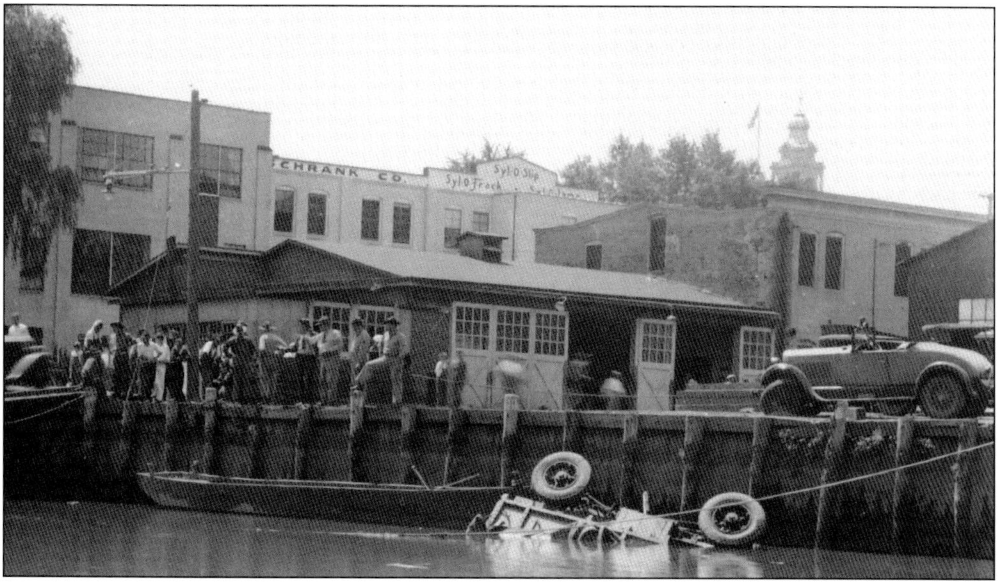

BAPTIZED IN THE COHANSEY. While putting the pontoon bridge into place, one of the army's trucks got too close to the west bank and ended up falling into the Cohansey River. The Schrank building and courthouse tower can be seen in the background in this view from the Connelly collection.

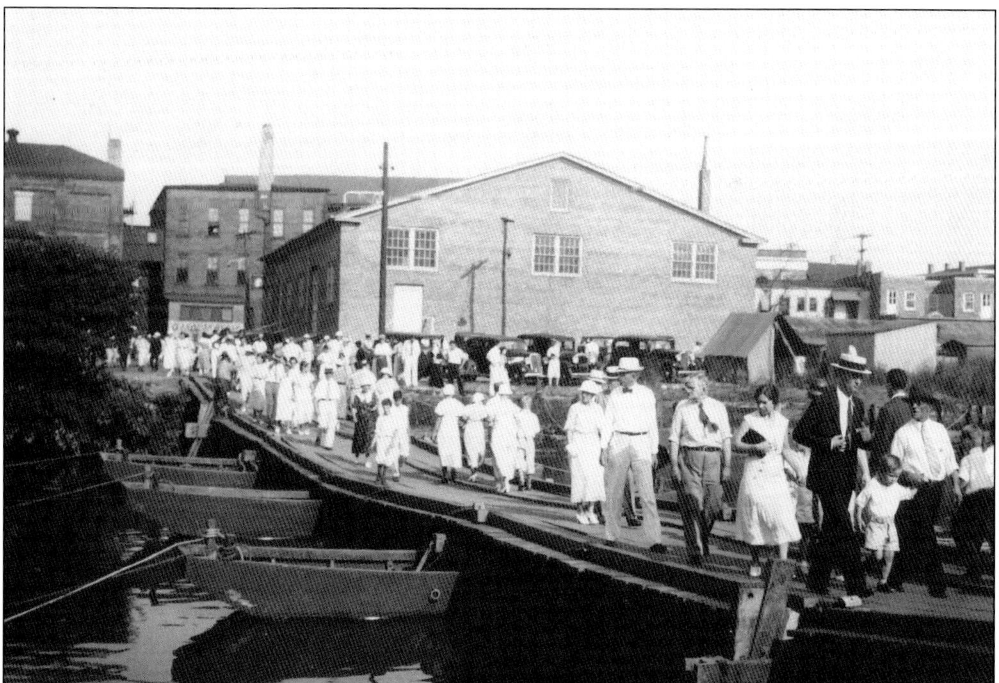

OUT FOR A STROLL. Following completion of the pontoon bridge, Bridgeton residents don their Sunday best to make the crossing and inspect the flood damage from a new perspective. Although it may appear flimsy, the temporary bridge could and did support motor vehicles.

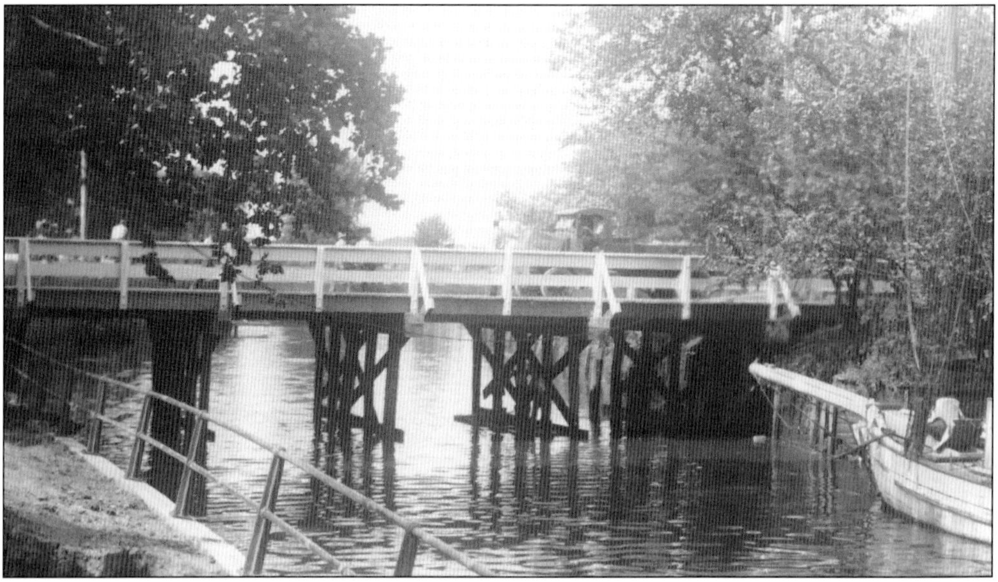

A TEMPORARY SOLUTION. One of the first bridges to be restored over the Cohansey River was this one at Washington Street, seen here looking north. It was not until 1936 that a permanent span was completed at Broad Street, and it still serves today as the War Memorial Bridge.

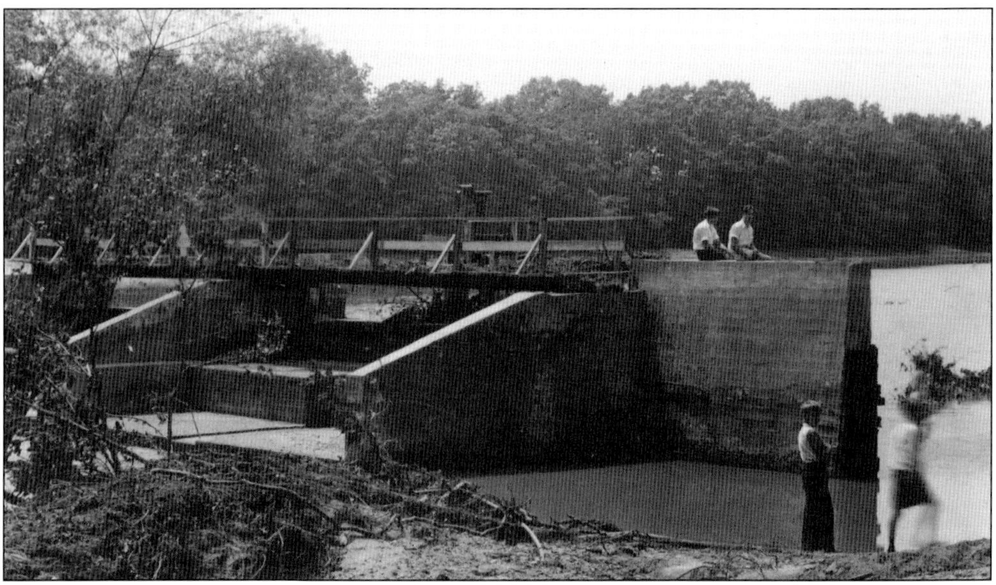

THE OLD DAM AT MARY ELMER LAKE. One of the causes contributing to the 1934 flood was the inadequate concrete spillway at Mary Elmer Lake, whose earthen embankment collapsed. Ironically, the spillway was restored, served another four decades, and then failed again during the flood of July 1975.

Seven

By Land, Sea, or Air

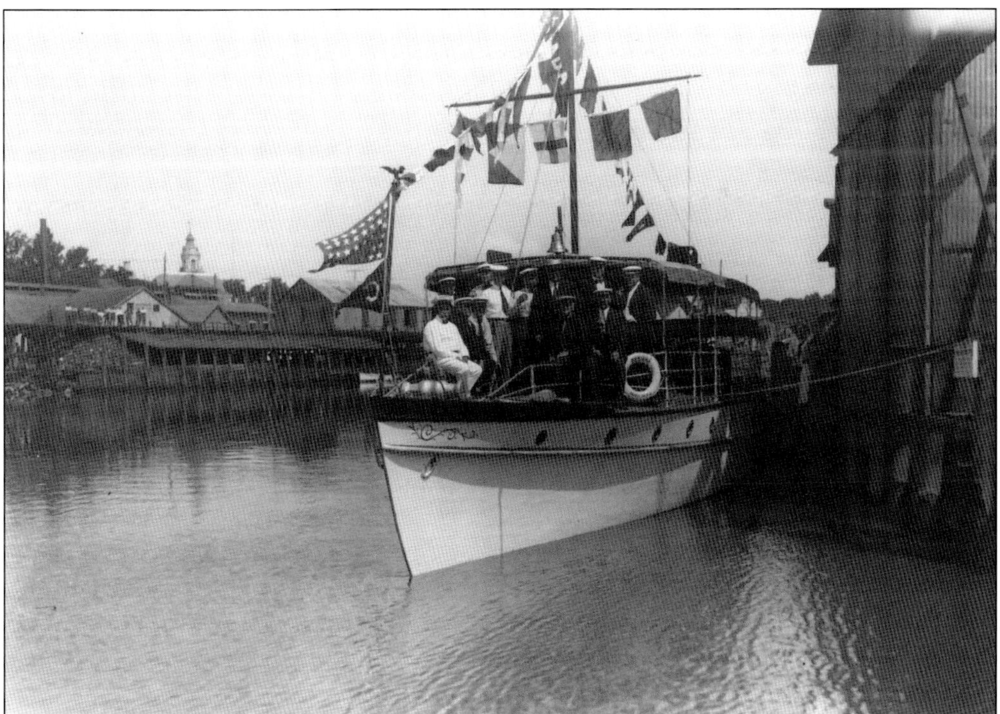

THE LABOR DAY BOAT PARADE. Clayton McPherson took this remarkable photograph of the *Mariada*, the flag boat of the festivities held on the Cohansey River in 1914. It was owned by glass magnates Richard and Robert More and navigated by Captain Elmer D. Mulford.

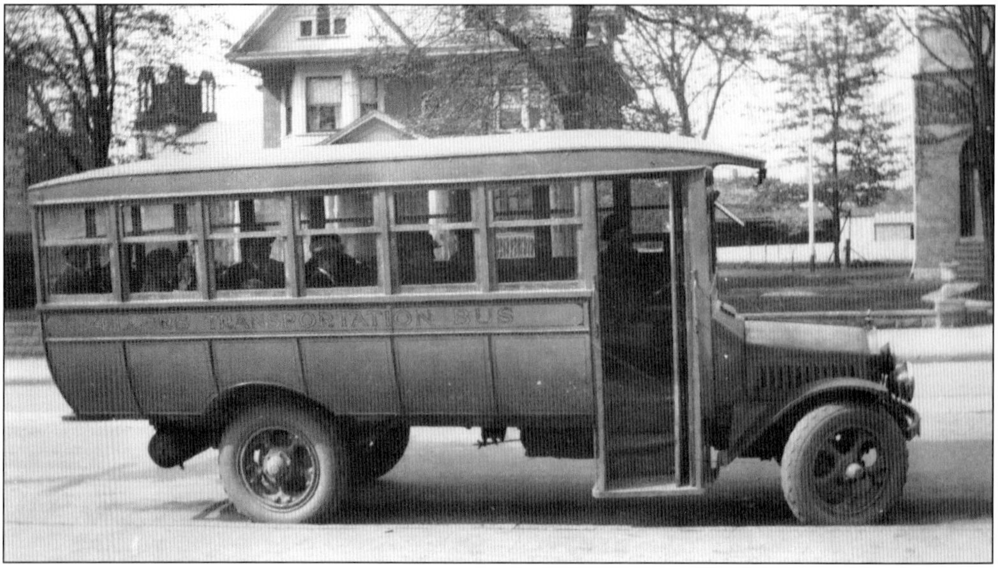

LEAVE THE DRIVING TO US. The 1920s was a transitional decade in many respects, and the various types of transportation used during this period reflected this state of flux. The local trolley car line received competition on the Bridgeton-Millville route from the Zellers Transportation bus, seen here on East Commerce Street.

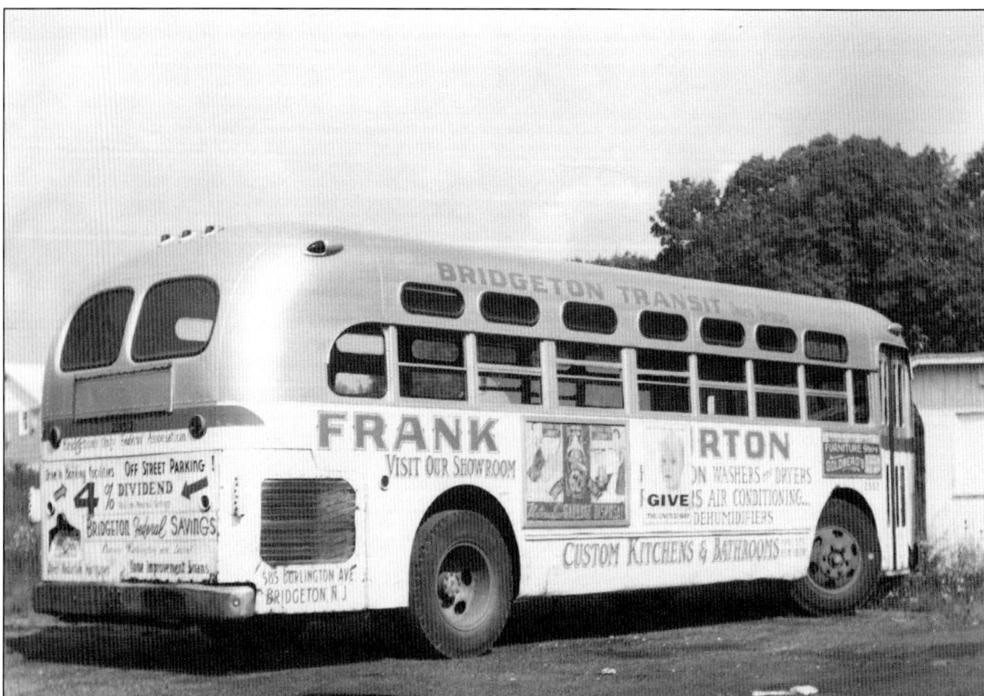

PORTABLE BILLBOARD. During the 1950s, the Bridgeton Transit bus line took every opportunity to make a dollar while carrying local residents. This vehicle sports advertising for Frank Burton Plumbing, Goldberg's Furniture Store, and Bridgeton Federal Savings.

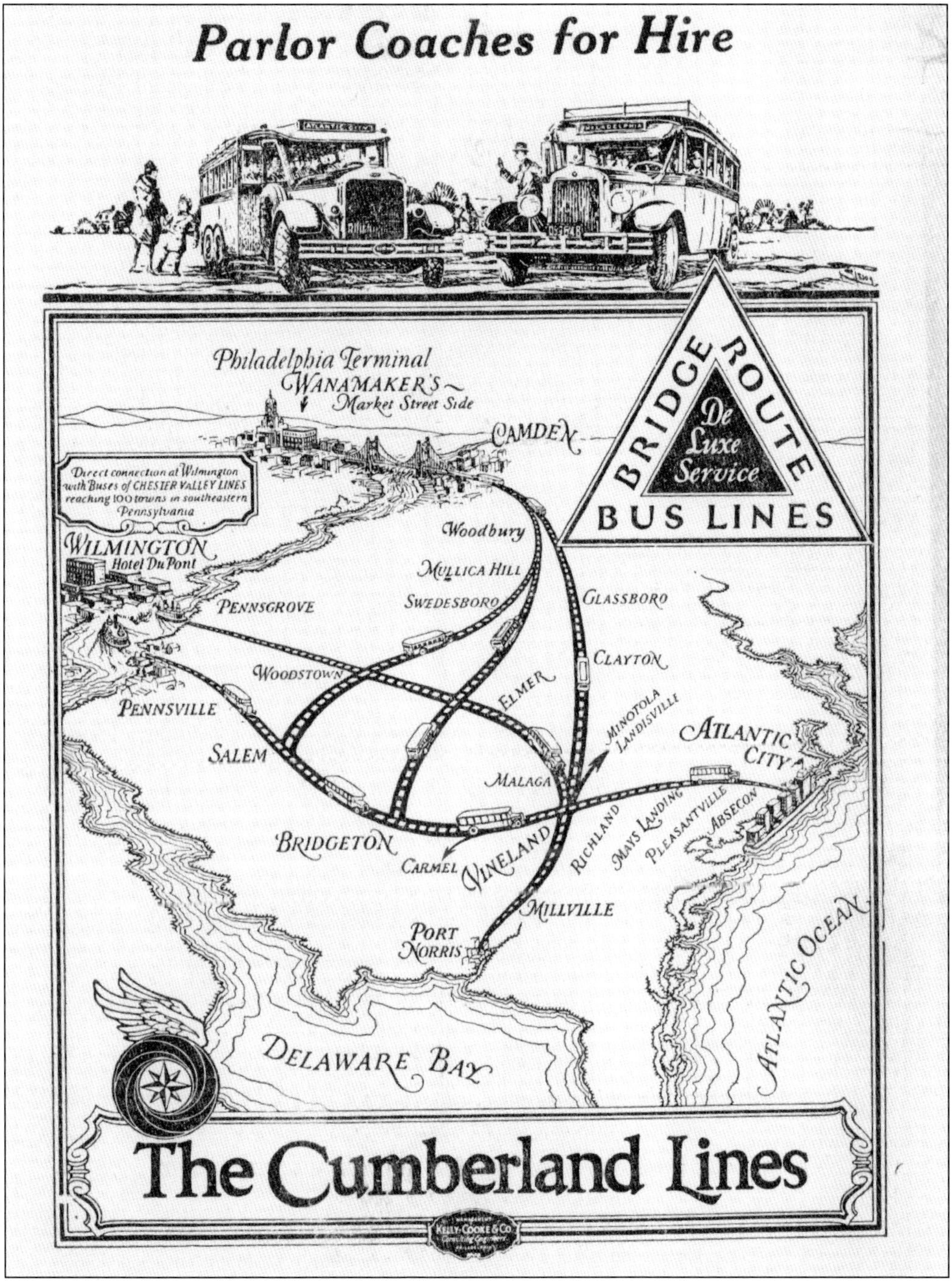

"THE BRIDGE ROUTE" TO PHILADELPHIA. With the opening of the Delaware River Bridge between Camden and Philadelphia in 1926, the Cumberland Lines bus company, headquartered in Bridgeton, offered direct service from South Jersey, as this 1927 timetable cover shows. When connections were made to Wilmington, Delaware, the ferry between New Castle and Pennsville still had to be utilized. Long distance passage over the route often included a meal at the Cumberland Hotel. Cumberland Lines, headed by Clayton McPherson, also operated a trolley division during this decade.

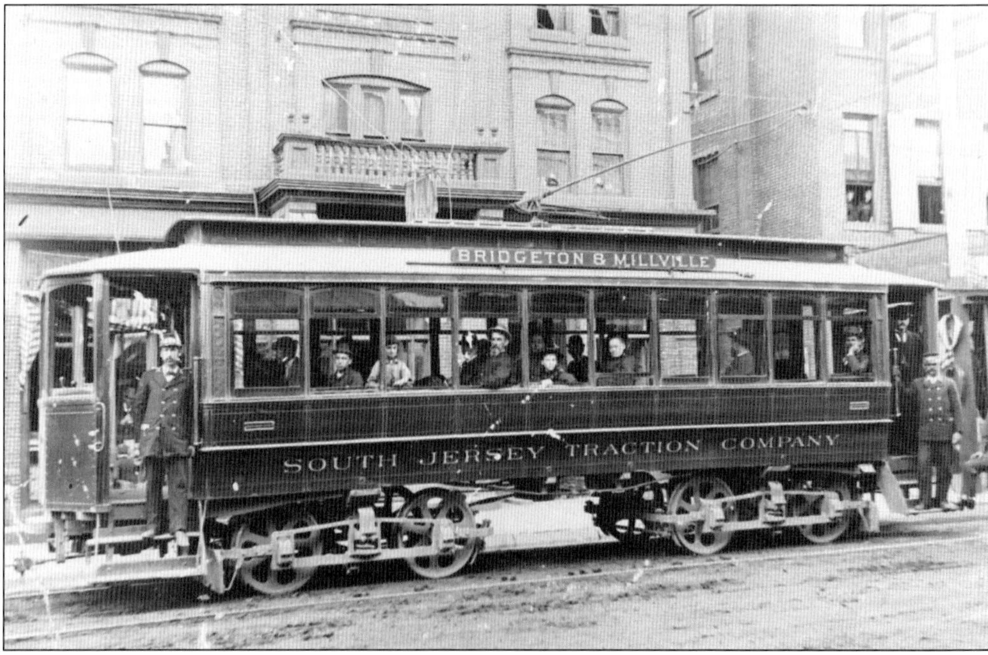

THE DAWN OF THE TROLLEY CAR ERA. Taken in front of the old Hotel Cumberland on North Laurel Street, this photograph was made shortly after trolley car service linked Bridgeton and Millville in 1893. During this era, the line operated under the name South Jersey Traction Company.

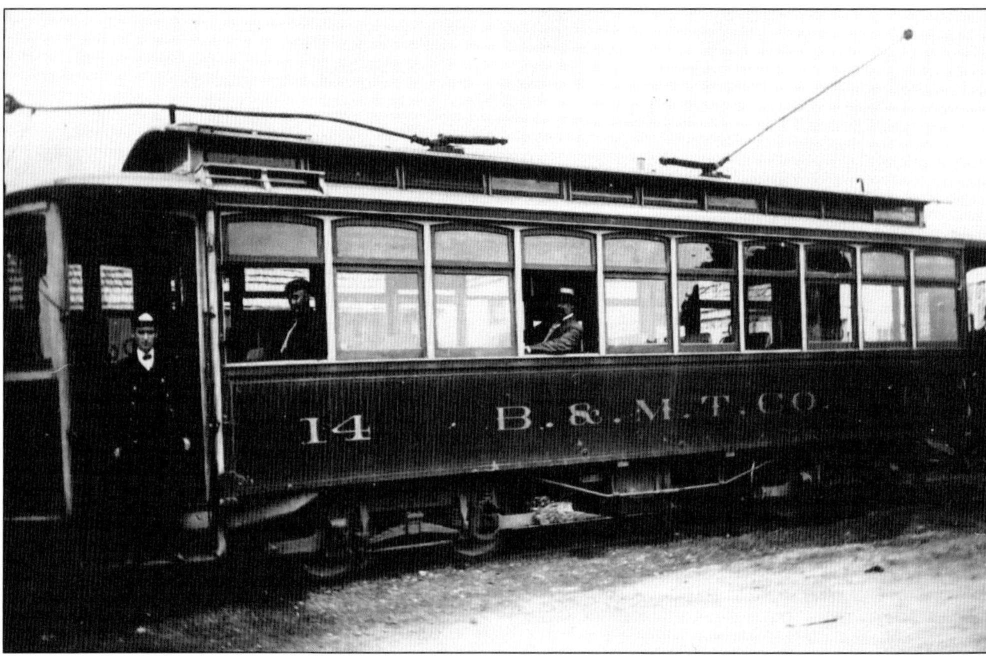

THE GOLDEN AGE OF TROLLEY CARS. In 1897 the South Jersey Traction Company name faded into history and the line became known as the Bridgeton & Millville Traction Company, a corporate entity that survived until 1922. Eventually, service was extended all the way to Port Norris.

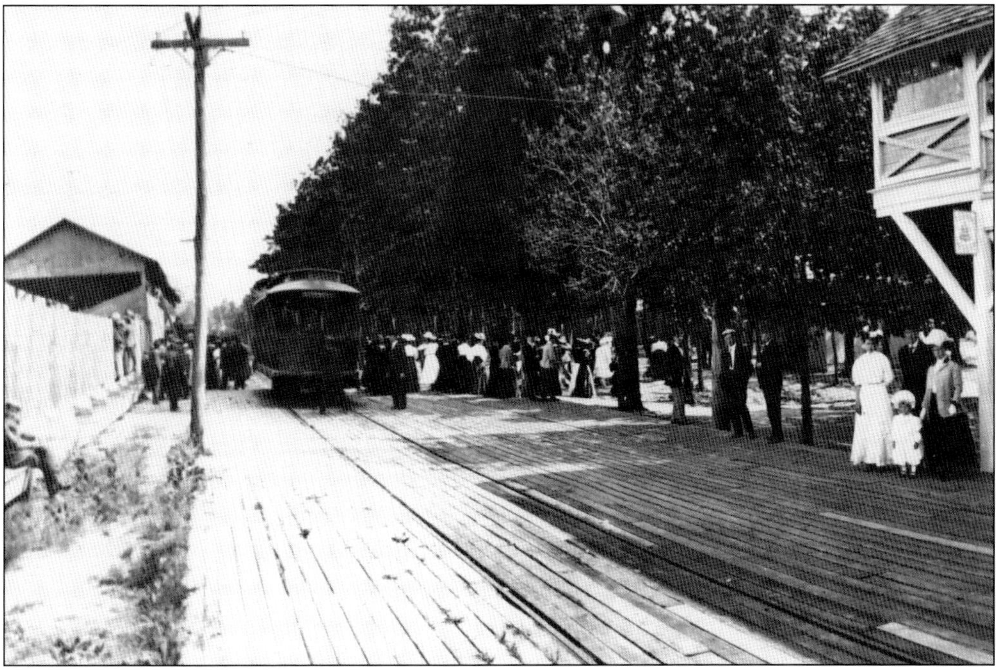

LET'S HEAD TO TUMBLING DAM PARK. The amusement park on Bridgeton's northern edge was a favorite destination before World War I and a good way reach it was by trolley. At left is the Bridgeton Baseball Association's field; at right is the trolley station.

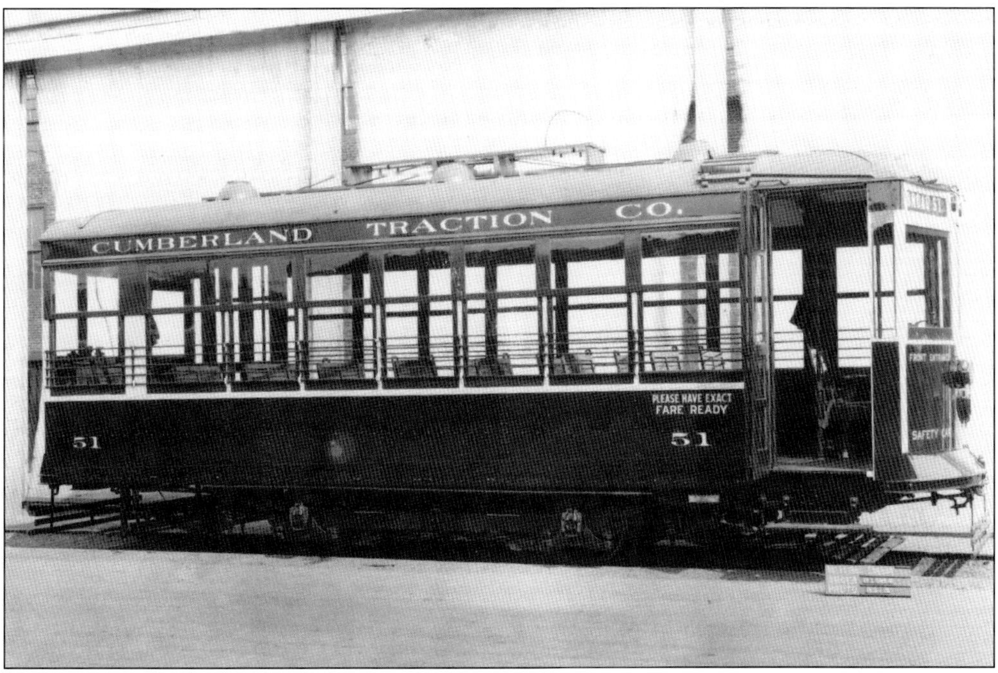

STATE-OF-THE-ART TECHNOLOGY. Increased competition from the automobile in the 1920s hurt the trolley companies. In response, Clayton McPherson, who in 1922 bought the line and dubbed it the Cumberland Traction Company, ordered this single-truck street car from Brill. It served from 1923 to 1931.

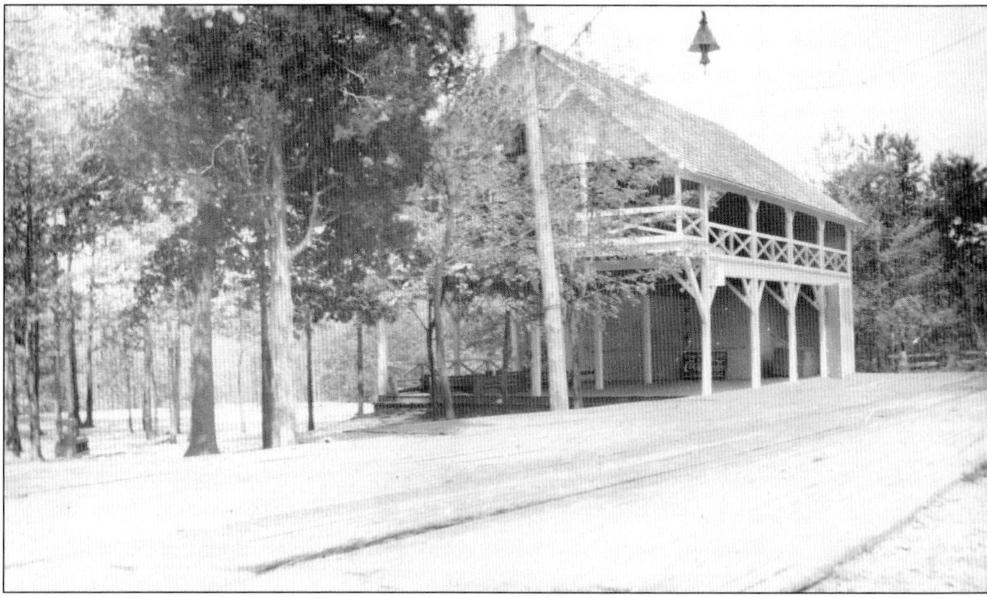

A RARE SIGHT. If not the oldest, this is perhaps the rarest photograph from the Pedrick collection. Dating from about 1910, it depicts the combination trolley station-confectionery stand at Tumbling Dam Park. Unlike most photographs of the site, it reveals the entire structure.

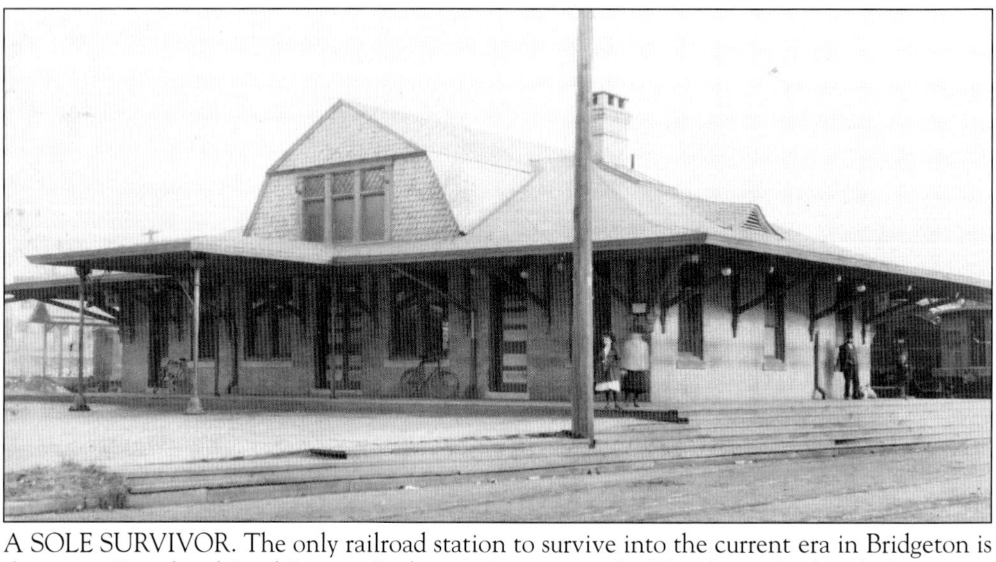

A SOLE SURVIVOR. The only railroad station to survive into the current era in Bridgeton is the one at Broad and Pearl Streets. Built in 1893 to serve the West Jersey Railroad, the station was later the site from which information was dispersed regarding the famous 1896 Red Men's wreck. Today it is the tourist center.

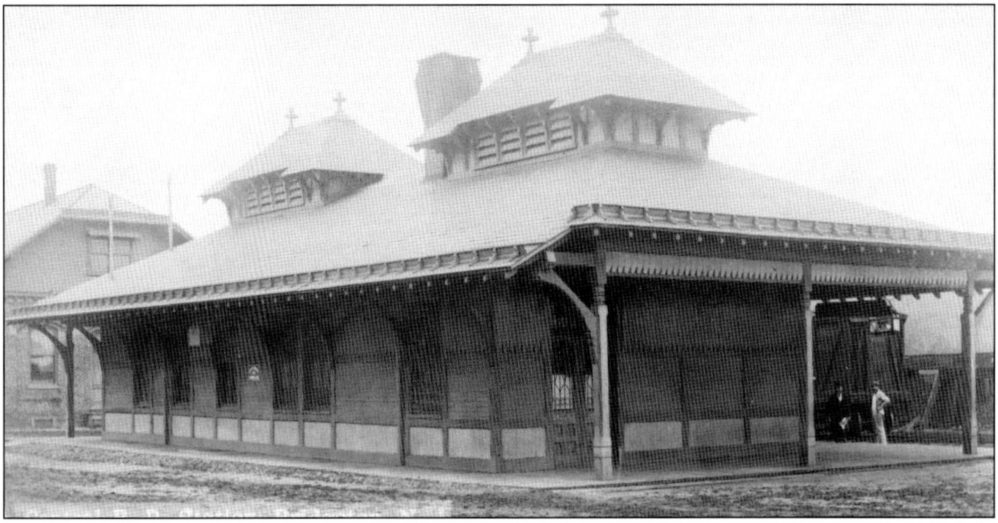

ON COHANSEY STREET. The Central Railroad of New Jersey, Bridgeton's rail link to New York, utilized this 1884 passenger depot attributed to famed architect Frank Furness. It was razed in 1951. The freight station in the left background, built the same year, burned in 1971.

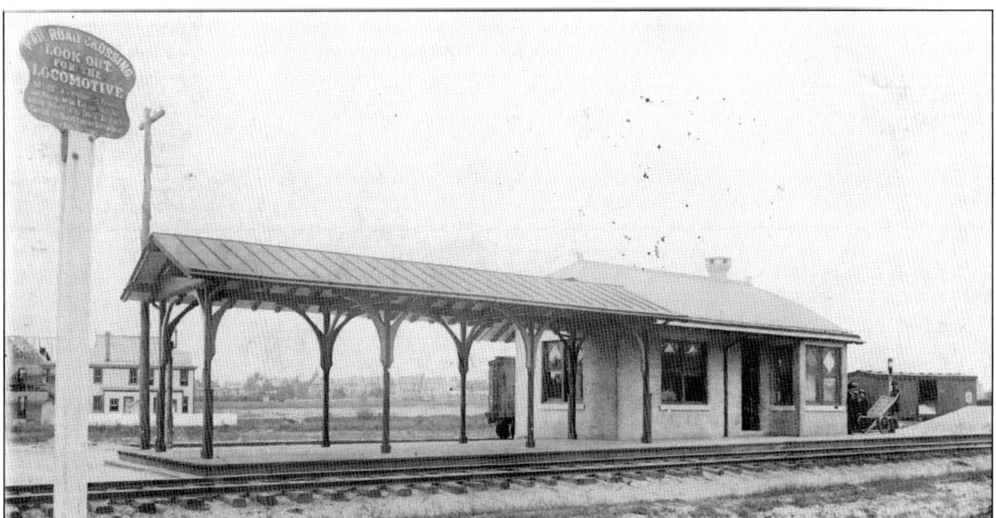

THE IRVING AVENUE STATION. Seen here in 1907, this was the West Jersey & Seashore Railroad station utilized by passengers boarding in east Bridgeton. Bridgeton enjoyed railroad passenger service from 1861 until the last regular run was made in 1952.

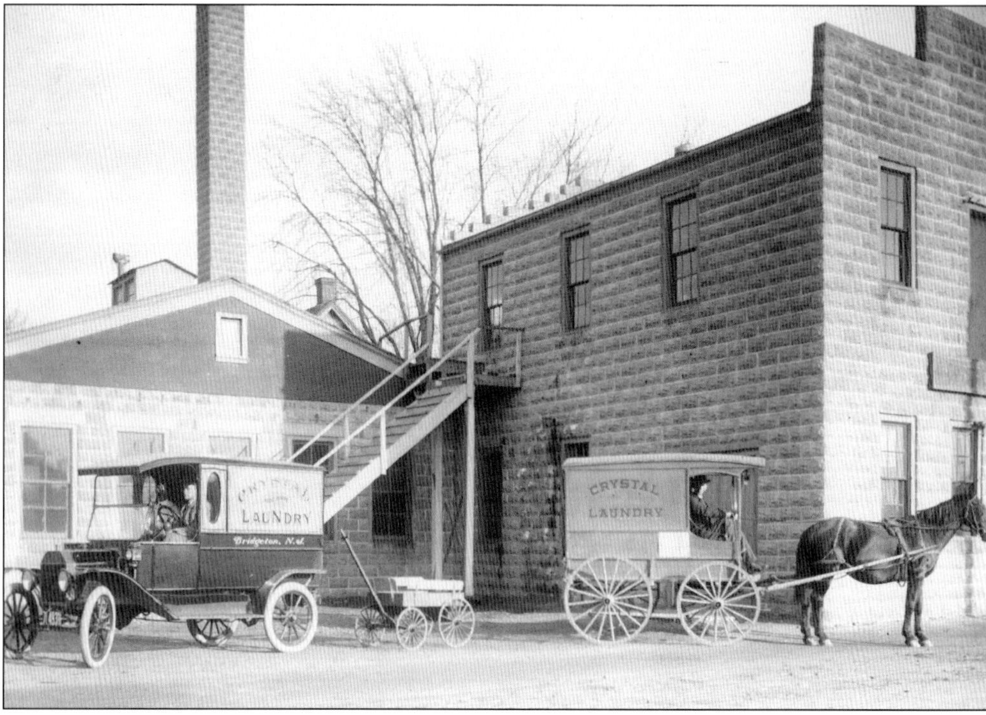

THE TIMES ARE CHANGING. Located at South Laurel and Mulberry Streets, the Crystal Steam Laundry was making the transition in motive power from horsepower to mechanized horsepower around 1915. Tracing its founding to 1888, the firm was owned by Preston Stratton when this photograph was made.

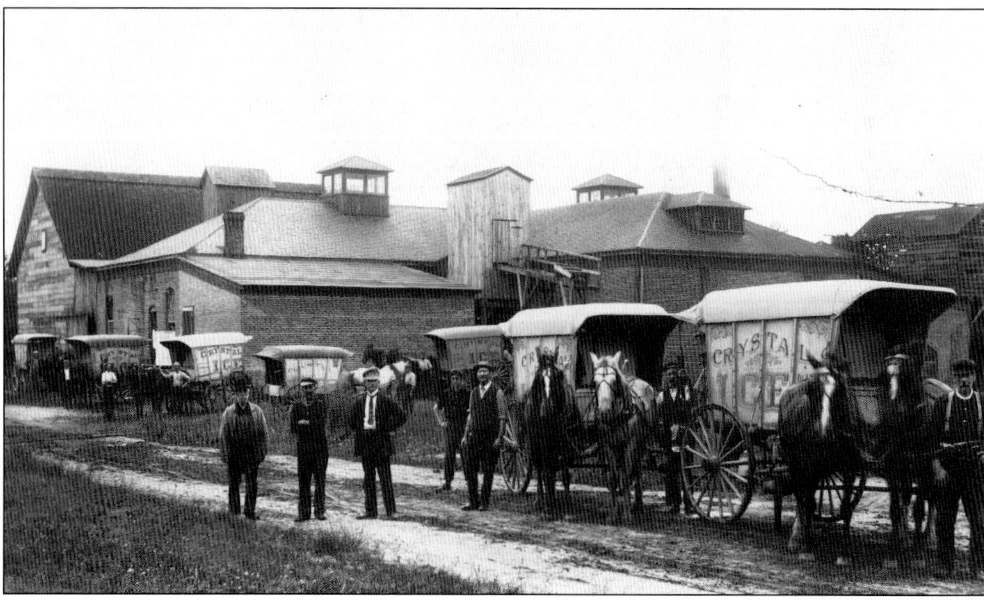

COOLING THEIR HEELS. Employees of the Crystal Ice Company relax along with their sturdy steeds at the ice plant on Elm Street. Beginning in the summer of 1896, this plant was among the first in New Jersey to use ice-making machinery of the modern type. The machinery still survives and is in use.

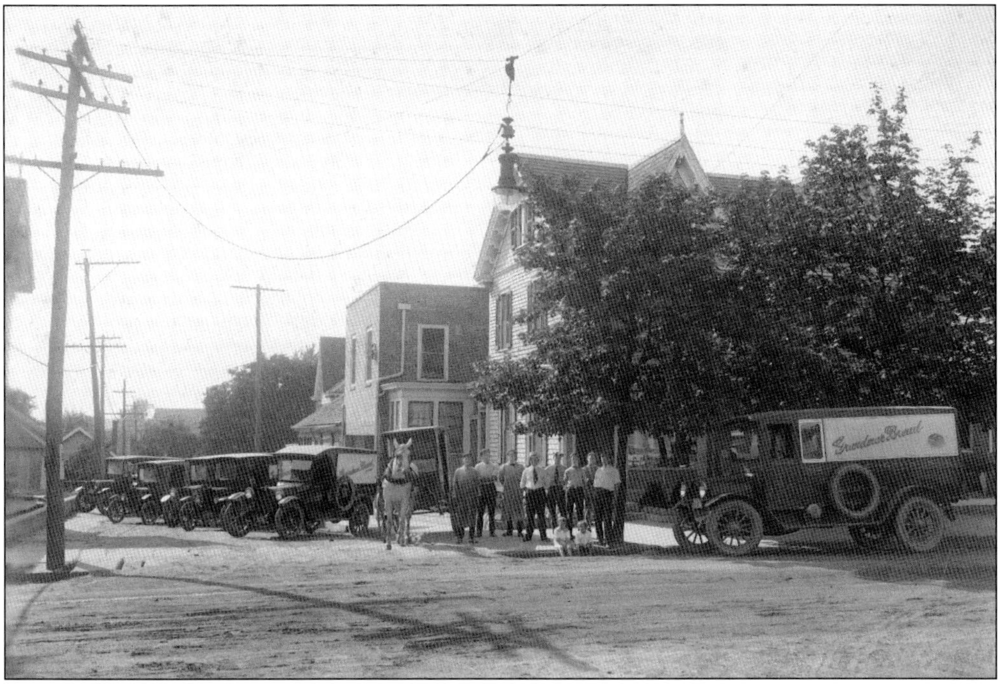

JUST LIKE GRANDMA'S BREAD. George E. LeStourgeon's Bakery at 240 North Pearl Street promoted its product as being like "Grandma's Bread" about 1920. During this time, LeStourgeon's was committed to using motor vehicles for delivery, but kept a horse-drawn wagon too.

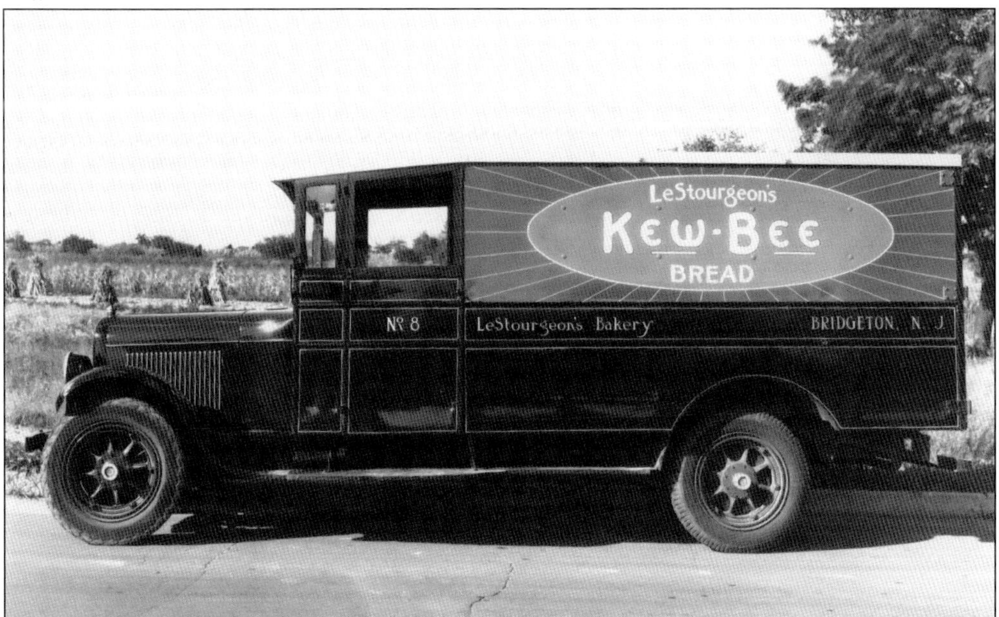

PRIDE OF THE FLEET. When George LeStourgeon's newest delivery truck, Number 8, arrived for duty in September 1932, he commissioned photographer J.T. Roberts to take a picture of it. The vehicle was painted to promote LeStourgeon's Kew-Bee line of bread.

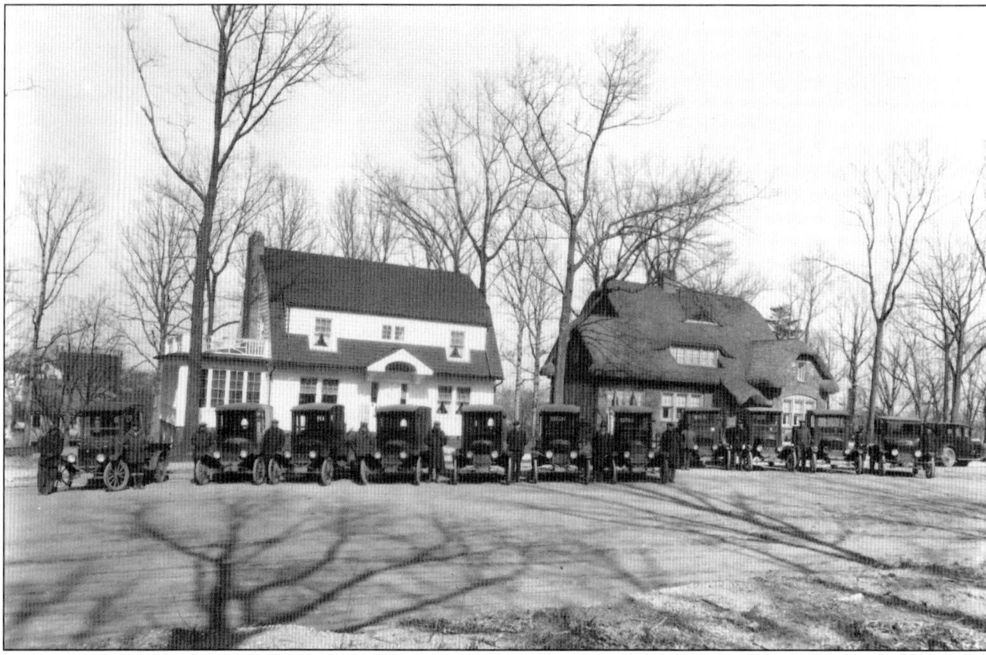

METER READERS' REUNION. Bridgeton Gas Light Company executive Jacob B. Jones was so proud of his service vehicles that he lined them up in 1926 before his Dutch Colonial-style home on Woodland Drive for a photograph by J.T. Roberts. At right is Archer Platt's famous "Gingerbread House."

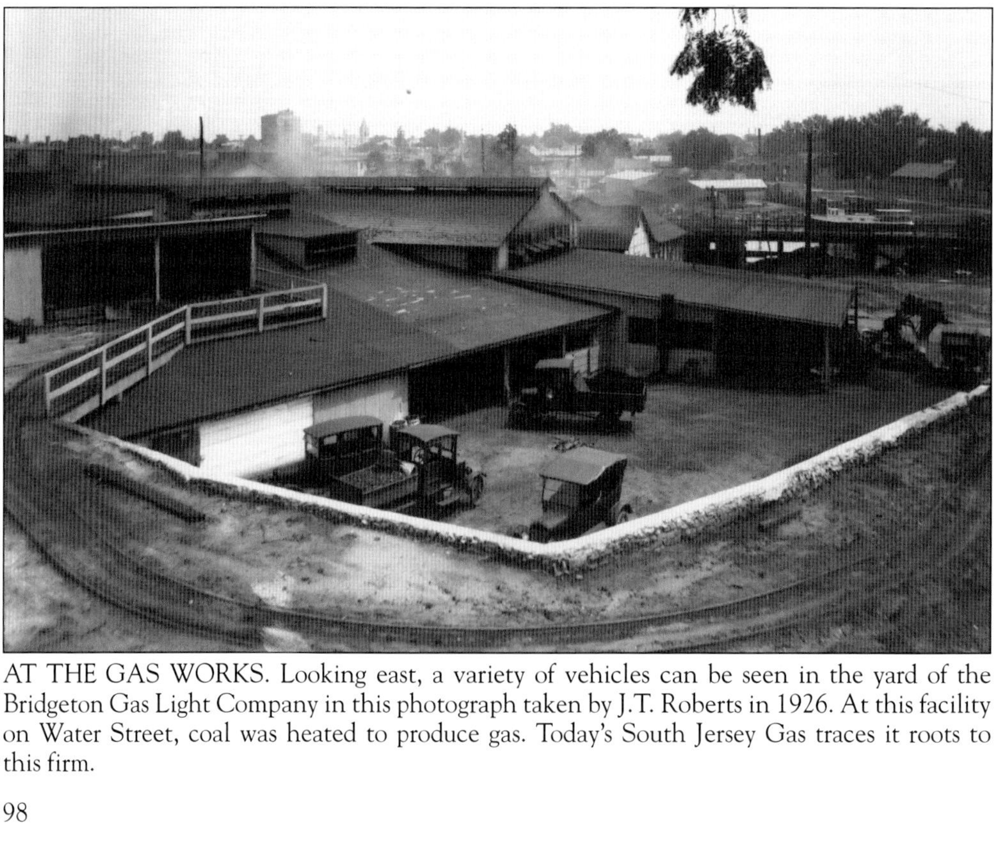

AT THE GAS WORKS. Looking east, a variety of vehicles can be seen in the yard of the Bridgeton Gas Light Company in this photograph taken by J.T. Roberts in 1926. At this facility on Water Street, coal was heated to produce gas. Today's South Jersey Gas traces it roots to this firm.

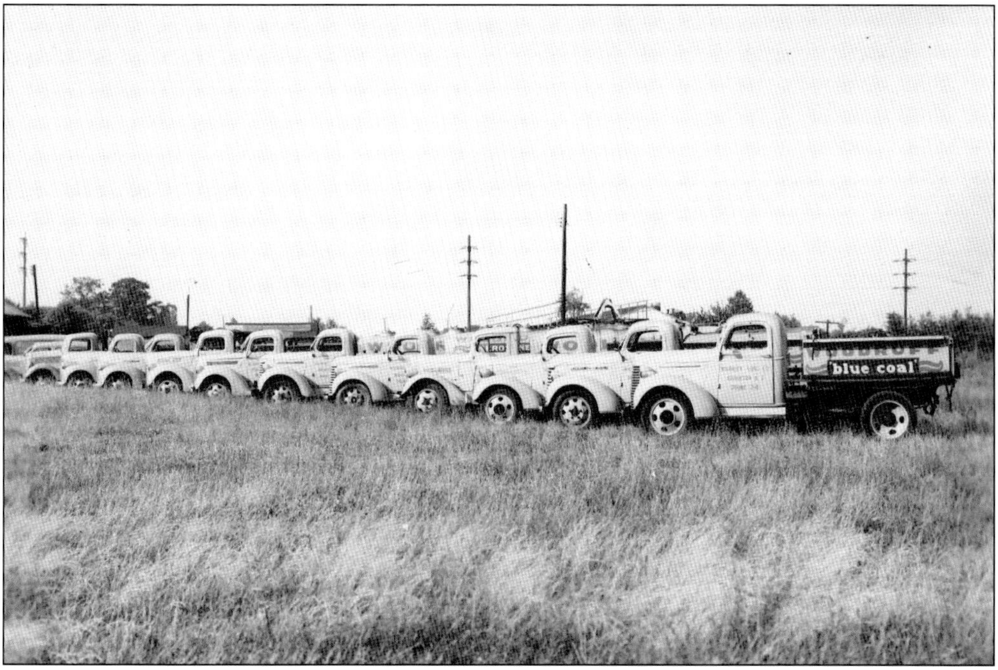

WHEN COAL WAS KING. The three-digit telephone number "214" on the sides of these vehicles belonging to what was then called the Woodruff Coal Company suggests that this photograph was taken in the 1940s. Reflecting changing consumer demand, the company later became known as the Woodruff Oil Company.

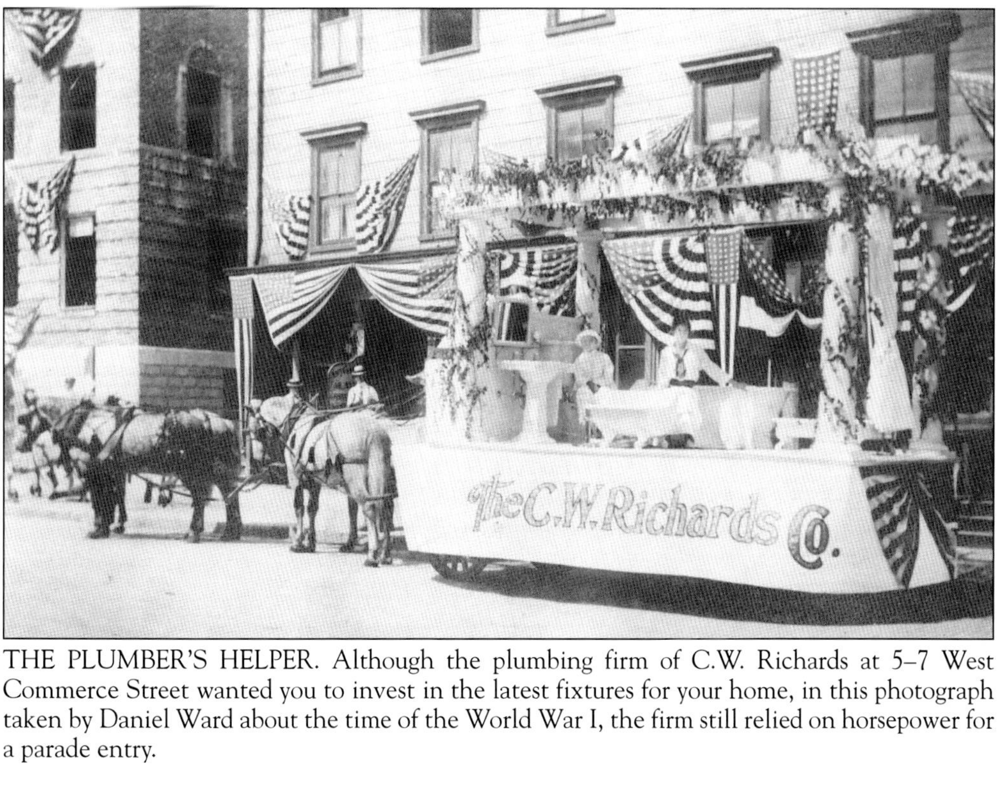

THE PLUMBER'S HELPER. Although the plumbing firm of C.W. Richards at 5–7 West Commerce Street wanted you to invest in the latest fixtures for your home, in this photograph taken by Daniel Ward about the time of the World War I, the firm still relied on horsepower for a parade entry.

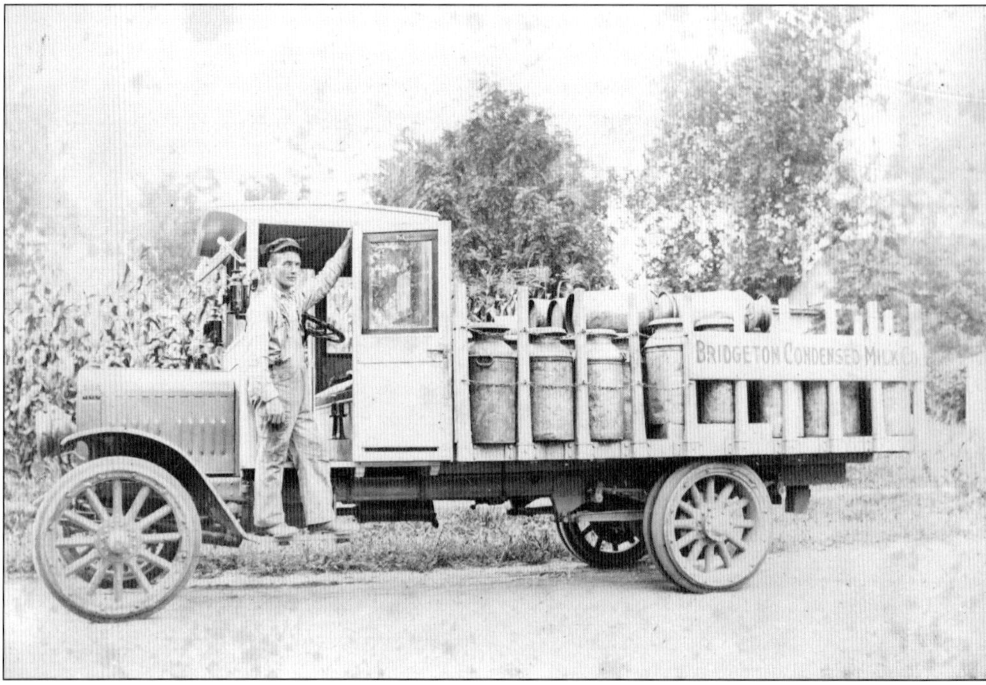

OF IRON MEN AND STEEL CANS. About the time of World War I, the Bridgeton Condensed Milk Company on Cohansey Street utilized this vehicle for bulk shipments. The muscular driver could wrestle the truck over rough roads as easily as he could load the heavy milk cans.

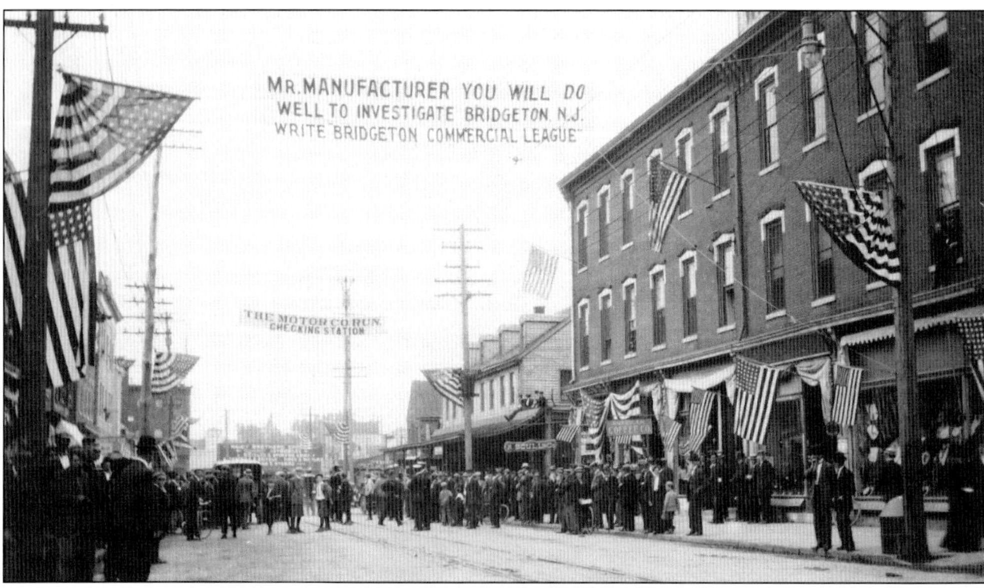

WELCOME MOTORISTS. A banner hanging over flag-bedecked South Laurel Street about 1910 proclaims, "The Motor Co. Run Checking Station," welcoming participants in one of the automobile rallies held during that era. Meanwhile, the Commercial League attempts to lure new business.

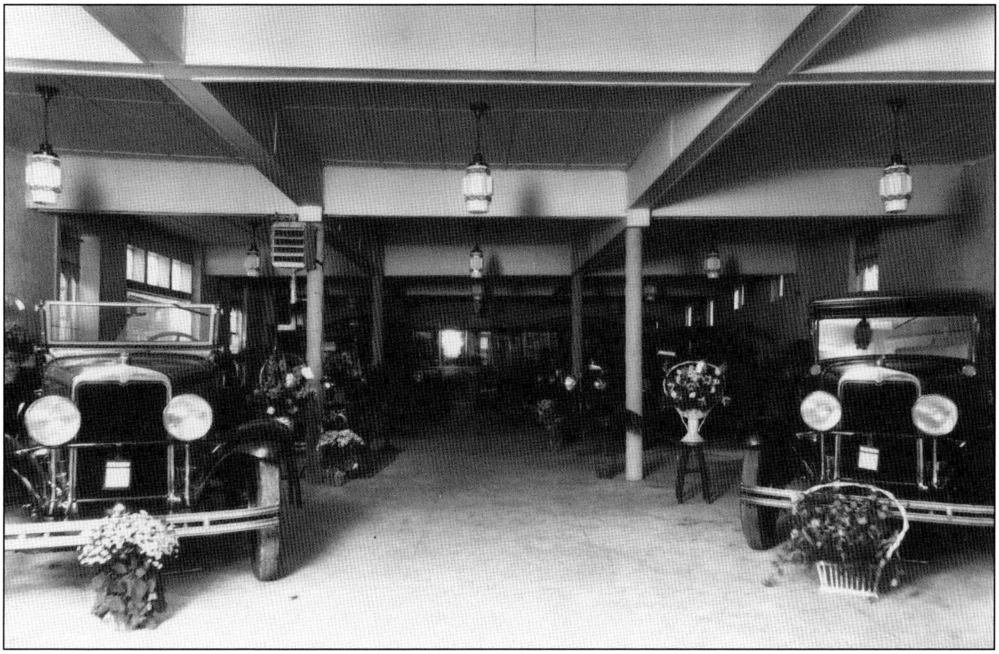

SEE THE U.S.A. IN A CHEVROLET. Benjamin and Joseph Scribner and David Lewis were justifiably proud when they had J.T. Roberts take this photograph of their new showroom at Pearl and Warren Streets on Saint Patrick's Day, 1930. Today Bob Novick continues this auto franchise tradition.

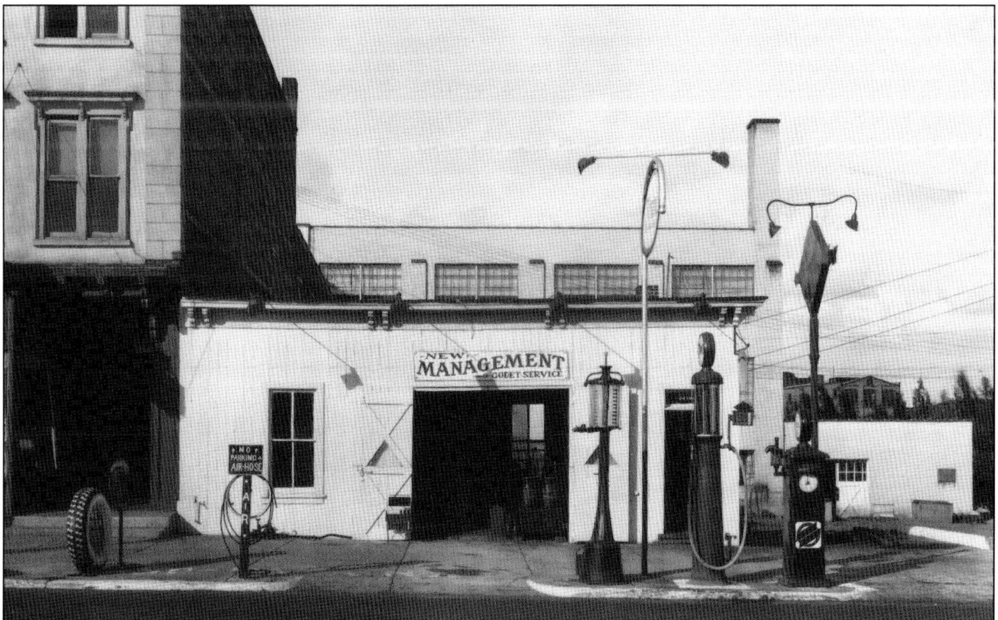

FILL'ER UP, SAMMY. Under a sign proudly announcing "New Management," Sam Godet opened a service station in October 1932 on Broad Street between the Schrank building and the Cohansey River. J.T. Roberts took the photograph. Sam and his wife Jennie also had a station on North Pearl Street.

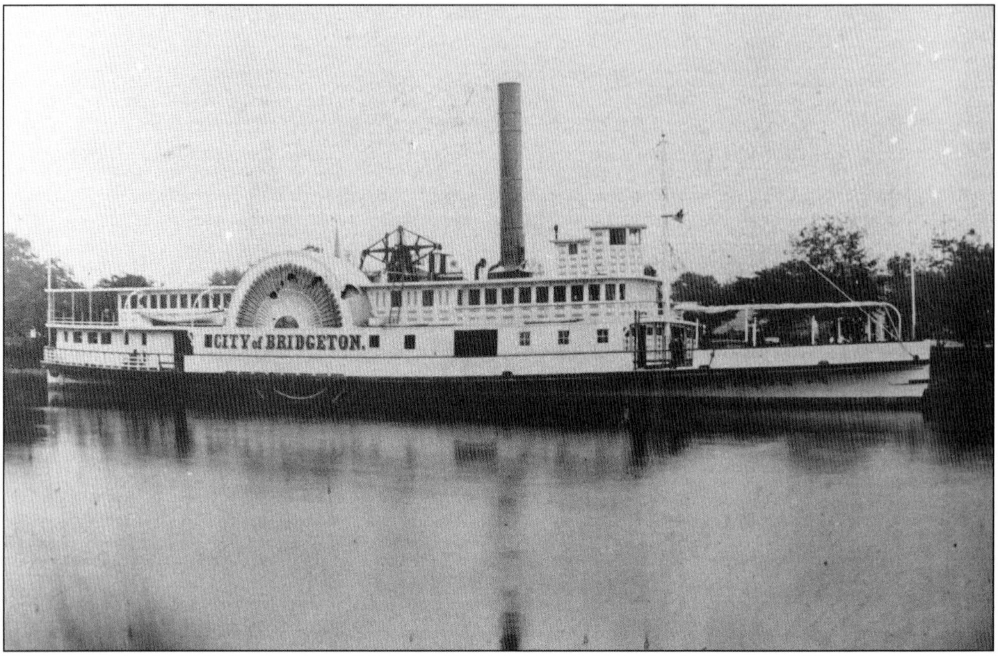

PRIDE OF THE COHANSEY. Among the oldest surviving outdoor photographs from Bridgeton is this one of the side-wheel steamer *City of Bridgeton*, which plied the route between her namesake port and Philadelphia from 1868 to 1876. Frank Stubbins rediscovered the rare photograph.

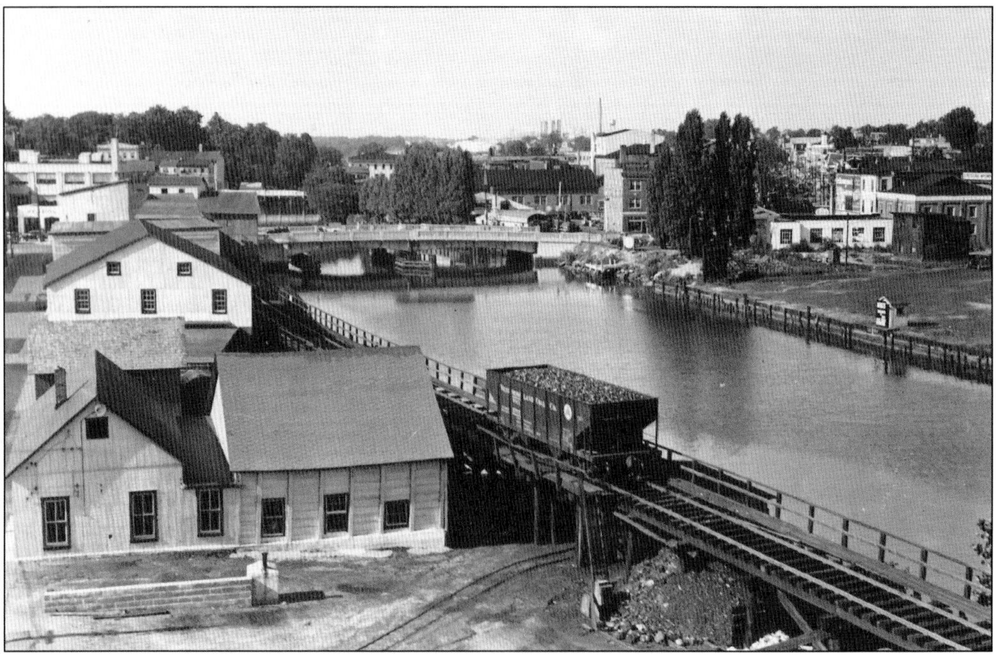

THE COHANSEY BELOW THE BROAD STREET BRIDGE. The father-son team of J.T. and Tom Roberts took this photograph from the west bank of the Cohansey River looking north about 1940. In the foreground is the rail line that served Woodruff Coal and the old gas plant.

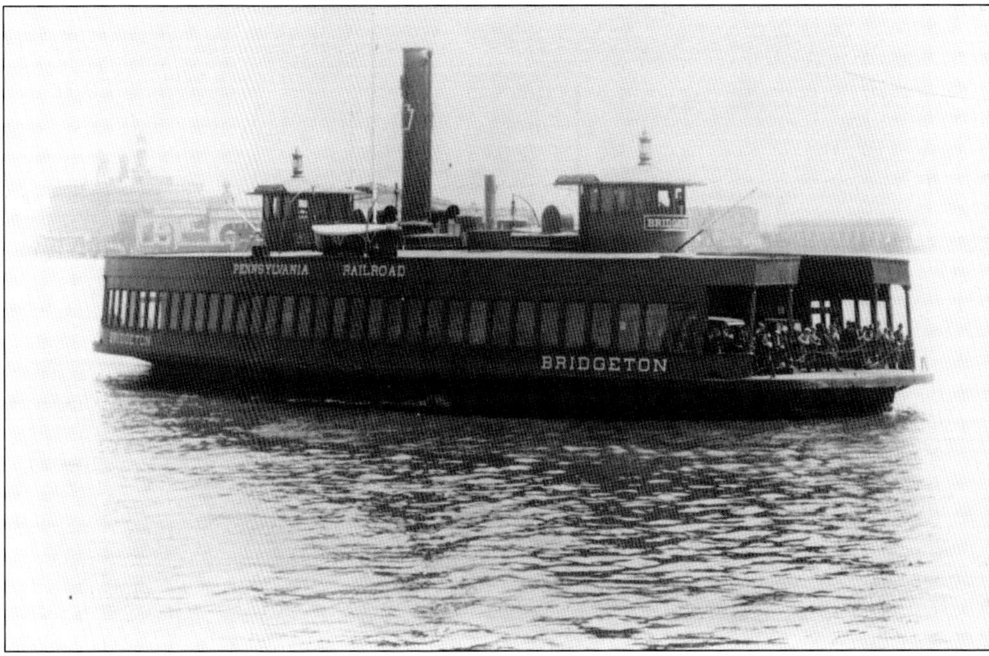

ON THE DELAWARE RIVER. Launched in 1913 for service between Philadelphia and Camden, the ferry *Bridgeton* is shown here making a crossing before World War II. From the MacDonald collection, the photograph illustrates that the owner named its vessels after prominent towns along the rail lines.

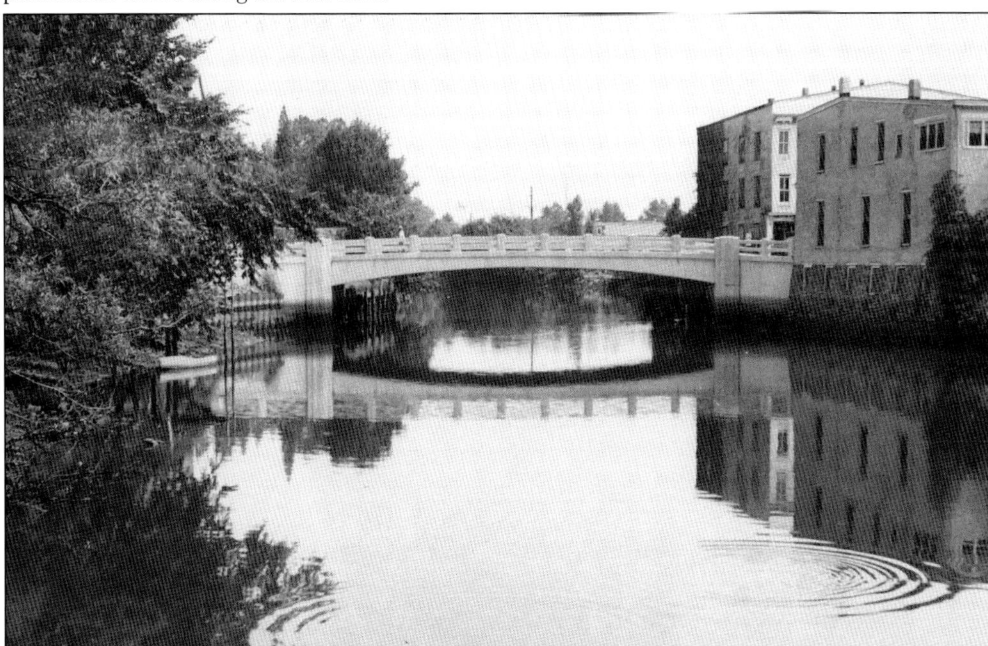

THE COMMERCE STREET BRIDGE. A span crossed this spot on the Cohansey River as early as 1716, while the bridge shown here was constructed in 1950. In 1955, the site appeared this way with the buildings on the east bank still surviving. The 1983 riverfront plaza project brought major changes.

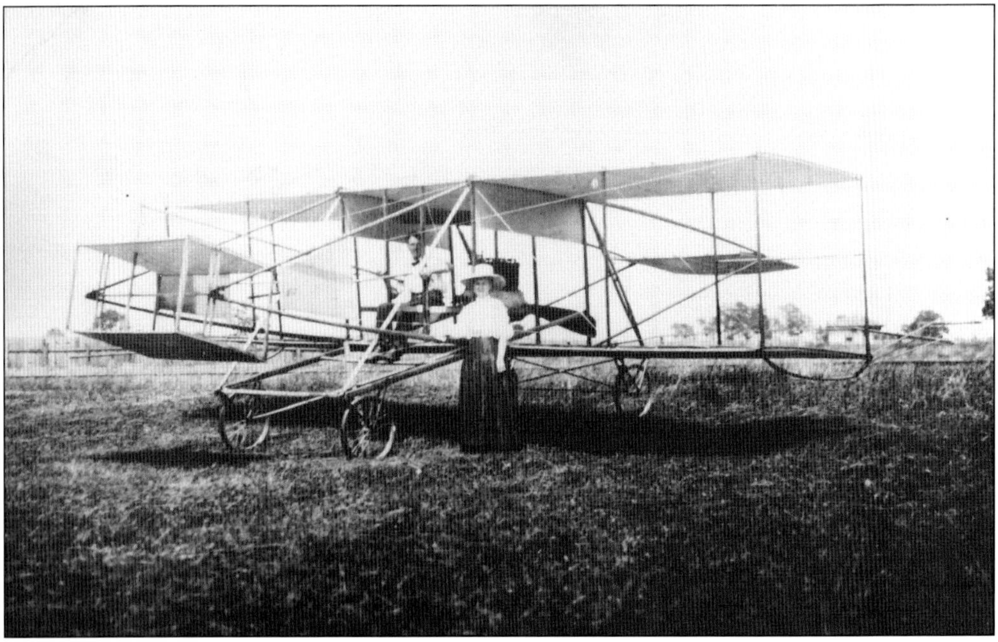

THE HETTINGER AEROPLANE. In 1909, local industrialist Henry Hettinger constructed this airplane, whose fabric-covered wings were sewn by his wife Mary. Hettinger made flights along the Cohansey River meadows, at the fairgrounds on Fayette Street, and then outfitted the plane with pontoons.

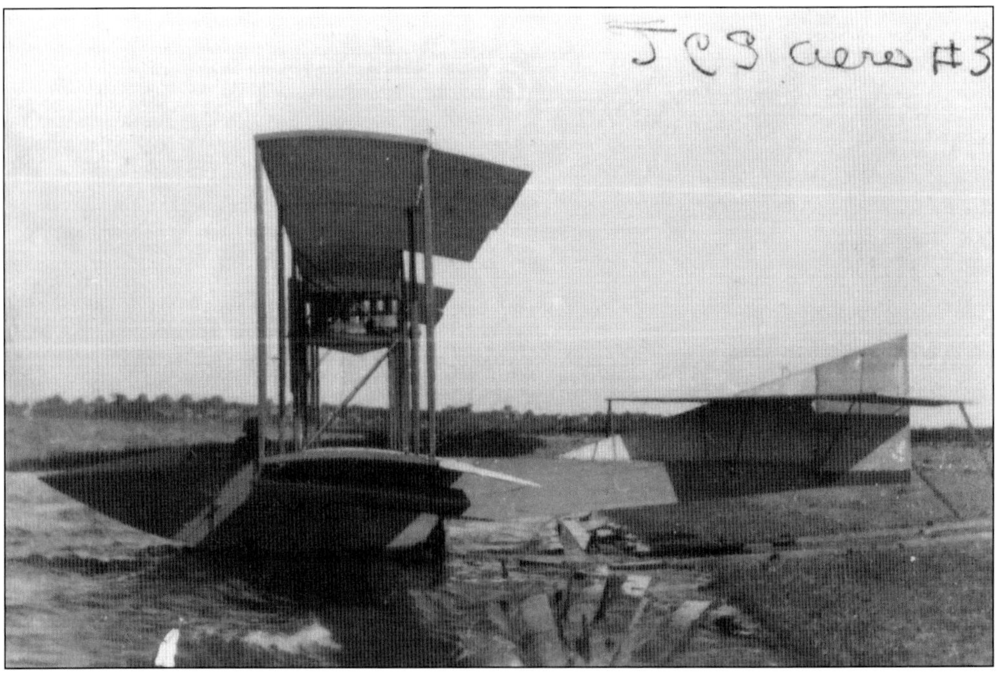

JOE SHOEMAKER'S AEROPLANE NUMBER 3. The scion of Bridgeton's Cumberland Glass manufacturing family, Joseph Clark Shoemaker, a 1903 Princeton grad, made his first solo flight in 1911. Several of his aircraft were preserved to become part of the Smithsonian collection.

Eight

Civil Guardians

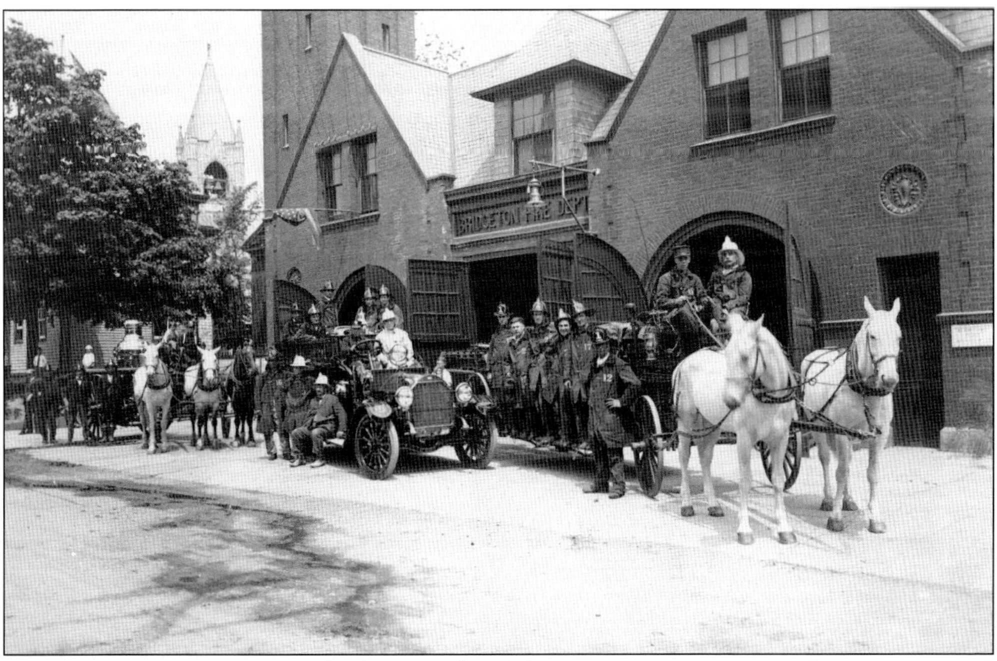

DAWN OF A NEW ERA. The latest in fire-fighting apparatus came on the scene in 1916 in Bridgeton when the city fathers purchased their first motorized unit, a Martin chemical truck. Here mechanical horsepower pauses next to the horse-drawn ladder wagon and LaFrance steamer.

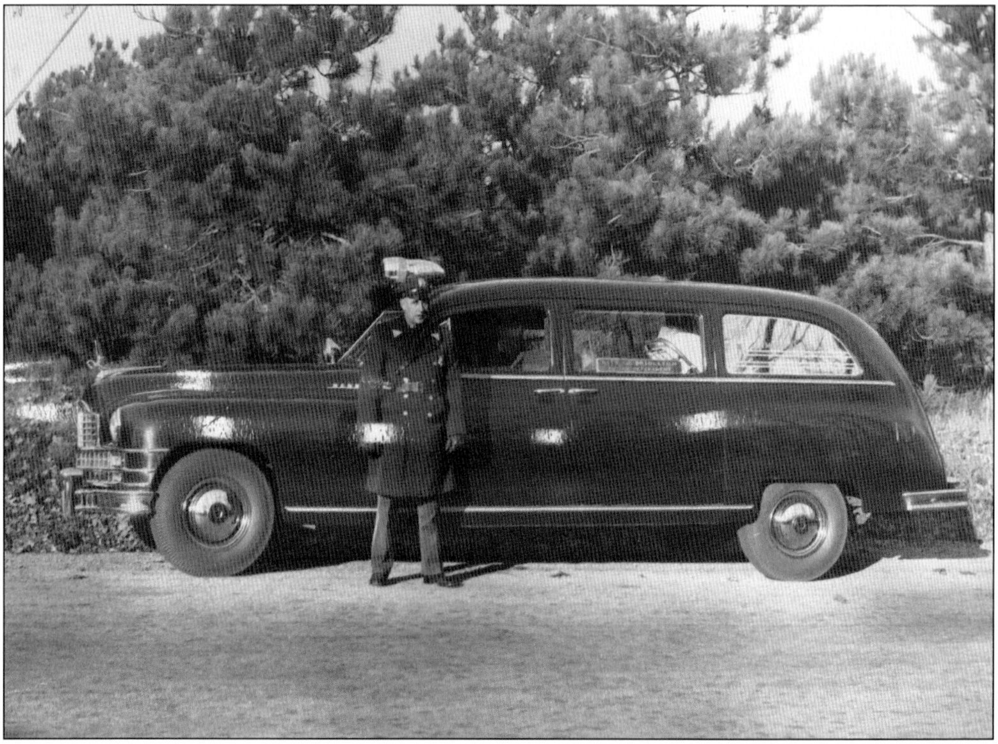

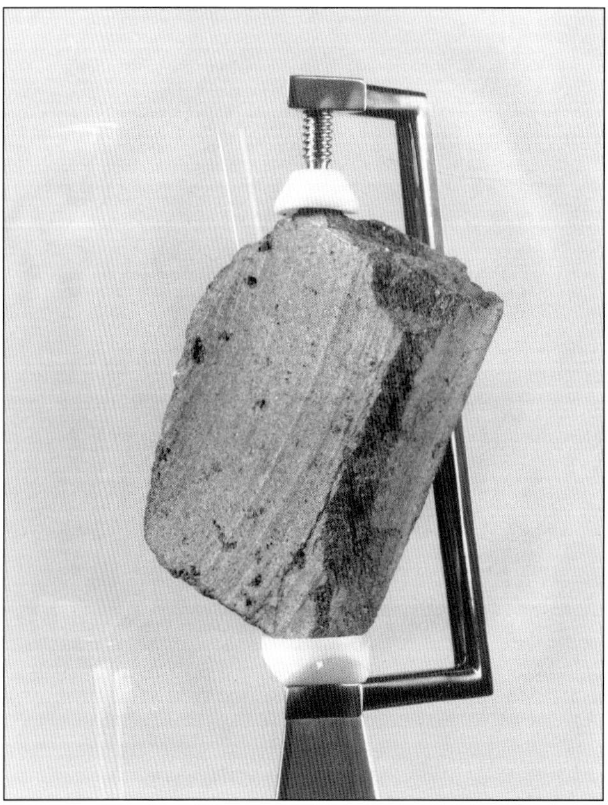

WE DELIVER FOR YOU. Police officer Chic Westcott stands in front of his department's ambulance, complete with fancy hood ornament, about 1941–42. During the World War II era, long before 911 came on the scene, you could reach the police department by telephoning 33.

YOU'VE GOT A PIECE OF THE ROCK. One of the most unusual jobs the Bridgeton Police Department had during its long history was guarding this 3.2-billion-year-old moon rock during its visit to the city park's Nail House Museum on Memorial Day in 1974. No heist attempts were reported.

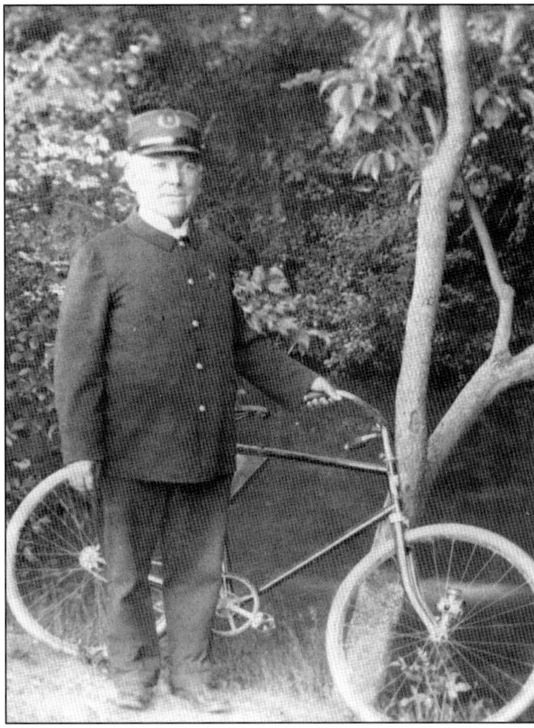

THE BPD BIKE PATROL IS NOTHING NEW. Officer "Shorty" Barton of the Bridgeton Police Department took to riding a bicycle, equipped with an axle-mounted headlight, to patrol the walk along the Raceway in the city park about 1915. In recent years, the BPD has returned to using pedal power.

THE BOYS IN BLUE. In 1938, about the date of this photograph at city hall, the BPD roster under Commissioner Mervin Beach included Patrolmen Hamlyn, Archer, Johnson, McGowan, Williams, Elwell, Husted, Knipe, and Woodlin, Special Officers Price and Leeds, and Sergeants Davis and Bacon.

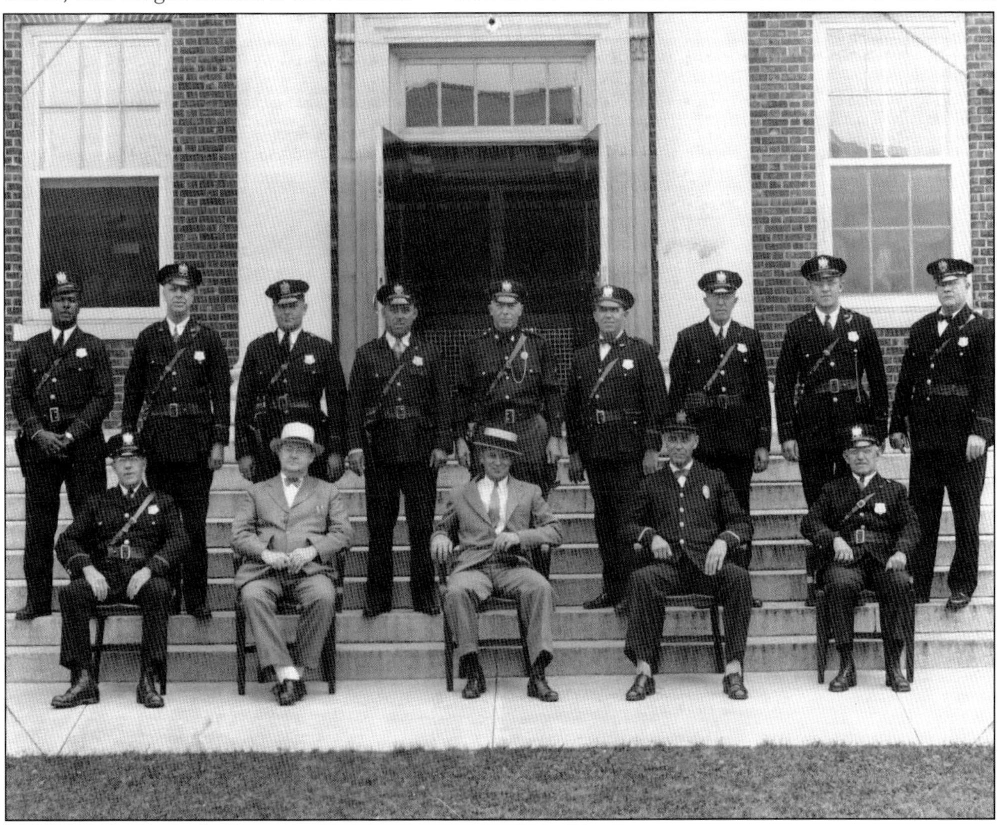

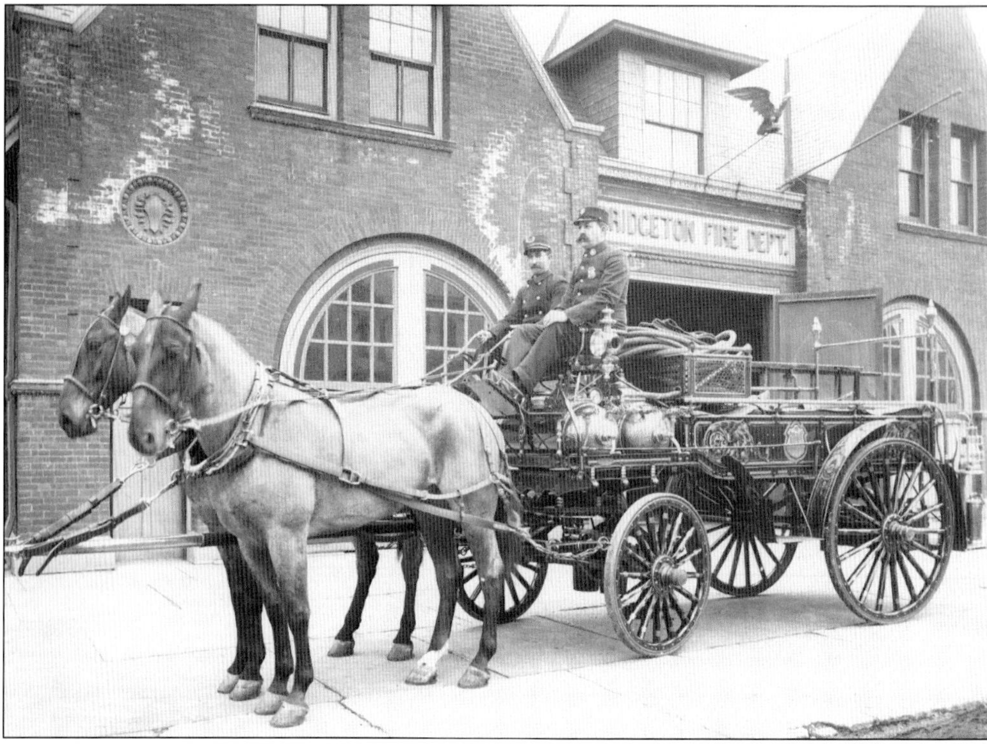

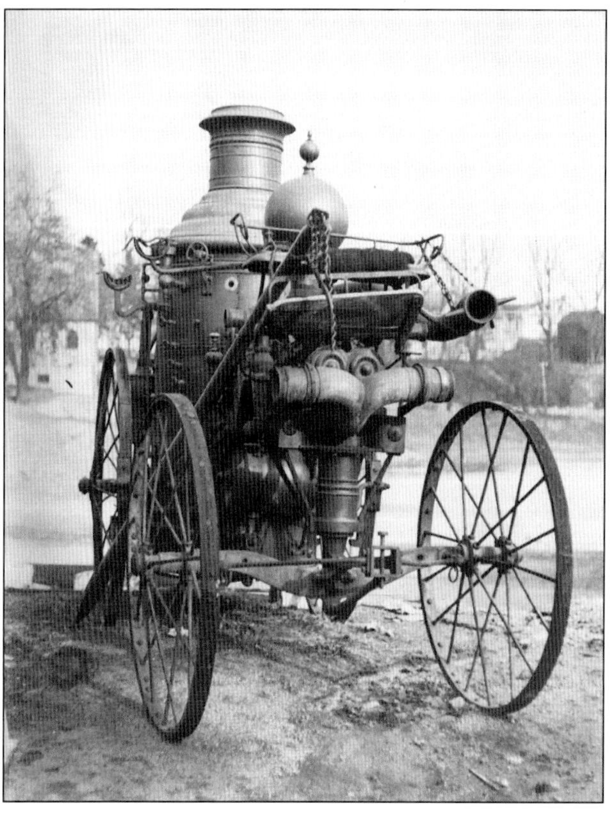

REPORTING FOR DUTY. Chief George Kinkle and Driver George Green pause for a photograph taken about 1905 by Harvey W. Porch in front of the 1898 engine house on Orange Street. Under the driver's seat can be seen the dual soda-acid tanks used to pressurize the chemical wagon's system.

THE END OF THE ROAD—ALMOST. Purchased new in 1877 and dubbed "Cohansey," the Silsby steamer lies forlornly in an abandoned state behind the fire engine house sometime after it was retired in 1915. During World War II it was almost sacrificed to a scrap drive, but was rescued.

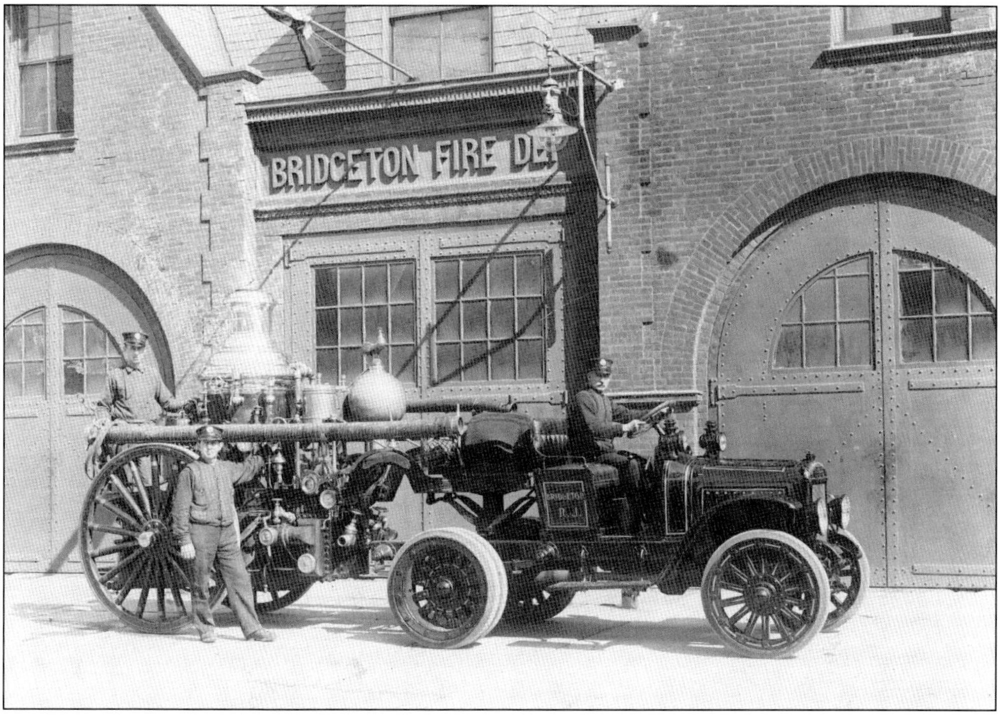

THE REO-LAFRANCE HYBRID. Around World War I, the Bridgeton Fire Department attempted to modernize its formerly horse-drawn vehicles by equipping them with internal combustion tractors. Daniel W. Ward photographed the combination Reo motor and 1890 LaFrance steamer.

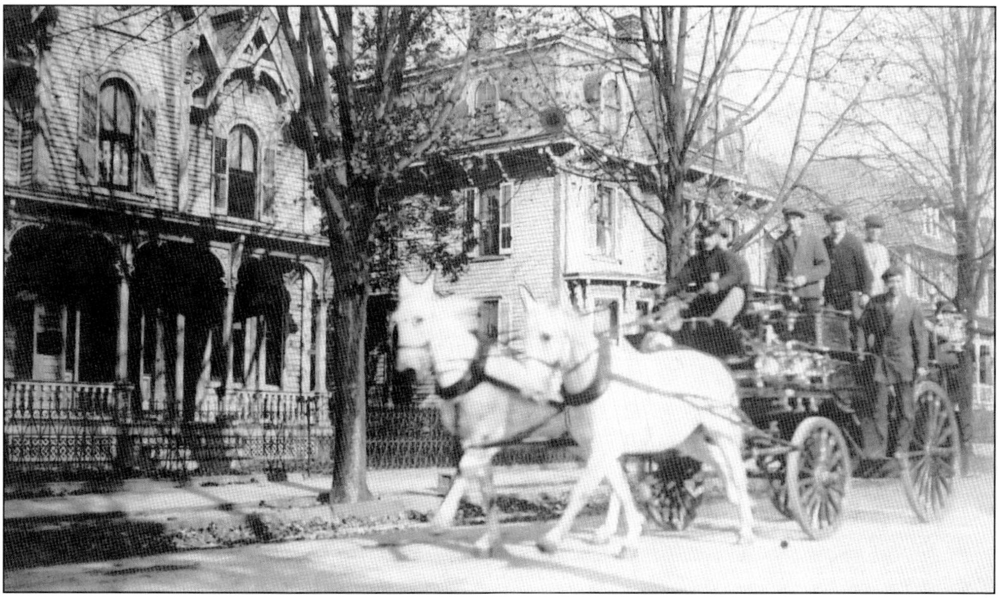

WE CAME, WE SAW, WE CONQUERED. This high-stepping pair of white horses pulling the chemical wagon of the Bridgeton Fire Department is headed south on Pearl Street just above Irving Avenue about 1910. At left is the home of Thomas U. Harris, the prominent Bridgeton banker.

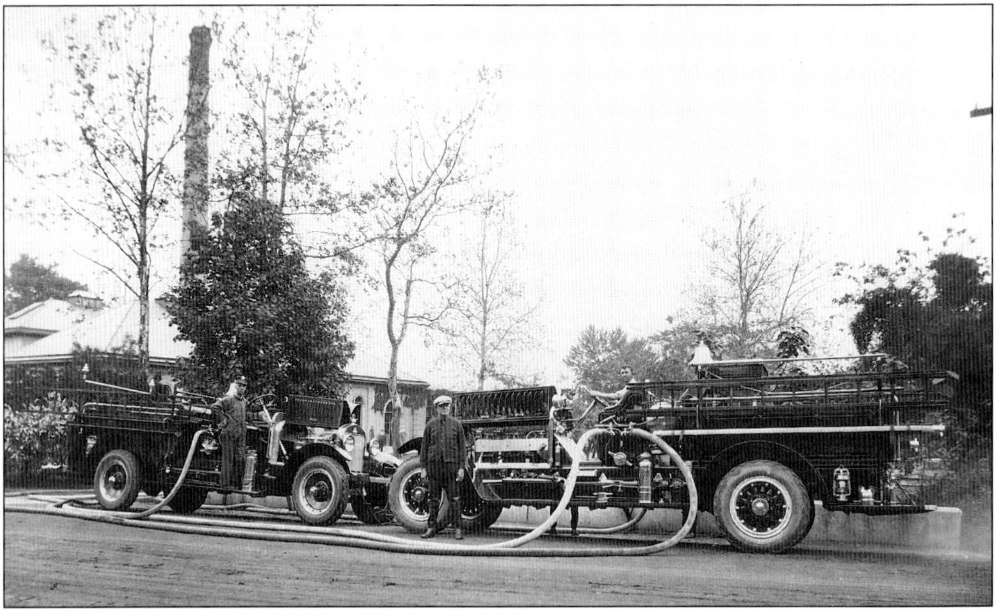

ALWAYS PREPARED. A pleasant spring day in the late 1920s encouraged members of the BFD to turn out for a drill with their most modern equipment in the Bridgeton City Park adjacent to the waterworks. Photographer Harvey W. Porch was on hand to capture the exercise.

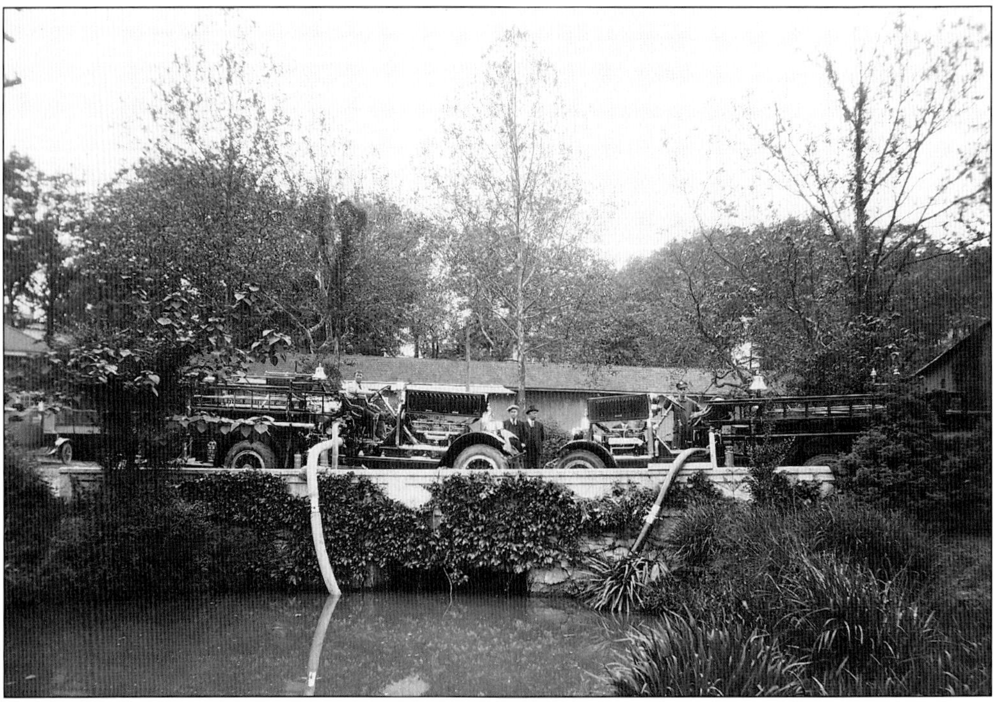

SHOW 'EM HOW IT'S DONE, BOYS. Demonstrating the technique used to draft water during fire-fighting emergencies in rural areas, members of the BFD lower hoses into the waterway connecting the Raceway and the Cohansey River. In the background can be seen the city park canoe houses.

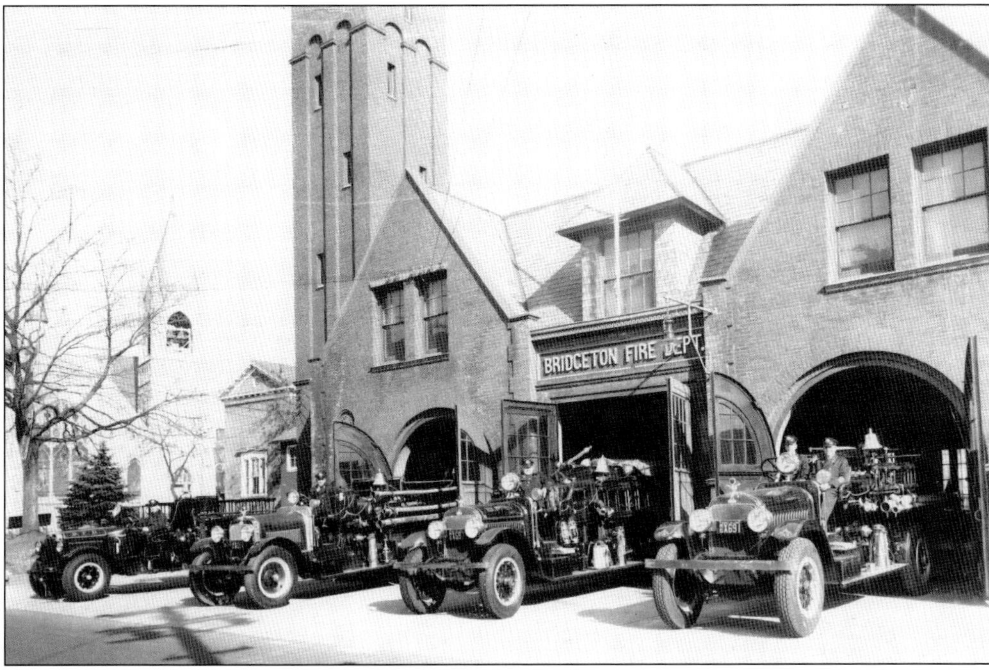

A GREAT DAY ON ORANGE STREET. America was in the midst of the Great Depression in 1938 when this picture was taken, but despite the financial crunch the Bridgeton Fire Department seemed to have the best available apparatus. The tower on the engine house was used to dry hoses.

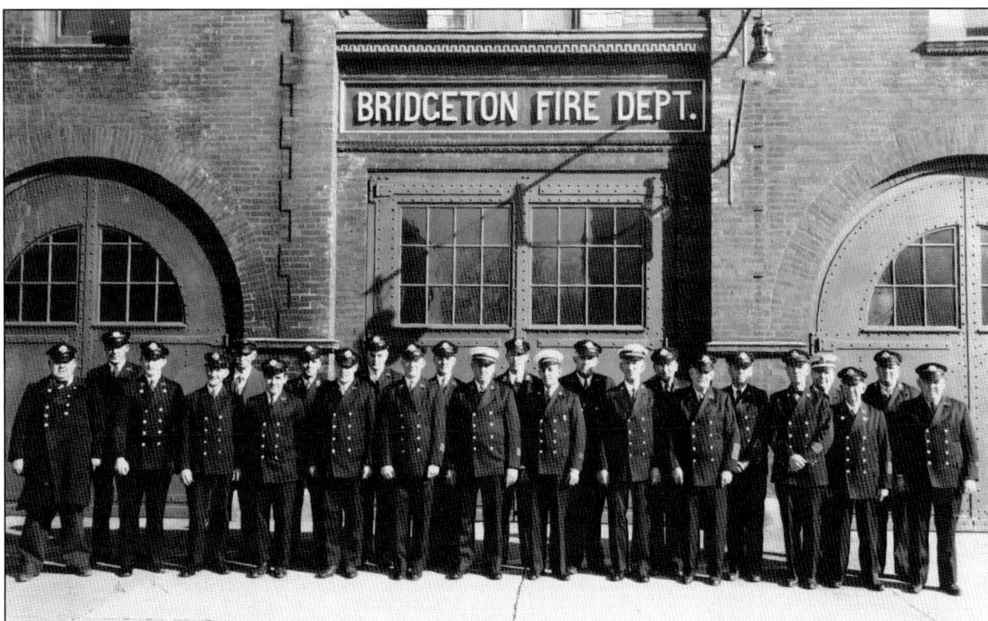

IN FORMAL DRESS. Some of the BFD members identified in this 1939 photograph include: ? Channels, B. Mead, E. Kellmayer, S. Vaughn, H. Shaw, ? Schaefer, R. Rainear, ? Johnson, B. Mulford, D. Elwell, W. Smith, J. Baumgarten, R. Husted, G. Facemyer, D. Blew, J. Mulford, ? Heller, and B. Mulford.

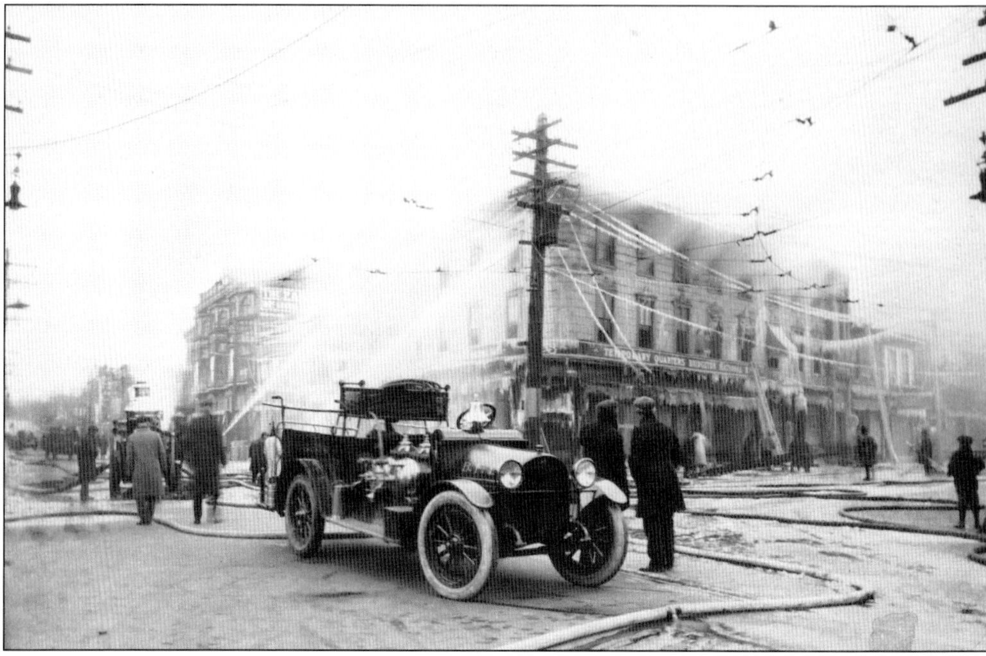

THE GROSSCUP-FEINSTEIN BUILDING BURNS. Among the most spectacular fires to hit Bridgeton was the one that took place on the northeast corner of Commerce and Laurel Streets on January 26, 1924. Dating from the Civil War era, the frame structure went up due to a fire in a restaurant's kitchen.

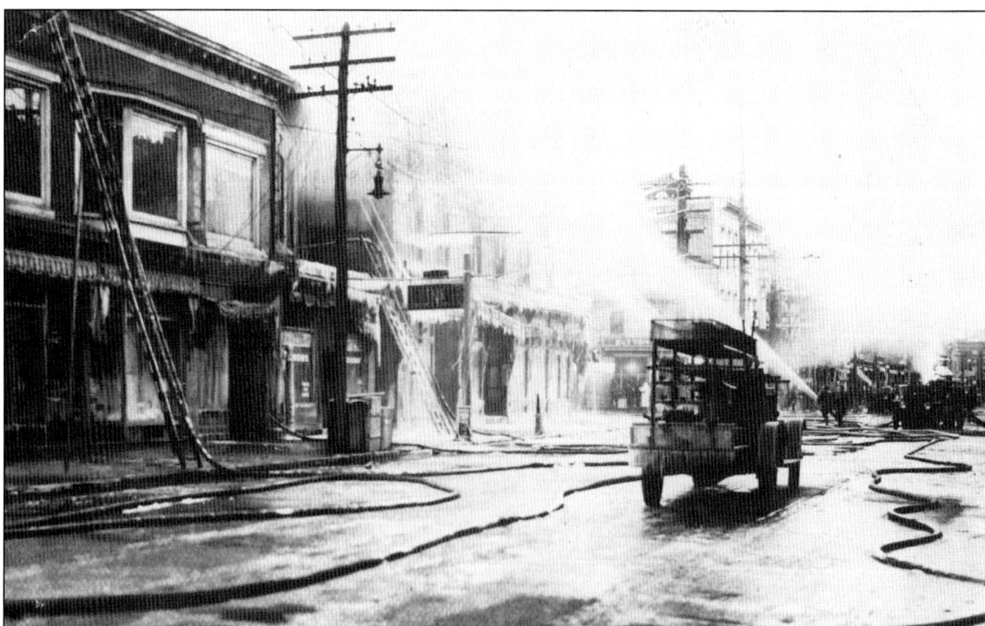

A GRIM SCENE RESULTS. Looking south along Laurel Street toward Commerce, a ladder truck stands by after its equipment has been deployed to fight the Grosscup-Feinstein fire. Meanwhile, hoses snake down the street to the intersection where firemen press them into service.

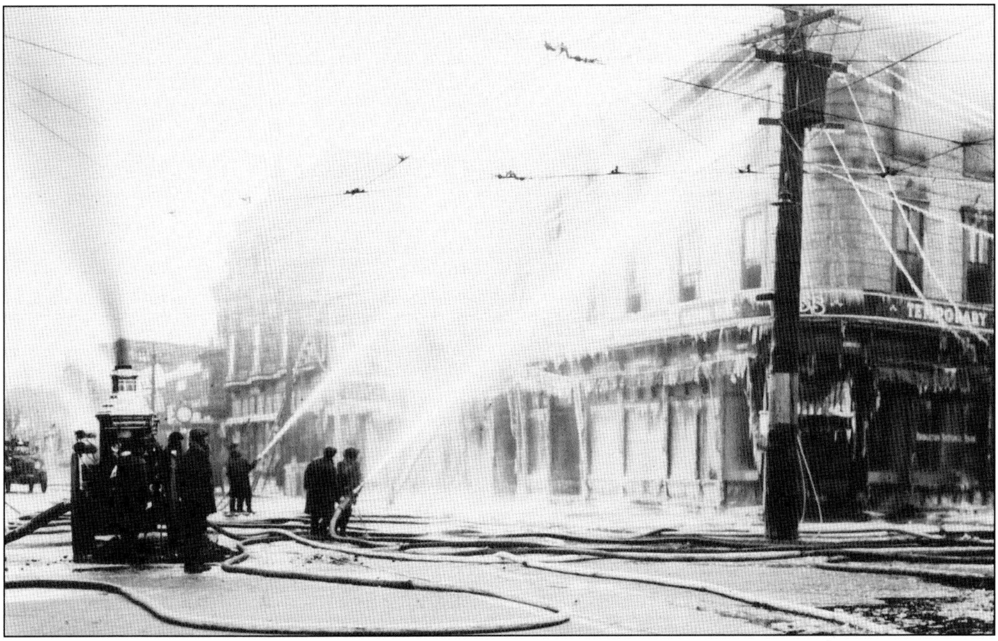

A STEADY STREAM OF WATER. The BFD continues to pour on water supplied by the Reo-LaFrance steamer that labors at left under a cloud of smoke. One of the building's occupants sacrificed to the Grosscup-Feinstein fire was the Bridgeton National Bank, which was then using the structure as a temporary headquarters.

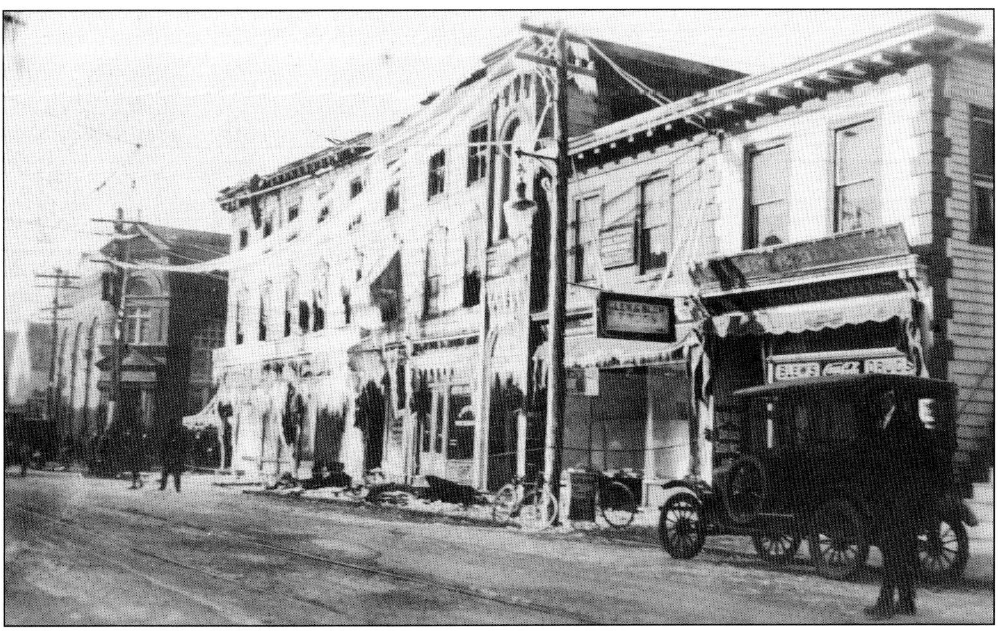

THE SCENE ON COMMERCE STREET. After the 1924 Grosscup-Feinstein fire died down, what remained of the ancient frame structure was encased in ice due to the freezing temperatures. This series of photographs is from the Pedrick collection.

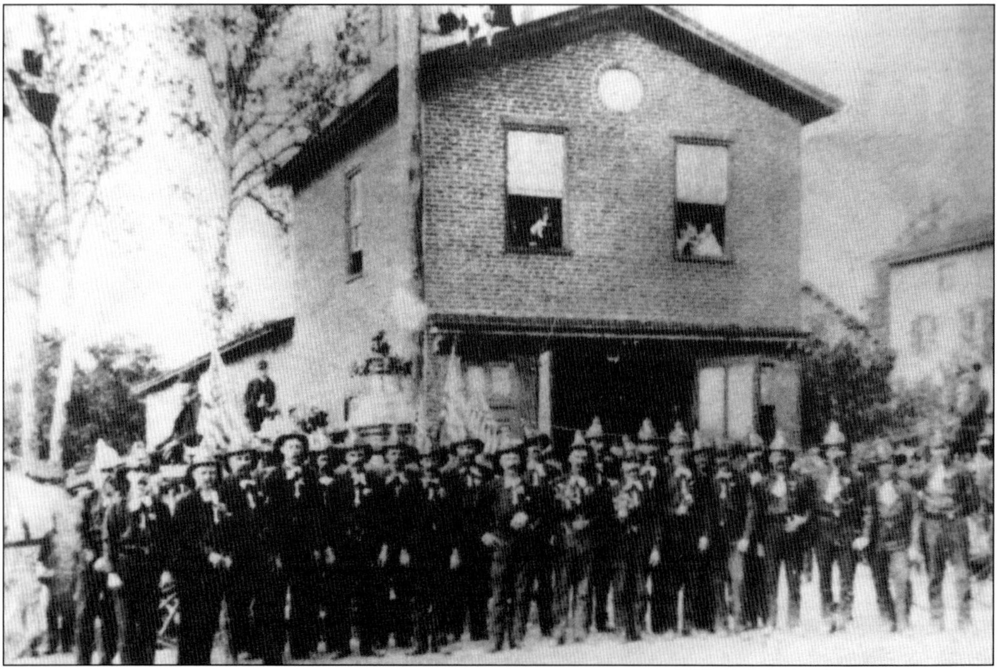

THE OLD FIRE ENGINE HOUSE. Members of the Cohansey Fire Company line up in front of the 1877 engine house at Washington and Cohansey Streets for a photograph about 1890. When this company first formed, it received support, including the loan of horses, from the nearby nail works.

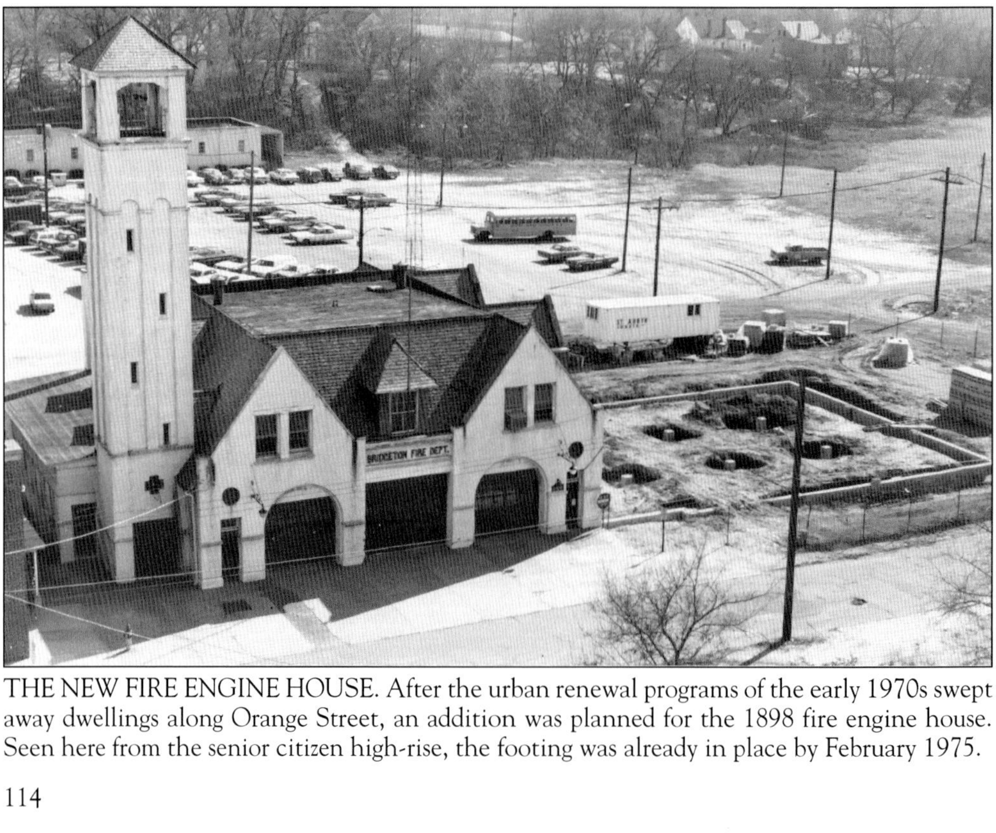

THE NEW FIRE ENGINE HOUSE. After the urban renewal programs of the early 1970s swept away dwellings along Orange Street, an addition was planned for the 1898 fire engine house. Seen here from the senior citizen high-rise, the footing was already in place by February 1975.

Nine

In Your Neighborhood

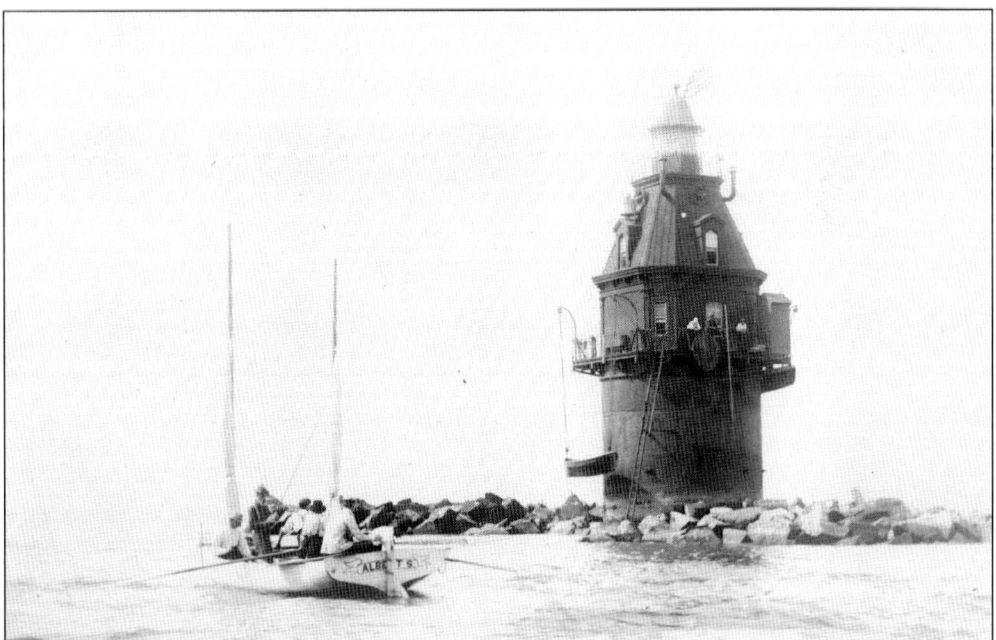

A LONELY RESIDENCE. A vessel makes its way past the Ship John Shoal Lighthouse just off the mouth of the Cohansey River as three keepers rubberneck in a photograph dating about 1910. Exhibited at the Centennial Exposition in Philadelphia in 1876, the beacon was installed at the site in 1877.

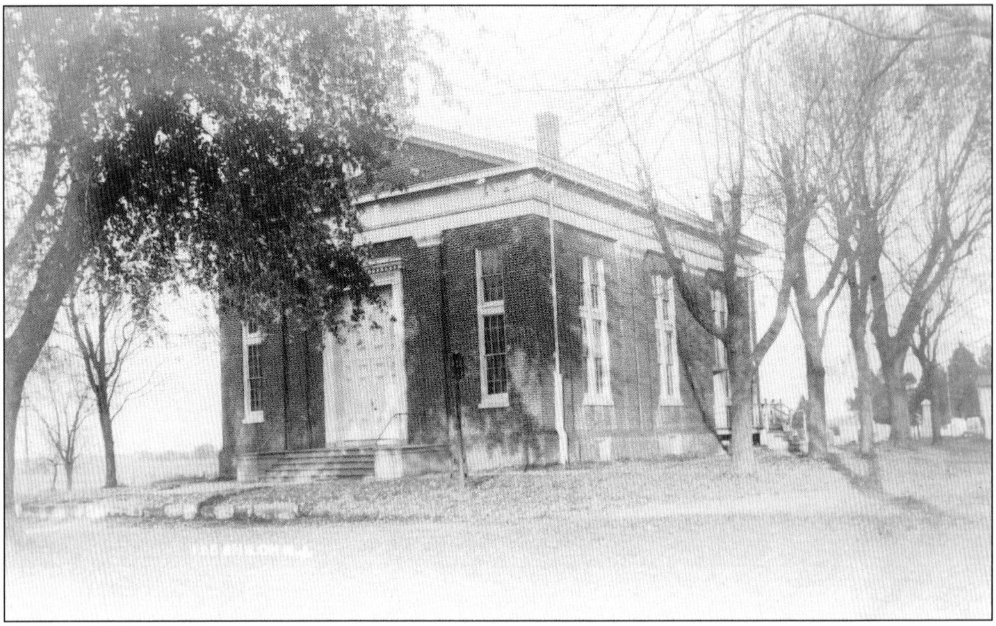

THE SHILOH SEVENTH DAY BAPTIST CHURCH. As its name implies, members of this congregation worship on Saturdays. The town and church take their names from the Biblical place where the Ark of the Covenant rested. The Neoclassical church, seen here in a *c.* 1910 photograph, was dedicated in 1850.

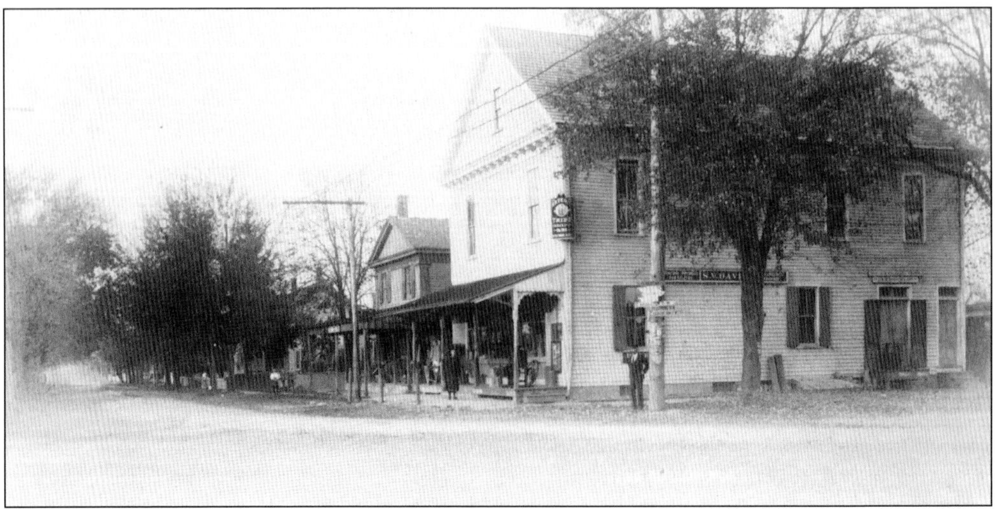

DOWNTOWN SHILOH. Things change very slowly in Shiloh, but the present-day Richardson's Store on Route 49 was the business of S.V. Davis when this photograph, now in the Turner collection, was taken in 1906. The local chapter of the Red Men met on the upper floor.

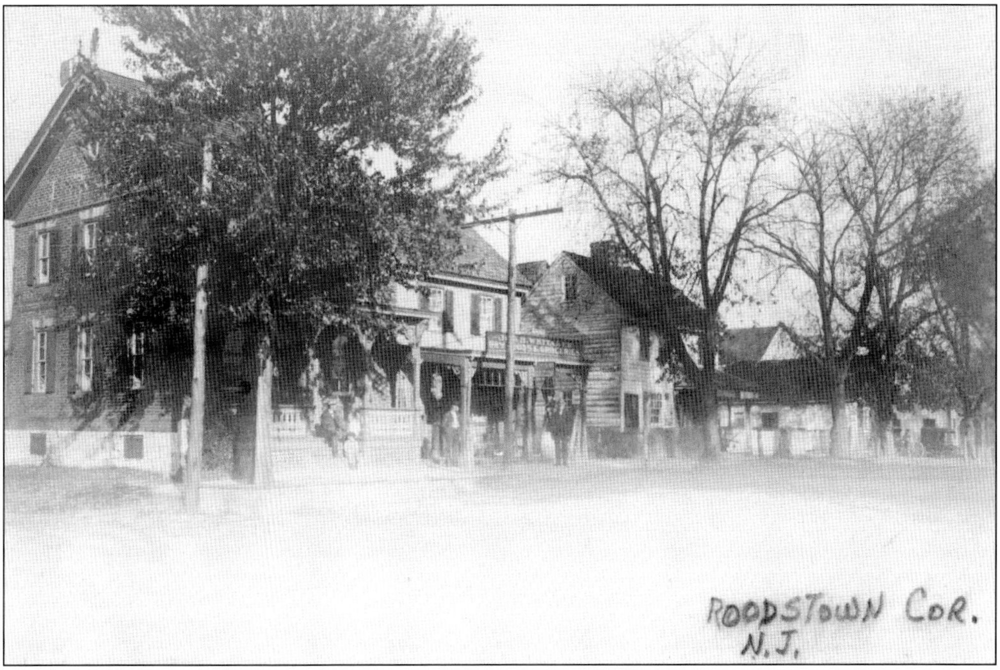

THE ROADSTOWN CROSSROADS. In 1770 Sheriff Ananias Sayre erected this fine brick home with the date worked into its gable end. By the time this photograph from the Turner collection was taken about 1905, the structure had a porch and wing added and served as the store of Joseph H. Whitaker.

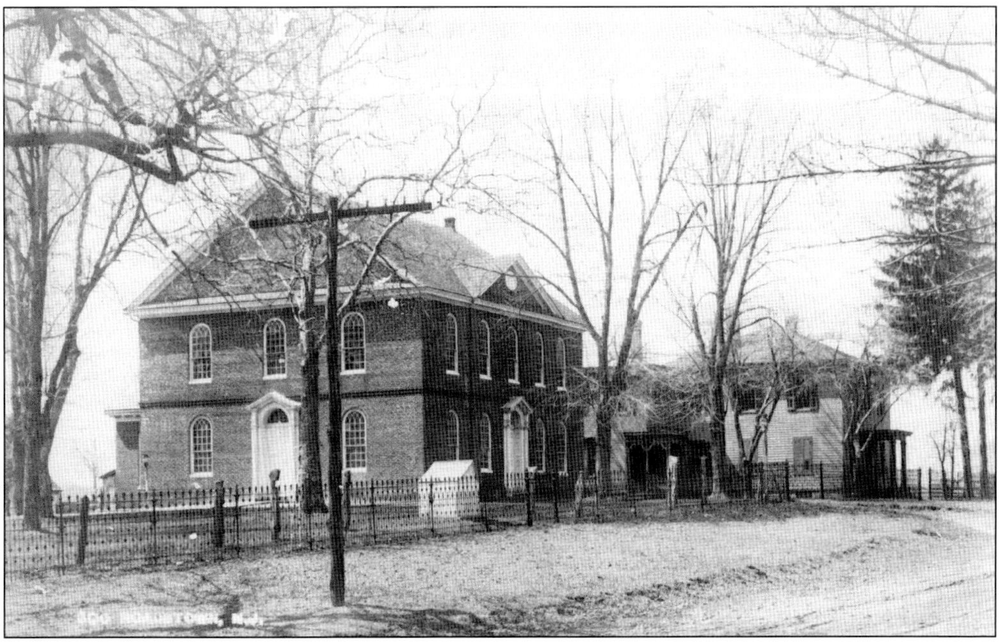

COHANSEY BAPTIST AT ROADSTOWN. Since the late 1600s, the congregation of the Cohansey Baptist Church has migrated from the banks of the Cohansey River in Fairfield all the way to Roadstown. The current church, seen here in a 1907 view from the Turner collection, was erected in 1802.

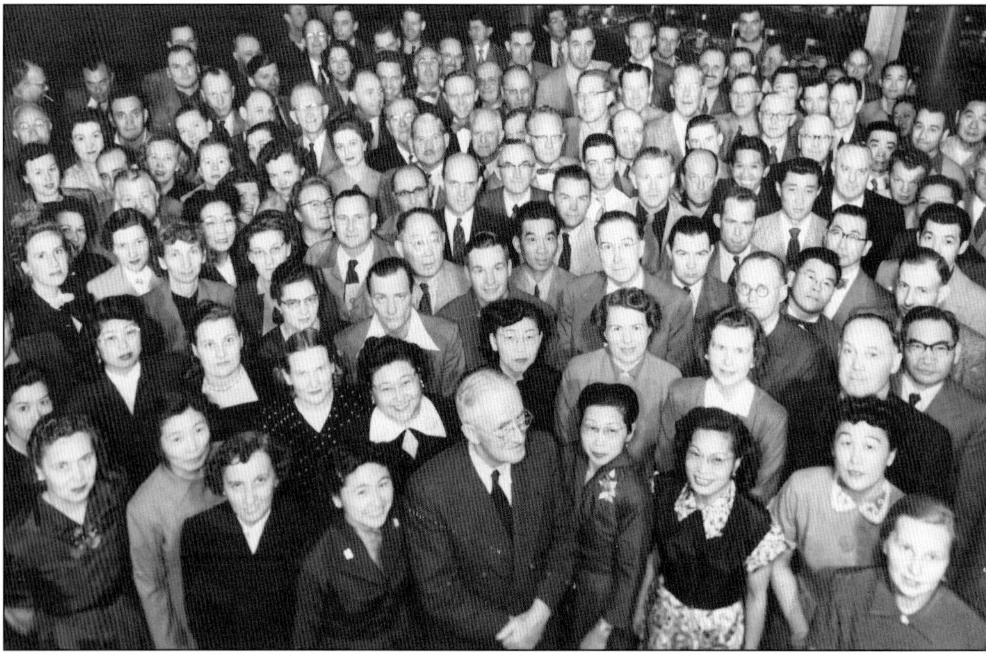

"C.F." AND HIS FLOCK. The legendary frozen food pioneer Charles Franklin Seabrook, better known as C.F., stands front and center surrounded by his employees, whose ancestors hail from the far corners of the world. The photograph was taken at a dinner in the plant cafeteria in 1954.

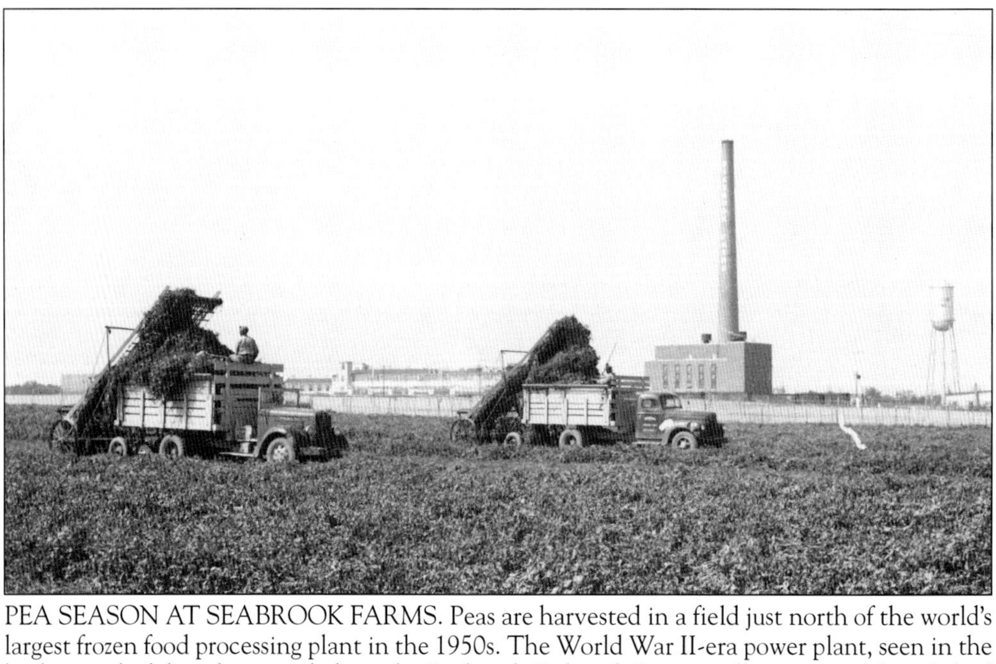

PEA SEASON AT SEABROOK FARMS. Peas are harvested in a field just north of the world's largest frozen food processing plant in the 1950s. The World War II-era power plant, seen in the background of this photograph from the Seabrook Cultural Center collection, was demolished in 1979.

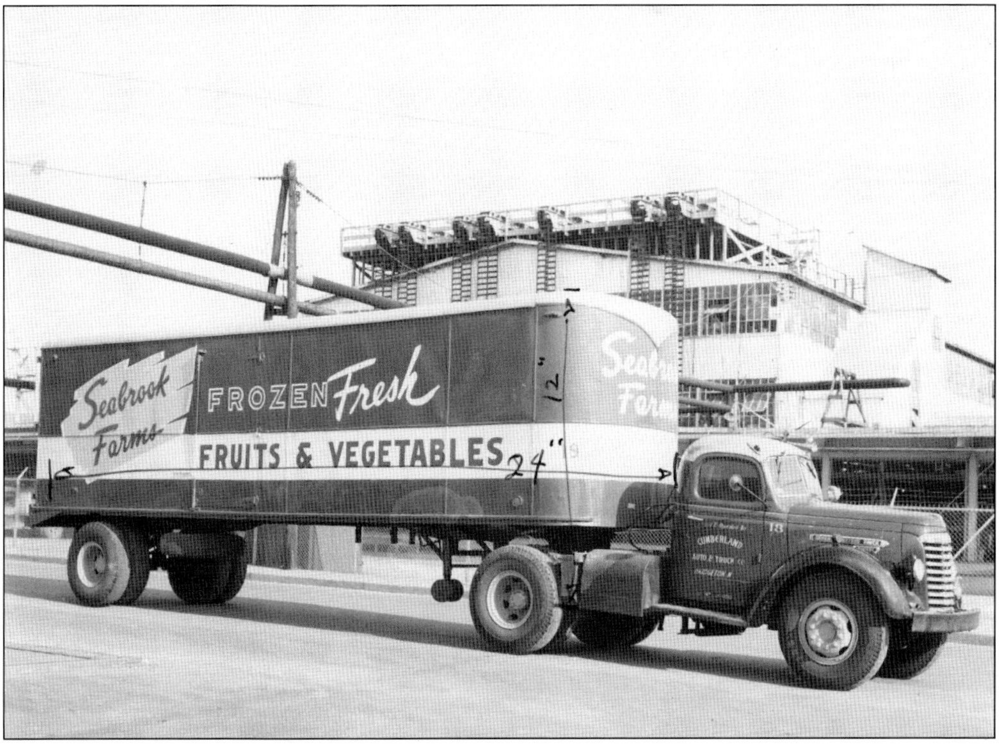

FROM SEABROOK TO YOUR HOME FREEZER. Cumberland Auto & Truck, one of several divisions of Seabrook Farms, operated a fleet of colorfully painted trucks to transport the company's products. This one is parked near the plant's front platform, where the pea and lima conveyors are visible.

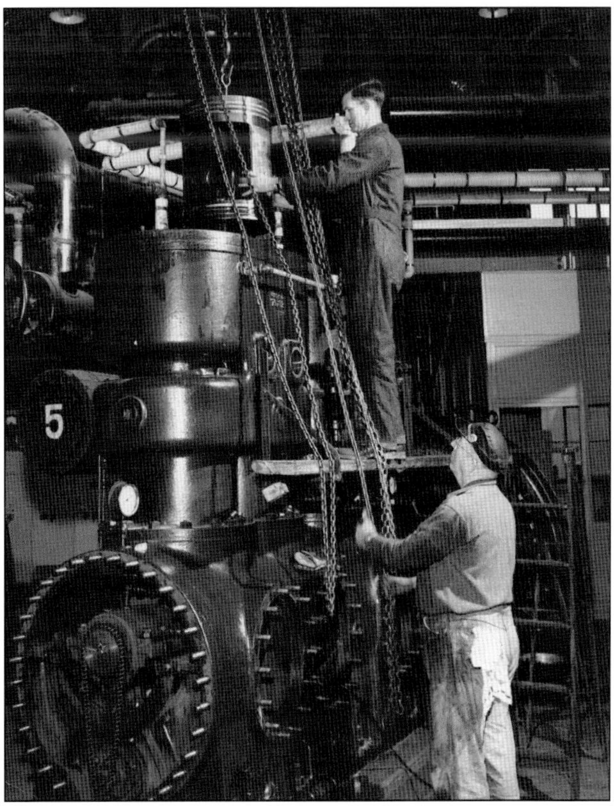

STATE-OF-THE-ART TECHNOLOGY. Seabrook Farms was always at the forefront of innovation, from the installation of overhead irrigation to the use of flash freezing, and it took skilled people to keep it operating. Herb Seibert and another employee install a huge compressor piston in the era after World War II.

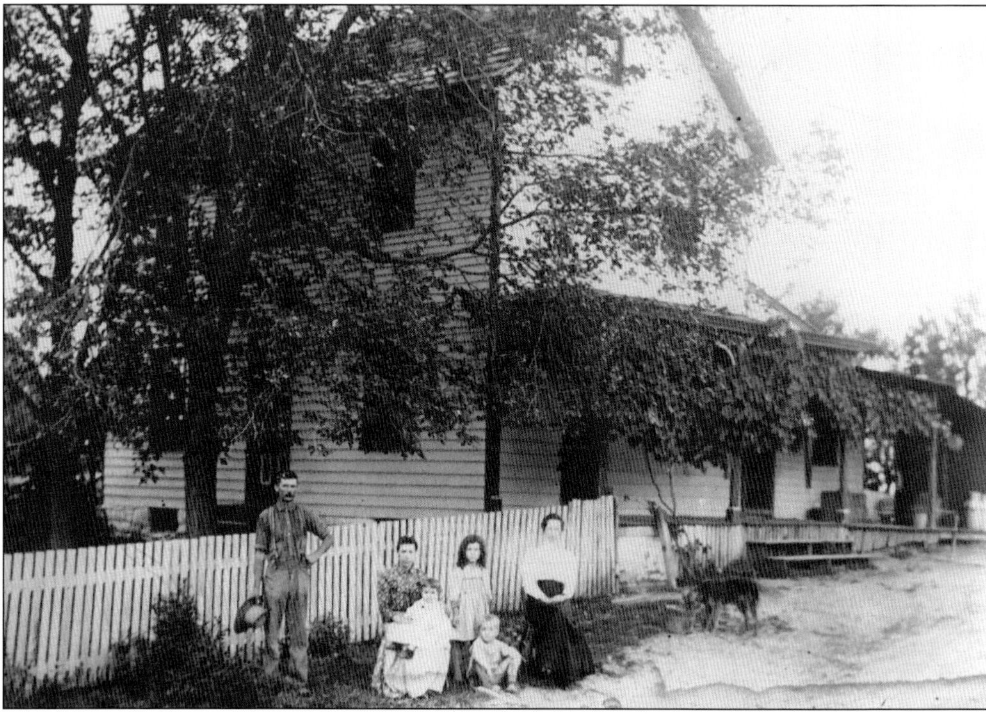

OUT COHANSEY WAY. The residents of Horse Branch Farm, near the village of Cohansey northwest of Bridgeton, assemble for a charming photograph in 1899. The picture includes Frank and Jennie Robinson, plus family members Warren, Elsie, Earl, and Frank's sister, Mary Walters.

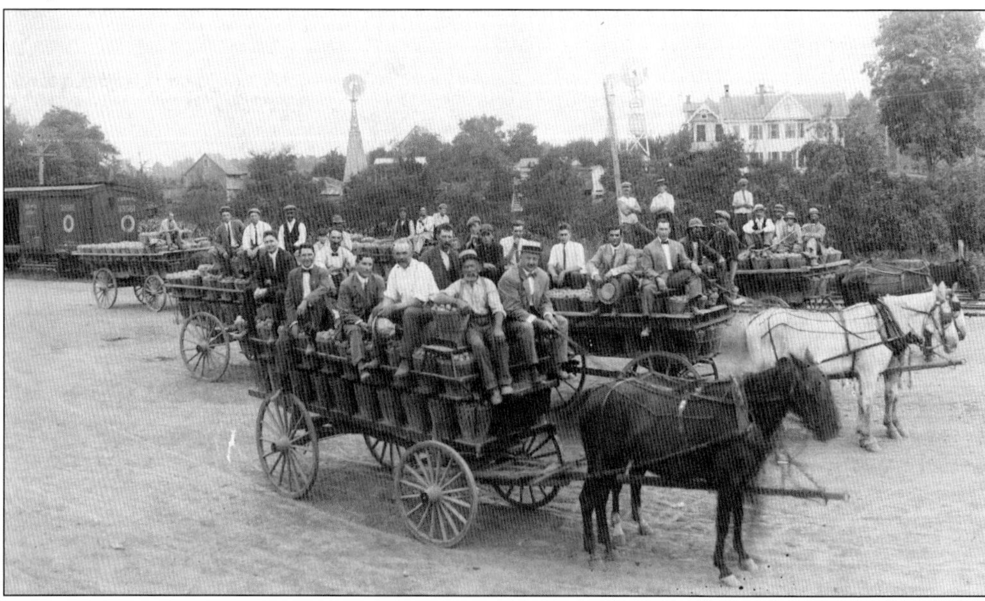

OFF TO THE MARKET. Bridgeton photographer Harvey Porch traveled out to the village of Deerfield Street north of town to take this photograph dating about 1915. Frank C. Robinson, seated highest in the nearest wagon, was among the farmers waiting to ship their potato crops by rail.

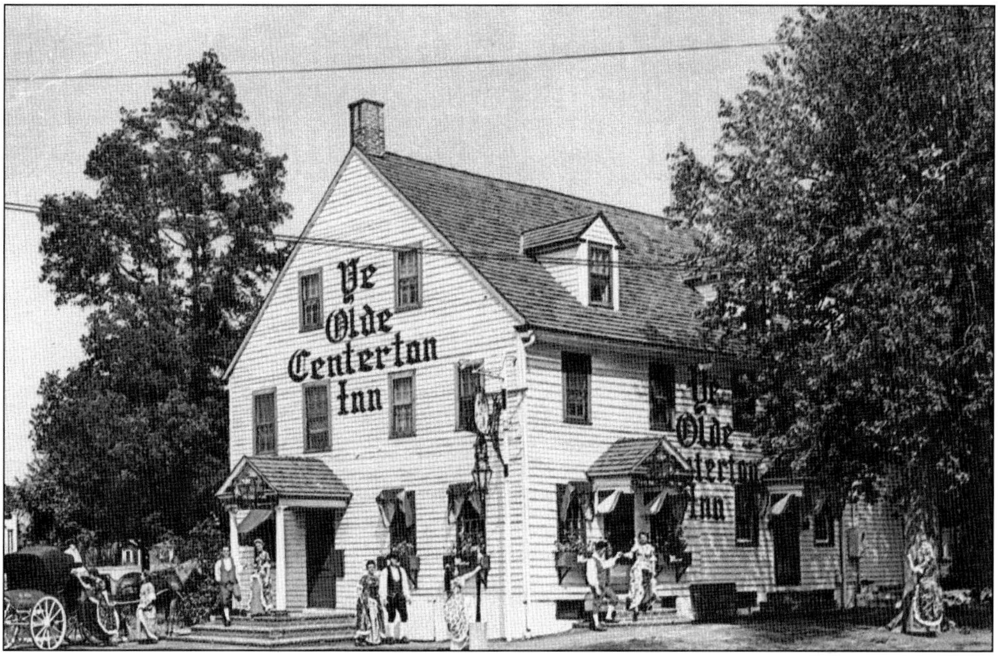

YE OLDE CENTERTON INN. A number of participants donned colonial garb to pose for this publicity photograph by Connelly-Moy about 1960 at Centerton, once known as Dayton's Bridge. The tavern, operated by Charles Dayton as early as 1763, is seen here with its original weatherboards.

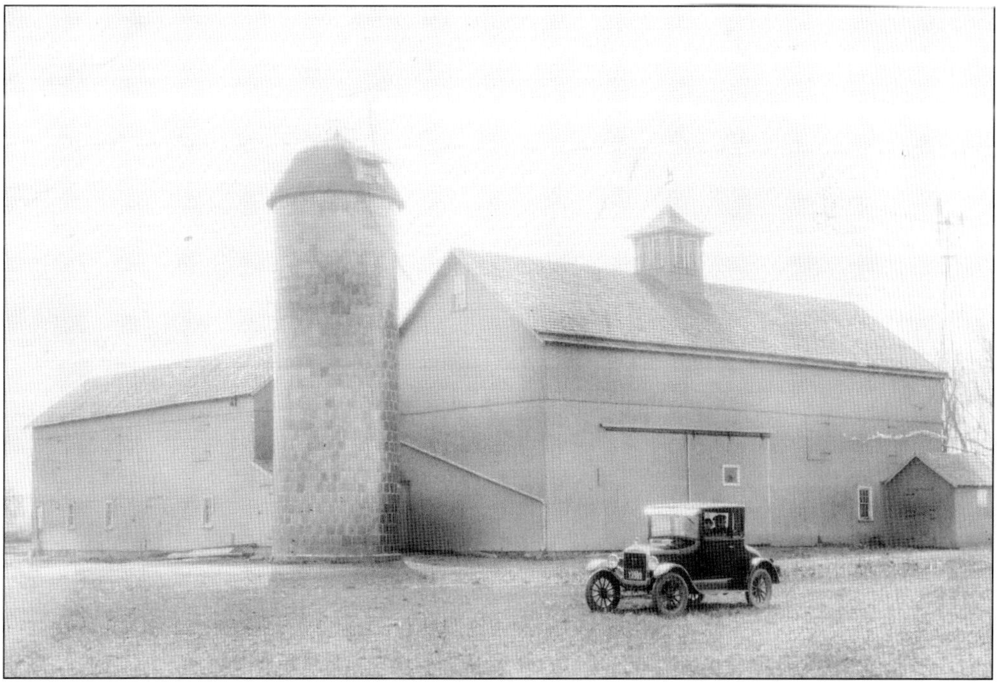

A VANISHING VISTA. The first round silo in New Jersey reportedly was built in the vicinity of Shiloh in 1901. This beautiful terra-cotta example and its owner's auto were photographed by Harvey Porch in the 1920s. Since the 1960s, these silos have become increasingly scarce.

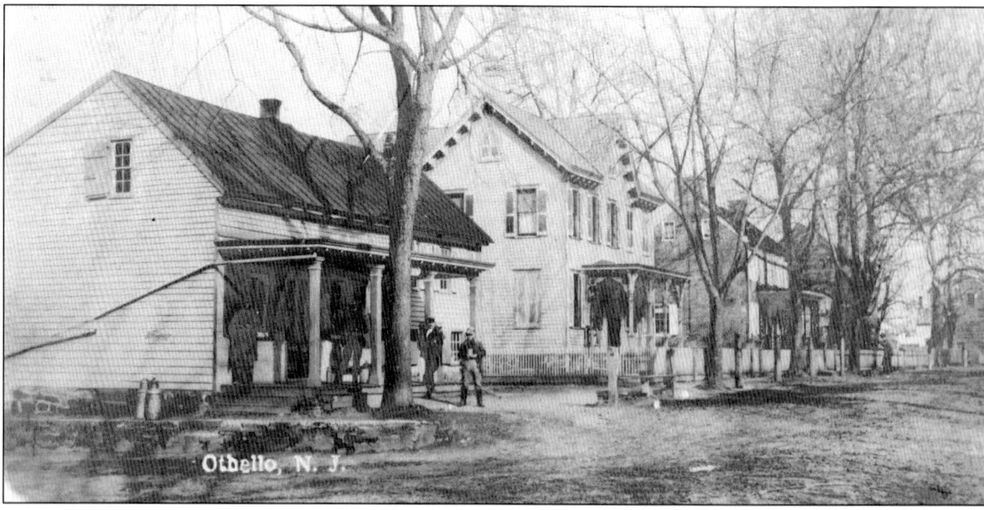

OTHELLO AT THE HEAD OF GREENWICH. Made up of Colonial and Victorian homes, Othello has changed little since this view from the Turner collection was taken about 1905. In the distance can be seen the home where the famed diary of Philip Vickers Fithian was rediscovered.

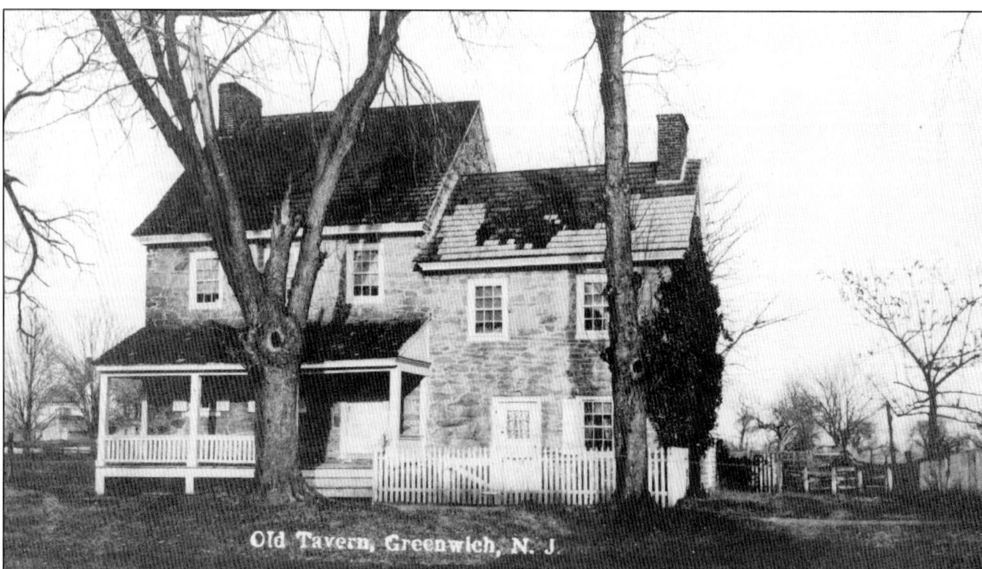

THE OLD STONE TAVERN IN GREENWICH. Depicted with the porch it once boasted, the Old Stone Tavern on Greate Street was where the courts met for the first few months when Cumberland County was established in 1748. Dating about 1910, this photograph is from the Pedrick collection.

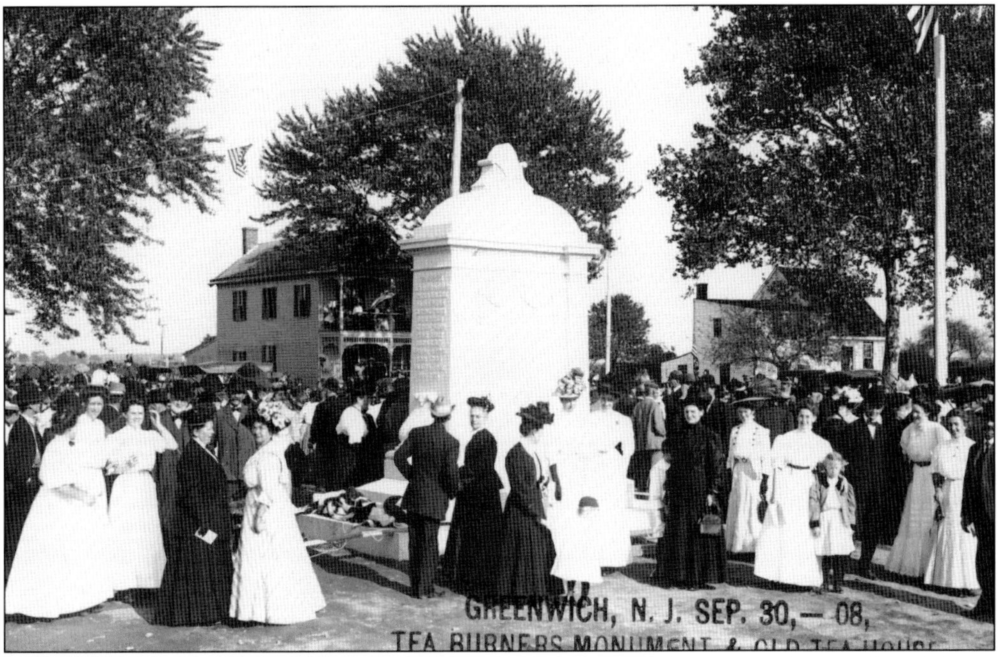

IN TEA BURNING TOWN. In 1774, a group of colonial patriots disguised as Native Americans gathered in Greenwich to burn a shipment of tea. The event was commemorated by the unveiling of a monument on September 30, 1908, much to the delight of onlookers, as this photograph reveals.

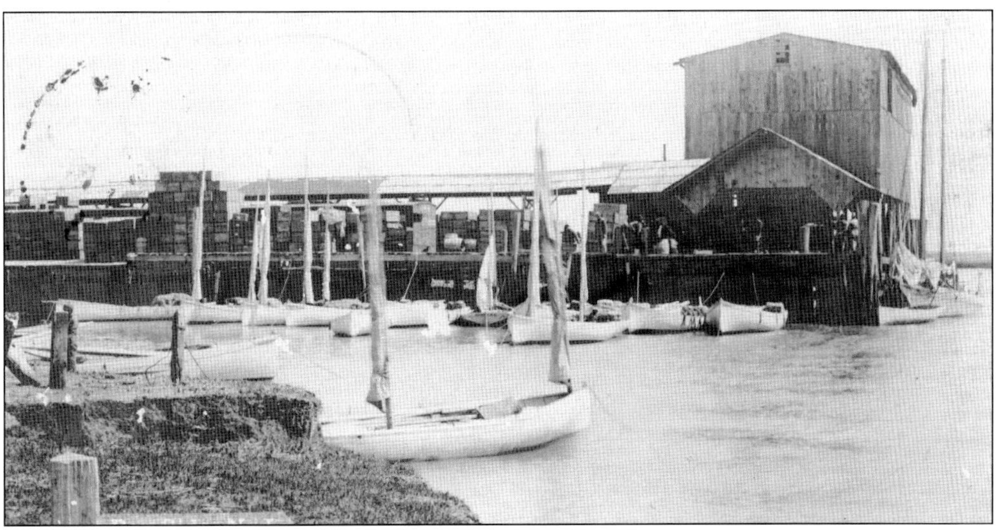

BAY SIDE ON THE DELAWARE BAY. Although today there are hardly more than a couple of fishermen's cottages and rotting pilings there, this *c.* 1907 photograph from the Turner collection reveals that Bay Side, also known as Caviar due to the village's shad roe industry, once had a population of 115.

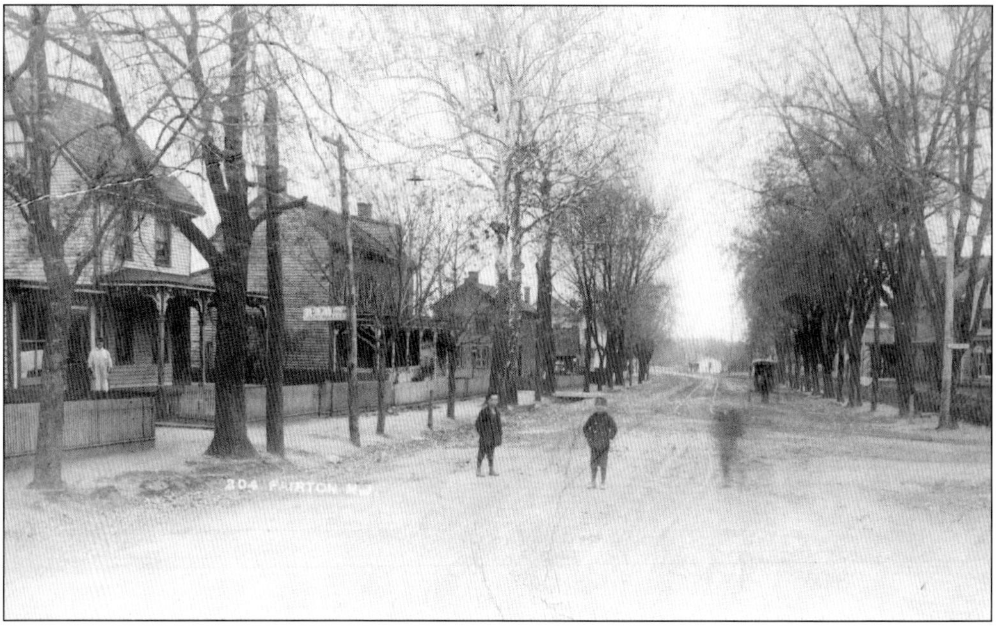

FAIRTON ON THE COHANSEY RIVER. This postcard from the Betty Lewis collection shows that the pace of life on Main Street was relatively slow on a winter's day about 1910. The business at left is the meat market of D.P. Taylor. To the right is the road leading north to Bridgeton.

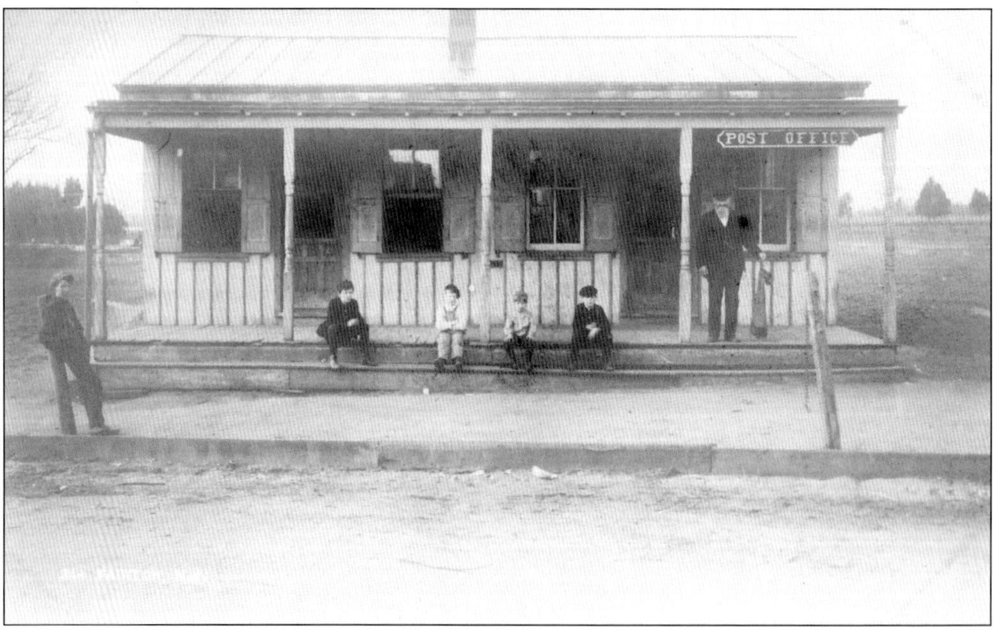

JUST HANGING AROUND. Enjoying time off from school, a group of kids lounges on the steps of the Fairton Post Office while the postmaster holds a limp bag, suggesting that business was relatively light. Just after 1900, about the date of this photograph, Fairton's population was six hundred.

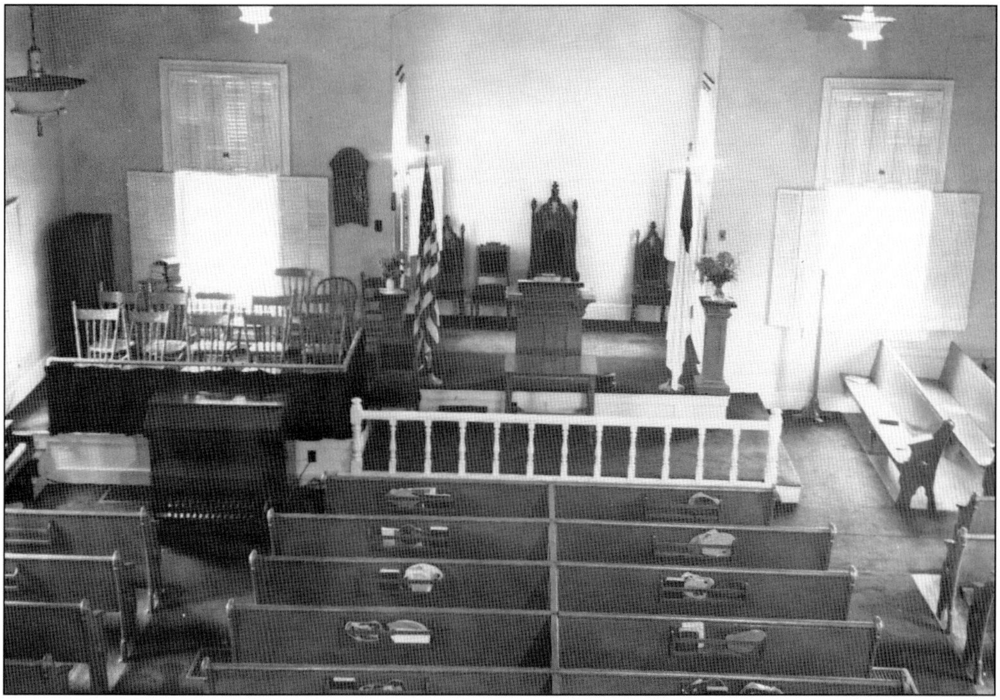

THE PRIDE OF GOULDTOWN. Central to the life of its congregation since it was erected in 1860–61 is the Gouldtown African Methodist Episcopal Church. This rare interior view by the Wright Photograph Service shows how the church appeared before World War II with its original shutters and seating.

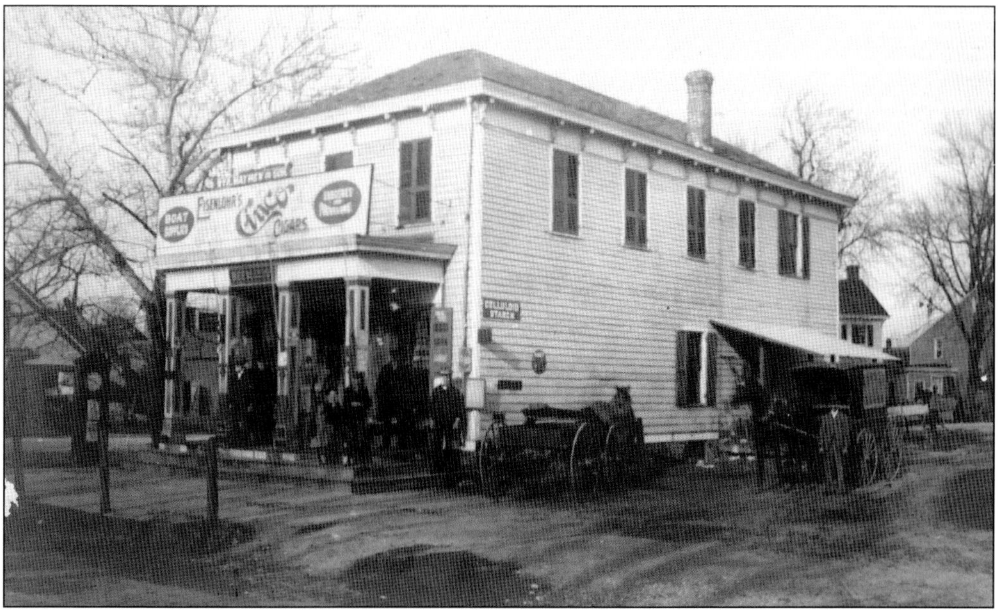

WHERE CEDARVILLE RESIDENTS SHOPPED. William A. Mayhew & Son's store was a thriving business in 1907, reflecting the town's role as one of the busiest commercial centers in the county. In the era before World War I, Cedarville boasted textile mills, sand plants, and canneries.

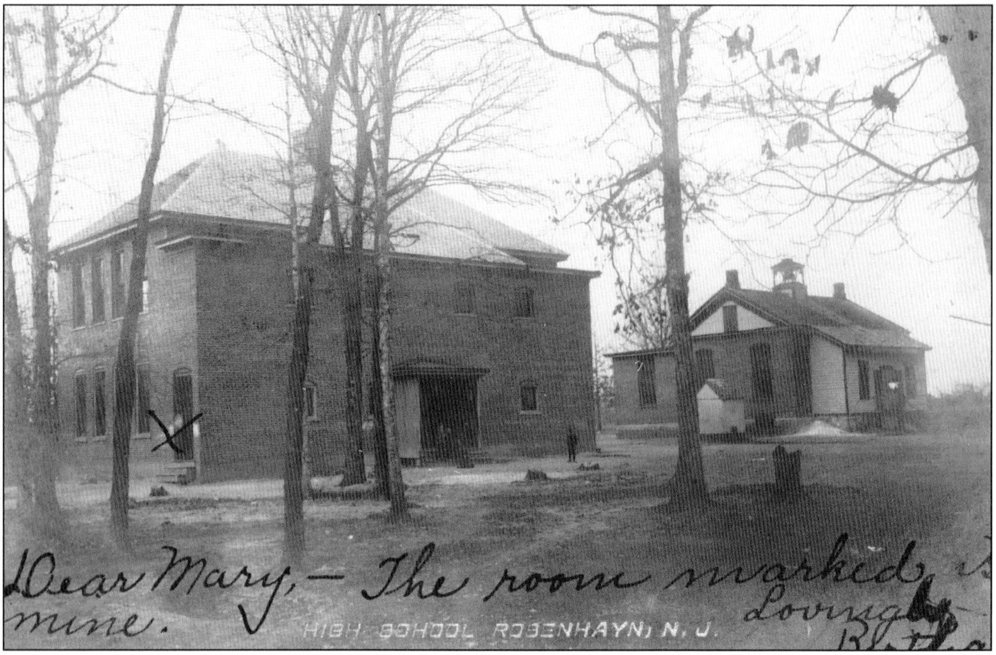

HIGHER LEARNING IN ROSENHAYN. Many find it hard to believe that Rosenhayn once boasted its own high school. But this 1907 postcard from the Pedrick collection shows that this structure, later the elementary school, served that purpose. Note the older frame schoolhouse nearby.

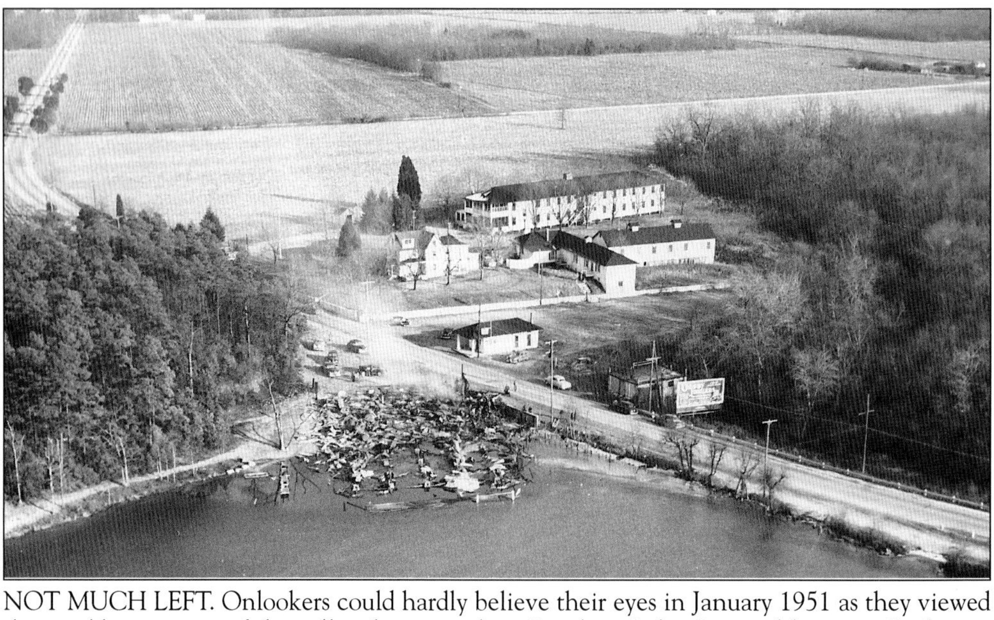

NOT MUCH LEFT. Onlookers could hardly believe their eyes in January 1951 as they viewed the smoldering ruins of the roller skating rink at Rainbow Lake. Located between Bridgeton and Vineland, the once-popular attraction lost patronage during the war due to gas rationing.

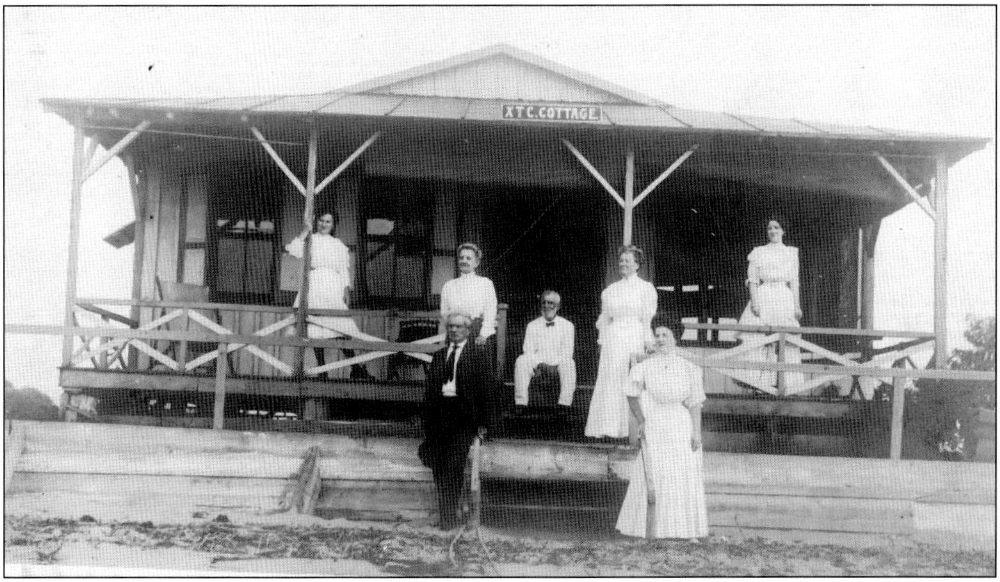

THEY'RE IN ECSTASY. A sign that a Bridgeton area family "had arrived" was that it could afford to erect a cottage at Fortescue on the Delaware Bay. Here a formally attired family gathers on the porch of their summer home dubbed "XTC," which perhaps suggested its occupants mental state.

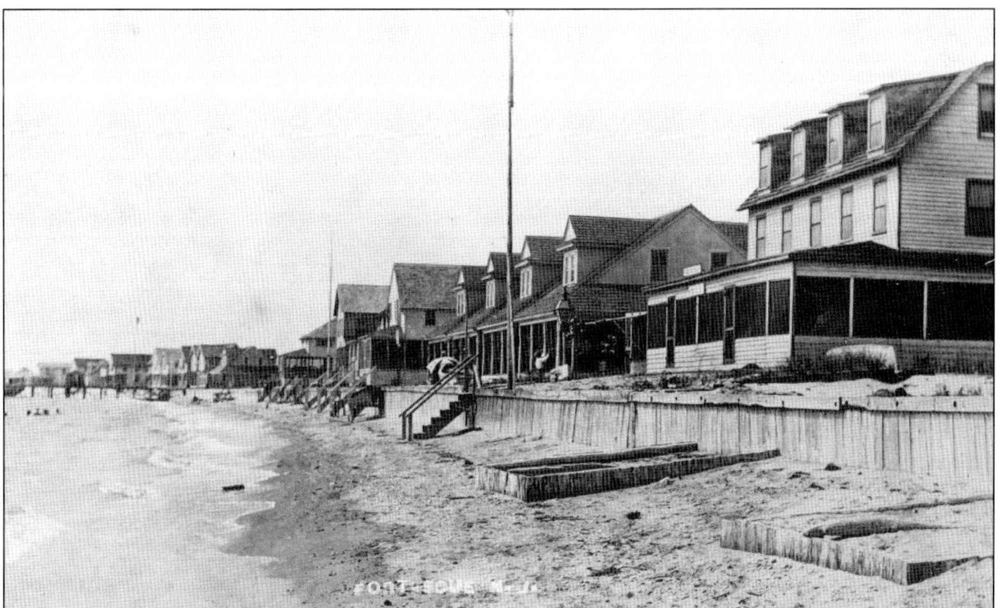

ON THE BEACH AT FORTESCUE. A view from the Pedrick collection dated 1912 shows that Fortescue was heavily developed at that point. A report from a half-dozen years later indicates that the summer population ranged from five hundred to one thousand. As early as 1911, a boardwalk ran along the beachfront.

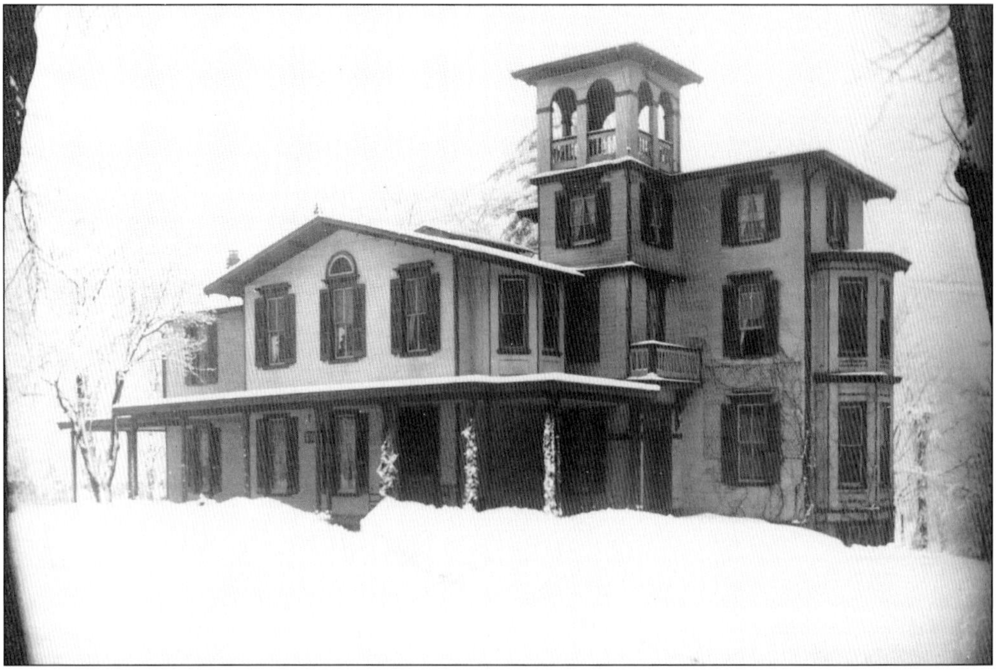

LOOKS RIGHT OUT OF TUSCANY. Among the finest homes in east Bridgeton was the Italianate villa of Robert C. Nichols, once president of the Nail & Iron Works. Constructed before 1875 and demolished after the turn of the century, it stood on East Avenue near the present playground site.

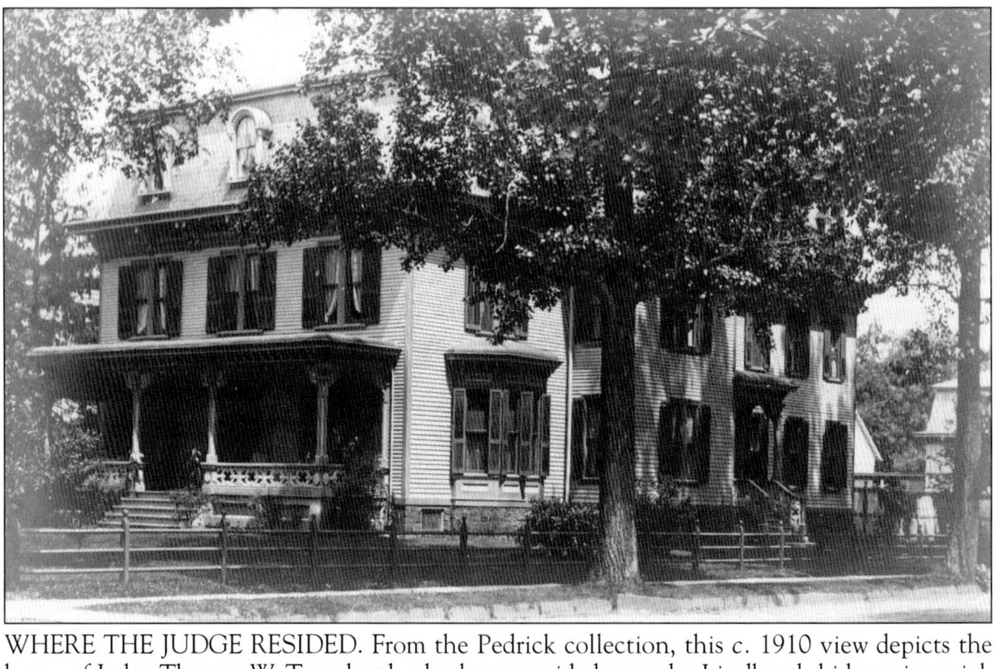

WHERE THE JUDGE RESIDED. From the Pedrick collection, this *c.* 1910 view depicts the home of Judge Thomas W. Trenchard, who later presided over the Lindbergh kidnapping trial. Shorn of its Second Empire trim, it still stands on the northwest corner of Commerce and Giles Streets.